Picture Yourself Drumming:
Step-by-Step Instruction for Drum Kit Setup, Reading Music, Learning from the Pros, and More

Jon Peckman

THOMSON

COURSE TECHNOLOGY

Professional ■ Technical ■ Reference

Image printed on DVD ©istockphoto.com/Jeremy Hohengarten

ISBN-10: 1-59863-330-9

ISBN-13: 978-1-59863-330-6

Library of Congress Catalog Card Number: 2006907928

Printed in the United States of America

07 08 09 10 11 BU 10 9 8 7 6 5 4 3 2 1

Thomson Course Technology PTR,
a division of Thomson Learning Inc.
25 Thomson Place
Boston, MA 02210
http://www.courseptr.com

THOMSON

COURSE TECHNOLOGY

Professional ■ Technical ■ Reference

Publisher and General Manager, Thomson Course Technology PTR:
Stacy L. Hiquet

Associate Director of Marketing:
Sarah O'Donnell

Manager of Editorial Services:
Heather Talbot

Marketing Manager:
Heather Hurley

Acquisitions Editor:
Megan Belanger

Marketing Assistant:
Adena Flitt

Project Editor/Copy Editor:
Cathleen D. Snyder

Technical Reviewer:
Curt Carbone

PTR Editorial Services Coordinator:
Erin Johnson

Interior Layout:
Shawn Morningstar

Cover Designer:
Mike Tanamachi

DVD-ROM Producer:
Curt Carbone

Indexer:
Larry Sweazy

Proofreader:
Dan Foster

*Dedicated in loving memory to my Dad, and
to my Mom, who is more of an inspiration to me now than ever*

Acknowledgments

THANKS TO:

Curt Carbone, for being my fearless other half on this project. I simply couldn't have done this without you.

Megan Belanger, for giving me this opportunity and her support and patience.

Jeff Belanger and Todd Lyon, for their advice and guidance.

Cathleen Snyder, for straightening me out.

Joseph Bastura, for saving the day by creating the music figures.

David Kuzminski and all at Conn. Valley School, for not only giving me the wonderful and rewarding opportunity to teach, but also to love it.

Matt Franklin, for letting me take his place.

The good folks at Peace Drums, for giving me the opportunity to showcase their excellent products.

My entire family, especially my sister Lynda, Rick and the boys, Justin and Dana, and all my friends, for their love and support during this challenging and sometimes difficult time.

Jim Chapdelaine and Chris Salonia, for their unwavering friendship and guidance. Where I would be without them is anyone's guess.

Todd Royce Morton, for being Todd Royce Morton. You're the best.

Vic Steffans, Fred Rossomondo, and Charles Houlihan, for being the best teachers that a young drummer like me could have ever had.

The late great Merle's Record Rack, for furthering my musical education.

Jeff Pitchell, Feathermerchants, and Pete Veru.

All the bands and musicians I've ever played with, who made me the musician that I am today (for better or worse).

My favorite drummers. Here are some off the top of my head: Bun E. Carlos, Tom Ardolino, Dave Grohl, Jim Keltner, and Ringo Starr. If you're not familiar with all the names on this list, then you don't really know how drums should be played, in my opinion. Check them out.

All of my students, past and present. Hanging out with you all is the best part of my job and sometimes even the best part of my life.

Paula, the love of my life. I wouldn't know where to start or where to stop. Now that the book's done, I suppose we should get married, huh?

About the Author

J ON PECKMAN is based in Connecticut and has been a professional drummer for 20 years and a teacher for 10. He currently teaches at Connecticut Valley School of Music and Dance in Portland, Connecticut, and can be found performing all over New England and beyond.

Table of Contents

Introduction xii

Chapter 1 **Where You'll Look into the Future,
Go Back to Preschool, Get Stuck, and
Learn How to Outsmart Your Parents** 1

Preschool for Lessons:
The Best Way to Use This Book and DVD Package 2

What You Will Learn by Using This Book and DVD Package 3

What You Need to Get Started 4

    Rhythm, Rhythm, Rhythm 4

    Sticks 4

Top Secret: For Your Eyes Only—How to Outsmart Your Parents 10

Life without Drums 12

Chapter 2 **Where You'll Learn How to Get
Set Up, Tuned Up, and Rugged Up,
and How to Accessorize Properly** 15

The Drum Set: Where Rock Lives 16

Things to Do before You Begin to Set Up Your Drums 17

Getting Set Up 19

Tuning Your Drums 20

    Tuning the Bass Drum and the Toms 20

    Tuning the Snare Drum 21

Bass Drum 22

Bass Drum Pedal 24

Hardware 25

    The Floor Tom 26

    The Throne 26

The Snare Drum 27
The Hi-Hat: Stand and Cymbals 28
Tom Toms 32
Cymbals 33
Accessories 36

Chapter 3   **In Which You'll Learn a New Language and Meet the "Big Three" 41**

Reading Drum Music: Stop Your Whining. 42
It's Just a Language 42
More Reasons to Learn to Read Music. 42
To Play or Not to Play: Notes and Rests. 45
The Framework: Staff, Key, Measures, Beats, and Time Signature 46
Quarter Notes versus Eighth Notes 48
Groove #1 50
Groove #2 53
Groove #3 54
Review 55

Chapter 4   **In Which You'll Count to 16, Get Filled In on Fills, Crash without Getting Hurt, and Learn What Your Left Foot Is For. 57**

Sixteenth Notes Equal Twice as Many Friends. 58
Fill 'Er Up. 59
Use Your Metronome When Learning Fills 59
Fill #1 59
Fill #2 61
Fill #3 62
Fill #4 63
Fill #5 63
Fill #6 64
A Crash Course in Crashing on a Crash 65
Your Left Foot: The Last to Join the Party 68

Chapter 5   **Where You'll Learn What to Leave
Out and How to Slice and Dice, and
You'll Meet Four Guys Named Steve** **71**

Sixteenth-Note Variation #1 and Groove #4 72

    Understanding "In Between" Notes 72

    Back to the Groove 73

    Déjà Vu 73

    Learning by Repetition. Learning by Repetition.
    Learning by Repetition... 74

    Hey, Brain—You're Fired! 74

    Using the Timer: Ten Minutes to Change Your Life 74

Sixteenth-Note Variation #2 and Groove #5 76

    Alone at Last: Isolating the Trouble Spot 76

    Groove #6: A Funky Combination, a Groove
    Sensation That Will Cause Elation All across the Nation 77

    Using Sixteenth-Note Variation #2 in a Fill 78

    More Fills Using Sixteenth-Note Variation #2 79

    Slicing and Dicing 80

Sixteenth-Note Variation #3 83

    Using Sixteenth-Note Variation #3 in Fills 83

Sixteenth-Note Variation #4 84

    Using Sixteenth-Note Variation #4 in Fills 85

Review: Four Similar-Looking Friends All Named Steve 86

More Slicing and Dicing 87

Making Up Your Own Fills: It's All in Your Mind 88

Adding Spice to Your Life and Crashes to Your Fills 89

Chapter 6   **The Triumphant Return of Your Left Foot** **91**

A Slightly Different Groove 92

The Declaration of Independence 94

Groove #6 with Open and Closed Hi-Hat 95

Sixteenth-Note Variations Using the Bass Drum: The Big Four 96

    The Big #1: Sixteenth-Note Variation #1 Using the Bass Drum 96

    The Big #2: Sixteenth-Note Variation #3 on the Bass Drum 98

    The Big #3: Using Four Sixteenth Notes to Create a Groove 100

    The Big #4: Sixteenth-Note Variation #4 on the Bass Drum 102

The Extra-Special "Congratulations, You've Reached the
Middle of the Book" Review That I Hope You're Happy About 104

Chapter 7   **In Which You'll Learn Why Over and Over,
Become Sharp, Get Lectured, Enter a
Brave New World, and Learn How to
Smoke and Throw** **107**

Practice Routines and Learning by Repetition, Learning by
Repetition, Learning by Repetition: Does This Sound Familiar? 108

Reviews: Keeping It Sharp 109

How to Set Up a Practice Routine 110

A Short Lecture 112

Triplets: A Brave New World 113

    What Is a Triplet? 113

    Watch Your Sticking 114

    Eighth-Note Triplets: Not Quite This and Not Quite That 115

    Sixteenth-Note Triplets: Not Quite That and
    Not Quite the Other Thing 115

Sixteenth-Note Triplets: The Happy Medium 117

Speed Kills 118

Slicing and Dicing with Sixteenth Notes and Sixteenth-Note Triplets . . . 119

Smoke and Throw 122

Review 124

Chapter 8   **Where You'll Meet Your Two New Best Friends
(the Quadruplet and the Flam), Join the
Secret Brother and Sisterhood of the
Flopping Fish, Slam Doors in Your House,
and Say Inappropriate Things at the Dinner
Table—All in the Name of Drumming** **127**

The Quadruplet 128

    How to Play the Quadruplet: The Secret of the Flopping Fish 128

    The Quadruplet with the Focus on Your Hands:
    A Lane, a Circle, and a Flopping Fish 129

    The Quadruplet with the Focus on Your Right Foot 131

    The Quadruplet: Putting It All Together 132

    Why Play Just One Quadruplet When You Can Play Two? 133

The Great and Mighty Flam 134
    A Flam Experiment: Go Slam a Door 134
    Follow the Leader to Flamsville 135
    Using the Flam as a Fill 137
Review 138

Chapter 9   **Where You'll Meet the Flam Tap, Make Combinations and Reverse Them, Learn How to Change Your Voice, Cross Over to the Dark Side, Receive Permission to Bail, and Find Out What a Paradiddle Is** **141**

More Fills Using the Flam Tap 143
Flam Taps and Quadruplets: A Killer Combination 145
Quadruplets and Flam Taps: Flip It 146
Re-Voicing: A Word I Made Up. 147
Crossing Over to the Dark Side: A Dark Version of the Quadruplet. 148
Telpurdauq Esrever: Reverse Quadruplet 150
The Reverse Quadruplet as a Fill. 151
       Permission to Bail 151
Forward and Reverse Quadruplets as Fills 152
A Flam Tap and Reverse Quadruplet Fill 153
Introduction to the Paradiddle 154
Review 157

Chapter 10   **Where You'll Break the Magic Circle, Learn a Bunch of Combinations, Eat a Bunch of Deluxe Cheeseburgers, Learn to Look Where You're Going, and Eat Some Broccoli with Style. . . . 159**

Using the Paradiddle in a Fill: The Magic Circle Is Broken 160
Sixteenth-Note Combination Combinations 162
    A Deluxe Cheeseburger: Three Combinations in One Groove 164
    More Deluxe Cheeseburgers 166
More Slicing and Dicing and Some Words on Style 170

Chapter 11   **Where You'll Take a Vow, Use Accents, Play in 3D, See a Ghost, and Express Yourself ... 173**

Using Accents—And I Don't Mean Talking Funny 174

Drumming in 3D: The Backbeat 175

Drumming in 3D: The Rimshot 177

Boo! Drumming in 3D: The Ghost Note............................. 179

Don't Push Me because I'm Close to the Edge. Drumming in 3D: The Hi-Hats 182

Drumming In 3D: The Bass Drum................................... 185

Chapter 12   **Where You'll Get a Quarter, Learn How Songs Work, Hitch a Ride, and Be a Volume Knob .. 189**

Hey...Got a Quarter? 190

Quarter Notes to the Rescue 191

The Ride Cymbal...Finally 195

The Ride Cymbal—Not So Much How as When 196

How Songs Work: The Short Version 197

Hi-Hats versus Ride Cymbals: The Winner Is You................... 199

> Half-Open (or Half-Closed) Hi-Hats, Ride Cymbals, and Infinite Possibilities................................... 199

> The Concept of Riding (and I Don't Mean in a Car) 200

The Hi-Hats: The Volume Knob of the Drum Set 201

Congratulations: You're Almost a Drummer 202

Chapter 13   **The Lucky Chapter: Where I'll Leave You with Some Last-Minute Advice 205**

Awareness of Arrangement 206

Dynamics 207

Location, Location, Location 208

The Last Note.. 209

1...2...1, 2, 3, 4 210

Pickup Artist 211

It's About Time 212

Hawkeye: The Nickname You Want 213

A Fond Farewell and a Last and Most Valuable Piece of Advice 214

Index 216

Introduction

AS AN INTRODUCTION TO THIS BOOK, I'd like to tell you a little bit about why I wrote it and who I wrote it for. As a drum instructor, I've worked with many different kinds of books as teaching tools. Some books are more focused on theory and technique, while others are simply filled with written exercises with very little other text. As I started to develop my teaching technique, I would find myself using several books at once and jumping around to introduce new students to the things I think they should learn in a particular order. When I was given the opportunity to write my very own book, I realized that I could finally put everything I would like to teach a new student in the exact order I wanted. So, in a way, I wrote this book for myself, I suppose.

Obviously, I wrote this book for anyone who is not only interested in learning to play the drums, but also likes to read books. I've noticed a lot of drum books that keep the words at a minimum and the notes and exercises at a maximum. Being an avid reader myself, I thought it would be an interesting idea to go into a little more detail in words while serving up relevant information about learning to play the drums. I've also tried to make the book entertaining and hopefully humorous for those who appreciate silliness and the absurd. In other words, I wrote the kind of drum book that I would have liked to read when I was starting out—so again, I suppose I wrote this book for myself. But maybe you're the kind of young aspiring drummer that I was and you'll relate to my style of writing and teaching. If you are, I sincerely hope you not only learn more about drumming than you ever hoped to, but that you also have the time of your life while learning and laughing. If you do, then this book was written for you.

I also wrote this book for all the parents of aspiring young drummers. While teaching at a school that does a small amount of retail, I've seen plenty of parents buy a drum set for their son or daughter and come back to the shop several times with questions about the various pieces of gear that make up a drum set. The drum set can be a baffling collection of things to anyone who is unfamiliar with them. Without a basic understanding of the various pieces and devices and their functions, you can only guess. What I've tried to do in this book and the DVD that comes with it is provide the clearest explanations of the gear and how to set it up. I've never run across a package that goes into the detail that I've tried to go into, and I hope that this package will shed some much-needed light on this subject. It is my sincere hope that the setup chapter alone will serve as a resource for student and parent alike.

In working with books as an instructor and also while doing research for this book, I've developed a strong opinion about instructional books, and I've allowed that opinion to shape my own book. I've noticed that many instructional books rush through the building blocks of drumming too quickly in an attempt to fill out the book with more advanced studies. I feel that more time and pages should be devoted to the building blocks so you don't build too many false expectations of what can be learned in any book. Private instruction is the most important part of anyone's musical education, and a good instructor can help you with all of your drumming goals from the simplest concepts to the most advanced. My hope is that by using this particular book to start your drumming education, enough attention will be paid to the basics so that you will have the sturdiest foundation possible when you finally seek private instruction. In other words, rather than dazzle you with depth and scope, I've decided to focus on the fundamentals without undue attention to techniques that I feel could be better addressed by a private instructor.

So, if you're not afraid to read and you're ready for a few laughs while you learn to play drums, turn the page and let's get started.

Where You'll Look into the Future, Go Back to Preschool, Get Stuck, and Learn How to Outsmart Your

Parents

PICTURE YOURSELF AS A PERFECTLY synchronized machine, laying down a solid rhythm that your band mates and your audience can feel down to their very bones. Picture yourself with the power to lock a crowded room of people into the rhythm of your heartbeat, and then increase their heart rates as you play faster and faster. Picture yourself as the very center of excitement on stage, the absolute controller of energy in the band, the actual heart of the band, without whom it's not alive. Now picture yourself packing up all your gear at the end of the night, while the rest of the band is out in the parking lot having fun or already halfway home.

Picture yourself as a drummer.

Why do you want to be a drummer? I'm sure that's not an easy question to answer, and it's one that you probably never thought you'd be asked. Ask it of yourself now. Do you have your answer? Now I'm going to blow your mind and tell you what your answer is. You want to be a drummer because at some point in your life, you saw someone playing drums and it excited you. Maybe it was at a parade, maybe it was at a concert or a party or a club. Maybe it was on TV. The drummer looked like he was having fun, and you thought to yourself, "Hey, I can do that." Now that I've seen your past, I'm looking into your future, and guess what? You *can* do that. You will.

Now let's get started.

Preschool for Lessons: The Best Way to Use This Book and DVD Package

THE OBJECT OF THIS BOOK is to give you a solid beginning to your drumming education, whether you're a young person or an adult. It is not meant to be the only source of information for you if you want to become a drummer. A teacher who gives one-on-one lessons is absolutely essential. You might not need a teacher if you were born exceptionally gifted in drumming and are a complete natural. In that case, I'd love to meet you because you are unbelievably rare. As a matter of fact, I don't know if I've ever met you in my lifetime. Although you might have a large chunk of natural ability, playing in a band with other people (and maybe sometimes in front of an audience) can be so entirely different from practicing alone that any advice or guidance from someone with experience is tremendously valuable. Because I will not personally be your private drum tutor (unless you're one of my current students, in which case I am—and if I am, why are you reading this book when you should be practicing *right now*?), I've packed this book with information that is important to know *before* you seek private instruction.

Lessons are an investment in both time and money, and I feel that by reading this book and following the instructions within, you will be given a solid foundation upon which private lessons will expand. Many of the topics that will be covered in this book would most likely comprise your first dozen or so private lessons. Rather than having only a half-hour lesson and then a week of practice to comprehend each building block of drumming skill, you can use this book to work on the basics at your own pace.

The DVD that comes with this book will visually demonstrate certain things that text cannot fully explain, such as setup tips or execution of certain things, such as patterns, fills, and so on. On the DVD you will also find coaching sessions in which I will help you to develop an effective approach to practice so that your frustration level when learning something new and challenging will be low. When learning something new, it's important to go at your own pace, concentrate, and really nail it, rather than giving it half a try, getting frustrated, and deciding to go join the soccer team at school instead. (Not that I have anything against soccer. You can be a goalie *and* a drummer. Rock on.)

By using this book and DVD together, you will learn the best way to tackle something challenging and get it right before moving on. Many times when learning drumming, you build on something that you learned in an earlier lesson, and you can't move on to the new thing unless you've fully learned the old thing. By following the method in this book and on the DVD, you will always be ready for the new thing because you've put time and effort into fully learning its precursor. Learning from the DVD will be very easy because you can simply rewind anything that you don't understand right away and keep going over it until you fully understand whatever it is you happen to be working on. And, as a bonus, if you get really frustrated you can put the DVD on and make fun of me or my hair or something. How cool is that?

What You Will Learn by Using This Book and DVD Package

▶ You will learn all about the drum set—what it consists of, how to buy one (or how to get someone else to buy you one), and how to set it up.

▶ You will learn how to read drum music, which will be a lot easier than you think as long as you can count to 24. If you can't count to 24, go find someone to explain it to you. I'll wait right here.

▶ You will learn about grooves and fills—what they are, how to play them, and, more important, how to make up your very own grooves and fills.

▶ You will learn the right way to practice. You will learn the quickest and easiest way to focus properly and conquer frustration when working on something new and challenging. Then, you will never be afraid to learn something new because you've proven to yourself that you can get results. This is a beautiful thing.

▶ You will be able to hear music and, using some techniques that I will show you, make a pretty good guess at what the drummer is doing so that you can try it out on your own. You will be able to hear drumming from a drummer's point of view instead of just a regular listener's, and this will give you the ability to play almost anything you hear (or at least give it a decent shot).

▶ You will learn all the little but important things that a good drummer can do to make any band that he or she is playing in sound better than it did when they were using that other dude or dudette. It's all in the details, and you'll be familiar with them all. And you will be the king (or queen) of the count-off.

When you complete this book and DVD program, you will have all the basic but important skills you'll need to get the most out of your private lessons when you take them. Then you can use your lesson time to concentrate on the specific style of drumming that you'd like to get into (classic rock, punk rock, funk, metal, hardcore, hip hop, country, or my favorite, deathcore bagpipe). When your new drum teacher realizes how well-informed and far along you are before you even start your first lesson, he'll probably get so excited he'll show you every trick he knows. That's what I would do.

What You Need to Get Started

YOU WILL DEFINITELY NEED a few things other than your own wonderful self to get started as a drummer. Some things are easier to get than others, and some things you might have been born with. Let's go down the list, shall we?

Rhythm, Rhythm, Rhythm

You'll need this because the drummer keeps the whole band in rhythm. It all starts with rhythm. In drumming, rhythm is everything. Some people respond to rhythm more than others do. If you were attracted to drumming in the first place, you are probably one of those people. If you were more attracted to melody, you'd be more likely to be a singer or a clarinet player or a bagpiper. If rhythm and drumming are the first things you notice when you hear music, then you've chosen the right instrument.

But what is rhythm? We can define rhythm as a pattern of sounds. A pattern, in musical terms, is something that you play over and over again. The drummer in a band often plays the same thing over and over many times to give the other members of the band a rhythmic framework that they can play on top of and along with. The drummer needs the most accurate sense of rhythm and the longest attention span of anyone else in the band, and these are things that can and should be developed. Many times we don't really notice the drummer in a band until he does something that strays from the pattern—something flashy or exciting—but what the drummer is doing when we don't notice him is his most important work in the band. He lays down the foundation upon which the rest of the band can rely.

Sticks

You'll definitely need sticks. They come in many sizes, models, and brands. I will explain the standard sizes to you. Standard means a size that every store will have. There are many brands of sticks, but every brand has standard sizes. You might see some models of sticks out there that are designed by and named after a drum hero of yours. It's not a bad idea to check some of these out. They might do the trick for you, but if you can only play using the extra-special brand named after some dude (or dudette), and your store runs out of them or you move and your new store doesn't have them, you're out of luck. The best idea is to pick a standard size or model that feels right to you. That way you'll always know you can get them, whatever store you visit. There are more sizes than the ones I'll talk about in this book, but these will give us something for comparing the special sizes and models.

Standard Sizes

▶ **7A. These are almost the lightest stick that you could use in a rock-type playing situation. If you are very young and any stick heavier than this feels too heavy for you, these should be fine. If you are over the age of 10, you'll probably want to go heavier than this. However, if you're interested in playing jazz (in which the drums are not generally hit as hard as in a rock-type situation), these might work for you. If you stick with playing the drums for a while, it's not a bad idea to have a pair of 7As tucked away in your stick bag in case you find yourself in a situation in which you have to play more quietly** than you're used to. If you try to actually play more quietly using your regular heavier sticks and you're still too loud, it's time to bust out the old 7As. The 7A would probably not be the stick to start with because if you get too used to the lightness of them, and if for some reason you have to use a heavier stick, that heavier stick will feel mad heavy, yo. And I mean heavy in a bad way.

▶ **5A.** These sticks are probably the best size to start with. If you start with these, you'll have room to go heavier or lighter if you want. When a student starts with me and he needs his first pair of sticks, unless he is very young or a very small person, I'll hook him up with 5As. If you start with these and you want to go heavier, you can always move up in size. As a matter of fact, this is the size I usually use.

▶ **5B.** These are the next size up from 5A, obviously. They feel much like a 5A but, you know, heavier. If you want to play in a heavier style while still using sticks that don't feel like you're swinging two baseball bats, these are worth checking out.

▶ **2B.** If you want to use sticks that feel like you're swinging two baseball bats, then go for it. If you're in a band that's so loud that you need to use these to be heard, best of luck to you and enjoy your hearing aid in a few years. I understand that sometimes when you're starting to learn to play drums you can really get into the loudness of the whole thing, and you just want to smash any drum or cymbal you can get near as hard as you can. I've been there. But not only can you damage your hearing, you will dent your drumheads and crack

your cymbals much faster if you use a stick that's too heavy. You can also develop tendonitis if you push too hard with sticks that are too big for you. Tendonitis is a condition that can end your drumming career. Get a medical encyclopedia and look up tendonitis. It's a bummer. Look up carpal tunnel syndrome too while you have that book out. You could wind up with either of these, or both.

▶ **3S.** Now you're just being silly. But seriously, drummers in drum corps usually use 3S sticks. A drum corps is a group of drummers that you might see in a parade or during the half-time show of a football game. (In a drum corps, one person plays the snare drum, one person plays the bass drum, etc.) They use heavier sticks because they use some different drumming techniques than drummers who use the drum set. These sticks usually aren't used on the drum set unless your goal is to play so loud that you drive everyone out of your life and destroy your drumheads and cymbals. (What are drumheads and cymbals, you ask? We'll get to those very soon. Anyway, I bet you already kind of know what they are.) Some people use these extra-heavy sticks when they practice on their *drum pad* so that later, when they use their regular, lighter sticks, they can really fly around the kit and play much faster than they could otherwise. I don't necessarily doubt this, but I never really tried it myself. I'm of the opinion (which I'll explain more in depth later) that there are no shortcuts to speed in drumming. Speed can be developed on any stick. Feel free to prove me wrong. I've been wrong before, but I can't remember when.

Figure 1.1 shows you some of the standard sizes of sticks.

Figure 1.1
Standard stick sizes

Other (or Non-Standard) Sizes

You'll sometimes see sticks made by one manufacturer or another that are named after a famous drummer. These are usually slight variations on a standard size, and they usually cost a little bit more because the person after whom they're named is just really, really cool.

It's certainly not a bad idea to check out a pair named after a drum hero of yours, but don't expect to magically sound as good as your hero by merely using his sticks. I know you're smarter than that, and I don't even know you. However, if I ever come out with my own model of sticks, then you'll know that they are magical.

You might also see sticks that are not named after someone, but also are not standard sizes. These are usually sizes that fall in between the standard sizes that I discussed a moment ago (see Figure 1.2). If you want to check these out, it's important to ask the salesperson which standard size they are closest to. For example, the salesperson might explain,

"Oh, these are like 5As but a quarter-inch longer," or "These are in between a 5A and a 5B." If you've tried a standard size and it never feels quite right, some of these in-between sizes are worth checking out. One of them might be the perfect stick for you.

Figure 1.2
Non-standard stick sizes

Ten Pairs of Sticks for a Dollar: Just Say No!

At some point very soon in your future, you might walk into a large music store and notice that there are some sticks named after the store that cost so little that it seems like the price must be a mistake. The mistake would be for you to buy them. I know it's tempting: Why would you want to pay up to $10 for one pair of sticks when you can get 10 pairs for the same $10? For one thing, drumsticks are made of wood, and wood can be very inconsistent. What this means to a drummer is that you can have three pairs of sticks that are supposed to be the very same weight, but they don't feel the same when you compare them. One pair might feel much heavier or lighter than another pair.

One thing that a name (or more expensive) brand offers you is greater consistency between pairs. In other words, higher-quality brands go to the trouble of making sure that every stick of a certain size feels as close to the same as possible. That's why they get the big bucks. When you buy the cheap sticks, even though they are all supposed to be the same weight, they can vary wildly. There's nothing worse than dropping or breaking a stick during a show, reaching into your stick bag for a quick replacement, and having the new stick go flying out of your hand because it's lighter than a butterfly's antenna.

The straightness of a stick is also an important factor. The first-class sticks are almost always as straight as they can possibly be. If sticks shaped like a banana (which the cheap sticks can often be) were easy to play with, we would just use really hard bananas instead of sticks. Try it if you don't believe me. You might think that the cheap sticks might last as long as the top-shelf ones, but they won't. You'll end up with a big pile of lousy broken sticks, while the good sticks will still be in one piece. Also, the cheap sticks can break while you're playing them, fly into your face, and kill you. I've never actually heard of this happening, but why take a chance with your life?

If the price of good sticks still really bugs you, save up some cash and wait until the good ones go on sale. It will be worth it. Or buy the cheap ones once, and don't say I didn't warn you. Actually, I must confess that I occasionally buy the cheap sticks for one reason only. I keep a few pairs stashed in my stick bag to give away to people who ask for a pair of sticks because they really enjoyed the show and they want something to remember it by. Or sometimes, if I'm feeling rowdy, I'll throw sticks into the audience. But I only give away or throw the cheap ones. I don't want to hurt anyone's feelings, but sticks don't grow on trees, you know…. Oh, wait. Yeah, they do.

Here's a Tip: Never Pet a Burning Dog
Drum sticks come with two kinds of tips—wood or nylon. Nylon tips are made of a hard type of

plastic. They produce a brighter, more distinctive sound when you use them on cymbals, particularly the ride cymbal. (I'll get to the definition of the ride cymbal very soon.) It's strictly a matter of preference of nylon versus wood. The best thing to do would be to buy a pair each of wood tips and nylon tips (if you can afford them) and experiment. If you much prefer the way the nylon tips make your cymbals sound, then those are the sticks for you.

There are only two possible drawbacks to nylon tips. They might cost a little bit more than wood tips, so be prepared to spend perhaps a dollar or two more per pair. That brings us to possible drawback number two. Now, I don't want to seem like I'm picking on the cheap sticks again, but cheap nylon-tip sticks are even worse than cheap wood sticks. A nylon tip is securely glued onto the end of the wooden stick that you pay top-dollar for. The cheap nylon tips are not glued on as securely. I guess they save money by using cheap glue. These tips can fly off without warning while you're playing, lodging themselves into the eye sockets of your screaming band mates. Honest, this actually happened to a guitar player I know. We call him Old Patch Eye.

When to Replace Your Sticks
It can be heartbreaking when your first new pair of sticks starts getting dents in the side of them, but this is normal. All drummers have felt this pain when starting out. Try to get over it and move on with your life. In most cases, a dented stick is perfectly usable, so rock on. Obviously, if and when they break, sticks need to be replaced. Sometimes, with wood tips, a small section of the tip can break off, and though the stick appears to be in one piece and playable, it creates a mushy and indistinct sound on your cymbals, particularly the ride cymbal.

That might not bother you too much (especially if you only own a few pairs of sticks and you don't have a lot of cash available to rush out and buy new ones), but I usually replace mine when the tips disintegrate. Sometimes a stick doesn't quite break when it should, but instead starts to shred and wear out in the middle. This is caused by hitting the cymbals on their edges. (This doesn't mean you shouldn't hit a cymbal on its edge. Certain cymbals are made to be hit on the edges.) Another cause of this peculiar sign of wear is the use of the rim shot, a special drumming technique that I'll go into later.

When your drum stick wears out and shreds so much in the middle that it starts to resemble an hourglass, you should replace it. It's just a matter of time before it breaks, and if it shreds too much you could get a splinter. Also, when a stick shreds a lot, the little pieces of wood that fly off can get stuck in the carpet and make a mess. You might not care about that, but wait until your mom or your significant other sees sawdust and wood chips in the carpet. As a matter of fact, you should probably set up your drums on a piece of carpet or rug that you don't much care about, because drumming can be a little bit messy. Sometimes, if a stick is really shredded and weak, I'll save it to break over my knee at a show when I'm sure everybody's looking. This is to show the audience what a tough guy I am and that I'm not to be messed with.

"Hey Man, Groovy Pad"

A drum pad is a device that drummers use to practice on, rather than an actual drum (see Figure 1.3). Drum pads come in a few different varieties. Some have a rubber playing surface, while others have an actual drum head to play on. The rubber type are generally the quieter of the two types, while the drum head type offers the advantage of a playing surface that more closely resembles an actual drum.

Figure 1.3
A drum pad

In my opinion, a drum pad is not absolutely essential when starting out. A pad comes in very handy when your drum set is not available (if you're on vacation, for example) and you want to hit something that was made to be hit (unlike the furniture), but it is no substitute for a drum kit. This book is for people who mostly want to play the drum set in a rock-type situation. The drum pad represents just one drum that you use two arms to play, while a drum set uses all your limbs (arms and legs).

If you just want to play in the marching or concert bands at school (which I think you should, by the way—I'll tell you why later), a pad is perfect to practice your parts if you're just playing the snare drum part. You might develop a warm-up routine at some point a little further along in your drumming career that uses the pad, so a pad is not a bad thing to have, but it's not entirely necessary. Many times students who are just starting lessons will buy a pad and never use it when they quickly realize that what they really need is a full drum set. If a pad is the only thing that you can afford (or that you can talk your parents into getting you), it's definitely better than nothing. When I was starting out, all I had was a pad for a year or two, but I played that thing to death. You might want to hold off on the pad for now and set your sights on the full drum set. However, this is just my own humble opinion. Your parents might get you a pad and promise you a drum set later, "if you're serious about this." I don't want to start trouble between you and your parents, but playing a single pad (or snare drum) doesn't fully prepare you to correctly learn to play a drum set. You can tell your parents I said so. I'll take the blame; I can handle it.

"But you don't know my parents," you're thinking. "They'll never buy me a drum set." Well, unfortunately, you might be right, but I'm going to give you some tips on how to work on your parents, as well as how to second-guess what their arguments for not getting you a drum set will be. Whatever you do, never let your parents see this next section. This is just between me and you.

Obviously, if you're an independent adult, skip this chapter. However, if you have a significant other that you report to, this info will come in handy for you.

Top Secret: For Your Eyes Only—How to Outsmart Your Parents

If you're an adult who doesn't need your parents' permission to buy a drum set, you can skip this section. And, if your parents have absolutely no problem with buying you a drum set, then you can skip this section. Before you do, though, can you ask them if they'll be my parents too?

BEFORE TRYING TO CONVINCE your parents to buy you a drum set, you have to outsmart them. You have to imagine all the reasons they'll give you about why they're hesitant to buy one for you. This section details some reasons that they might give you and possible solutions or answers you can use to help them to see things more clearly. I've tried all of these, and they all worked (eventually).

1. "How do we know what to get?"

This is an easy one. Refer your parents to the section of this book that will answer that question. You can do some research on your own, too. Go to a big music store that will let you take a catalog or sales book home. Looking through it will give you an idea of what packages they offer that might work for you. The prices will tell you which ones are at the top of the line. Most drum companies offer several different lines, from absolute beginner (usually not the best quality) to professional. It's generally a good idea to go

for the best-quality set that you can possibly afford, so keep your eyes peeled for sales. A good sale might give you an opportunity to get a better-quality set than you could normally afford.

It really pays off to do some good research and have a clear picture of what you're looking for before you go to the store to buy. Depending on how big the store is, you might find yourself being pressured into buying something more extravagant or expensive than you need. The more you know about what you want going in, the better. When you do your research beforehand and your parents see how much you know about drums, they'll see that you're serious about your new passion. If you're not going to be doing the talking, make sure you tell your parents beforehand as much as you can about what you're interested in. Or better yet, lend them this book so they can read it and understand as much as you do about what you need to buy.

One thing to keep in mind when going to a store to check out drums is the size of the store—and I don't mean square footage of the building. If it's really busy and crowded, and it takes you a long time to get the attention of someone who works there, that can be a bad sign. If something goes wrong with your drums or you need to go back and ask questions after you've bought them, the store might not give you the quick, personal attention you deserve. An advantage to a smaller, local store is better and more personal service. They might not offer prices as low as a giant store, but sometimes the advice and support that they can give you is worth more than money.

2. "They're too expensive."

True enough, but there are alternatives to a brand-spanking-new expensive drum set. You could check out a used set. I played used drums for years and years before I could afford my first new kit (which I'm still playing to this day). There are many places to look for used drums, such as the classifieds in your local newspaper, music stores that buy and sell used gear, or even auction sites on the Internet. If you ask all your friends whether they know of anybody looking to sell a used kit, you might get lucky. You could also ask your parents to ask around at their job or maybe put up a flyer on a bulletin board there. Ask around at school. Your new used drums might be even closer than you think. Another unexpected benefit of buying used drums is that you might make a drum buddy or meet somebody who could hook you up with a good teacher or who might be a teacher themself.

3. "What if you decide you don't want to play anymore after a month, and we're stuck with drums collecting dust, just like the bagpipes you wanted last year?"

Hopefully you'll want to stick with drumming for a while, but if you change your mind about staying with it, you can always sell them later for close to what you paid for them, depending on how well you take care of them. I don't want to give you a lecture and sound just like your parents, but they're right about this one. You should try your very best to take care of your drums, whether they're brand new or used. Drum heads will always wear out and have to be replaced, but if you take decent care of the drums, cymbals, and hardware, they will retain their value pretty well. Be careful when moving them, don't drop them, and give them a cleaning once in a while. If you tend to be a slob (like I am), then this will take some extra effort, but when your parents see how serious and dedicated to your new passion you are, they will be like putty in your hands.

4. "If we get you drums, you'd better behave for the rest of your life."

This is the toughest one to hear, but if you're serious about drumming, you'll agree to do whatever it takes, including behaving for the rest of your natural life. You might have to promise to stop picking on your little sister or to empty the garbage every day or to mow the lawn without complaining. You might have to agree that your new drums are your next two or three birthday presents combined. You might not get the next video game that you want. You might even have to get a summer job if you're old enough. It can be a sad fact of life that you might be at the mercy of your parents for a while, but you'll have to seriously ask yourself whether you can take what they might dish out. Only you can answer that question, but at least you won't be mowing that lawn for nothing. Getting the drum set you want might take a small sacrifice. One of my students with really long hair wanted a double bass pedal very badly. His dad promised him the pedal if he got a haircut, and the next week he showed up at lessons with really short hair and a new pedal. When my parents bought me one of my first kits, they actually made me sign a contract with them, promising to shower at least twice a week and to keep my room clean forever. To this day, I still keep my room clean.

Life without Drums

WHAT IF YOU JUST CAN'T GET DRUMS right now? Do you give up hope and pursue some other interest? Not necessarily. You can still get on a drum set occasionally and try it out. Maybe you have a friend who has drums, and he'll let you have a try. You could be a little bit sneaky and become friends with someone who you otherwise can't stand because that person or a family member has a drum set that he or she will let you have a try on. (I actually did this when I was starting out. When I see this person around town now, he still thinks I actually liked him, not his older brother's drums.)

You can still sign up for lessons even though you don't have drums of your own. In fact, this can be a perfect opportunity to have a try at real drums and decide whether you're really into them before you go and buy a set of your own. A lot of my students start out this way. Just make sure when you sign up for lessons that you'll be taking your lessons on a real drum set, not a drum pad set.

Suppose you actually end up with a drum kit? What then? Turn the page, that's what.

Where You'll Learn How to Get Set Up, Tuned Up, and Rugged Up, and How to Accessorize

Properly

T HE DRUM SET (or *drum kit* or just plain *kit*) is where all the action happens. When people talk about their drum kit, they're not just talking about the actual drums, but all the other things besides drums that make up the kit. I'll talk about all of these things in these next sections.

The Drum Set: Where Rock Lives

A basic drum kit consists of the following:

▶ **A throne**

▶ **A bass drum and bass drum pedal**

▶ **A snare drum and a snare drum stand**

▶ **A hi-hat stand and hi-hat cymbals**

▶ **One or two mounted toms and the mounting hardware**

▶ **A floor tom (a tom with legs rather than mounted on the bass drum)**

▶ **At least one crash cymbal with a cymbal stand**

▶ **A ride cymbal with a cymbal stand**

As I said before, this is a basic setup. You might encounter a kit that has more or fewer toms or more or fewer crash cymbals and maybe some other special kinds of cymbals, which I'll tell you about later, but I'll use this basic setup as an example to show you how to set it all up. You will find a detailed setup sequence in this book's DVD that should clear up any problems or questions you may have about setting up your kit.

How many pieces in your kit? What does that mean, anyway?

Here's a bonus tip about how drummers talk about their kits. You'll often hear them talk about a four-piece kit, a five-piece kit, or a seventeen-piece kit. What they are referring to is the number of actual drums they have in their kit. They are not including the number of cymbals they have in their number count. This can be a good thing to know if you happen to be looking in the paper for a used kit. For example, if it says "five-piece drum set," that means it has five drums. If it doesn't say how many cymbals the kit comes with, that will be a question for you to ask whoever is selling it.

Things to Do before You Begin to Set Up Your Drums

ONCE YOU FIND THE SPOT in your house or garage where you're going to set up your kit, take some time to locate (or go out and buy) a rug to put down on that spot where your kit is going to be (see Figure 2.1). The best kind of rug to use will have rubber on the bottom and rug on the top. Next time you walk into a restaurant, check out the rug that you're supposed to wipe your feet on when you walk in. (You do wipe your feet, don't you? Of course you do.) Not the welcome mat that's outside, but the rug that's just inside. That's the kind of rug I'm talking about. (Unless you walk into the only restaurant in the world that doesn't have the kind of rug I'm talking about and you think I'm crazy. What's he talking about now?) You can find these rugs at Home Depot or a similar store. They shouldn't be too expensive. Get the size that looks as if it will be big enough to set up your drums, obviously. This whole rug issue will be covered on the DVD. Check it out if you're having any problem whatsoever picturing what a rug looks like.

You use a rug for two reasons. The first reason is because if you set up drums on a wood floor with no rug under them, they will slide all over the place when you play them, driving you crazy. If you ever take your drums out of the house to set them up somewhere else, always (and I mean always) take your rug with you. Treat it as the most important part of your kit. I guarantee you, the first time you don't bring your rug will end up being the one time that you definitely need it. Bring it every single time, or else you'll be frantically searching around for a nearby restaurant from which you can "borrow" one.

Figure 2.1
A rug

There might already be a rug or carpeting on the floor where you're going to set up your kit, which might make you wonder whether you still need a special drum rug. You do, and here's why. Drumming can be messy. Oil might drip from your pedal onto the rug; those little wood chips that I talked about before might be flying around and landing on the rug; and blood, sweat, and tears might even fly if you're really rocking out. Or you just might spill your drink.

Your mom or significant other will not be happy when he or she sees what rocking out has done to their carpet or rug. Your days of rocking might come to a sudden halt, and your days of vacuuming the rug will begin. Be a considerate drummer and use your own rug. Then commence rocking.

Before you start to set up your kit, locate the drum key among the pile of shiny metal stuff (see Figure 2.2).

You'll need this small tool for a couple of things. You never want to be without one of these around, and you probably shouldn't have just one. If you lose the one that you have, you'll absolutely have to go out to the music store and get another one, so I would suggest that the next time you're near the music store, you go in and get an extra one or two, whether you need one or not. (I actually have one on my keychain so I'll almost never be without one. Unless I lose my keys, but that will never happen, right?) You need this little tool to turn the rods that tighten or loosen the drumhead on the drum. This is called *tuning the drum*, which you will learn to do shortly. The second use for a key is to tighten various things on the hardware or stands.

If you go to tighten something that's too small to grab with your fingers, you'll probably need your trusty key. If you don't have one handy, just find me. I have one on my keychain. Hey, wait. Where are my keys?!

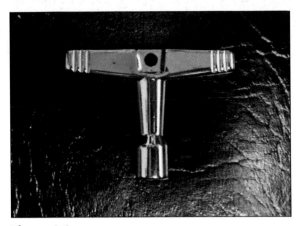

Figure 2.2
A drum key

Getting Set Up

THIS SECTION OF THE BOOK will give you some very general pointers on how to set up your kit. For more detailed instructions on how to best set up your kit, check out the "Getting Set Up" chapter on the DVD that came with this book. If you buy a brand-new kit, often the drumheads will not be on the drums when you get the kit out of the boxes. Included in the "Getting Set Up" chapter of the DVD are instructions for putting the heads on the drums.

A Crash Course on Drumheads

There are two heads on each drum, top and bottom. Drumheads differ in various ways, such as color, single-ply or double-ply, or sound characteristics, but the most important difference is weight or thickness. The bottom head on the toms is usually of a lighter type than the top because it's to add tone to the drum, not to be hit like the top or *batter* head. On a snare drum, we find the greatest difference between top and bottom heads. The bottom snare head, usually called the *snare side head*, is very thin.

Drumheads come in not only many varieties of type and color, but also several degrees of quality. The best-sounding and most durable heads are the most expensive, and, in order to keep the cost of the full kit down, the heads that you get with your drum set might not be the best quality, depending on the line of drums that you get. These heads are fine when you're starting out, but when they break, replace them with a quality name-brand head, such as Remo or Evans. You should immediately hear the difference in sound.

Tuning Your Drums

ONCE THE DRUMHEADS ARE PLACED on the drum, they need to be tuned. As you'll notice when you watch the DVD, I don't fully tune the drums until after the kit is completely set up. On the DVD, you'll see me assembling the floor tom and the bass drum from scratch, which includes the process of putting the heads on, but not necessarily tuning them. For the purposes of the book, however, I've explained the process of putting on the heads and tuning up the drums in the same section.

Tuning the Bass Drum and the Toms

Place the drumhead on the drum shell first, and then place the rim over the head. You'll notice that the rim has holes in it. The rods (long pieces of metal with threads on one end and another end that your drum key fits onto) fit through the hole and down the outside of the drum and into the threaded hole at the top of the lug.

The *lugs* are the pieces attached to the outside of the shell of each drum. The drum key is used to tighten or loosen the rods on the drum to change the pitch. It's best to get a general pitch that's somewhere in the middle of the range of pitches that the particular drum you're working on is capable of. To do this, use your drum key to loosen all the rods on both the top and bottom heads until they are as loose as they can be. This will give you a starting point from which to tune the drum.

If your drums came with the heads not on them, put the heads on the drums and tighten the rods into the lugs just enough so that they are threaded into the lug, but not so tight that there's any pressure. (Again, check out the DVD if you're having trouble picturing any of this.) Then pick any rod and begin to tighten it just enough so that you start to feel some resistance. Then, go to the rod across the drumhead from the one that you've just tightened, and tighten that one as close as you can to the same amount of pressure as the first one. Pick another rod and do the same thing that you did to the first two. Then go to the rod opposite of that one, and do the same. It's very important that you always go to the rod that's across from the one you're working on when tuning up your drums.

If you tightened up all the rods on one side of the drum first, before going to the opposite side, your head will end up sitting on the drum like a seesaw, with one side of the head tightened down and the other side up too far away from the lugs to be tuned properly. If you follow this procedure with all the rods on both the bottom and top heads of the drum, you're ready to begin tuning.

Choose any rod and tighten it up just enough so that any wrinkles that you might see near the area of the drumhead that you're working on smooth out. Once those wrinkles smooth out, repeat the procedure with the opposite rod. As you continue this procedure for all the rods on the drum, try to pay attention to how much you're tightening down on each lug. Ideally, you want to apply as close to the same amount of pressure to each and every rod as you can. If you do this to all the rods on both the top and bottom of the drum, your drum will then have a pitch or note that you can work with.

It takes a little bit of experimentation to get the perfect pitch for each drum. If you have three toms in your kit, you'll notice that they are all different sizes. If you tune each tom to its ideal note, they will all naturally fall in a descending order of pitch. In other words, they'll go from higher to lower pitch according to their sizes.

Tuning the Snare Drum

You'll follow a different procedure when tuning the snare drum than you did for the other drums in the drum kit. When tuning the toms or the bass drum, you want both the top and the bottom heads of the drum to be at more or less the same pitch. When tuning the snare drum, you should tighten the bottom head (the head with the snares lying against it) as tight as you can within reason. There's no need to tighten the head so much that the drum implodes, but the tighter the bottom head, the better the snare response. So, tighten that bottom snare head as much as you can without making a strength test out of it, and you should be good to go.

To tune the top head of the snare drum, follow the same procedure that you did to tune the top head of any of the toms. Remember to always tighten the rods from one side to the other, just like with the toms. To get a nice, crisp snare drum sound, you can tighten each rod somewhat past the point where the wrinkles on the head disappear.

Experimentation is the key to finding the snare drum sound that you like. Some drummers like a very high-pitched sound from their snare drum, while other drummers prefer a lower, tubbier sound or anywhere in between these extremes. It's really a matter of personal preference when it comes to snare sounds.

A good way for you to determine what kind of snare sound you might be looking for is to listen closely to the sound of the snare drum in the music that you like to listen to. Is it medium-pitched? High-pitched or low? This will at least give you a snare sound to shoot for. You can always change your snare sound as your tastes change. When I was first learning to play drums, a very high-pitched snare sound was quite popular, so that's the sound I used for years. After a while, I got sick of that sound so I started tuning my snare lower until I arrived at the sound that I prefer now. My current snare sound is at a pitch just a little higher than average. Experiment to find your own sound.

Bass Drum

THE BIGGEST DRUM IN THE KIT is called the *bass drum*. You might hear some people call this the *kick drum* (but usually only really cool people). It is placed on its side and has little legs called *spurs* attached to it (see Figure 2.3). These are to keep the bass drum from moving when you're playing it.

Figure 2.3
Spurs on the bass drum

Spurs are fairly easy to figure out. You want to try and make sure that the drum is level (or flat) when you're done tightening up the spurs.

Now it's time to hook up the *pedal*. If your drum kit comes with the heads not on the drums, you might want to take this opportunity to throw something in the bass drum, such as a small blanket or pillow. This is to muffle the sound. If you don't have anything in the bass drum, it will ring out too much when you're playing it, sounding very boomy. This is not usually the best sound for you to start out with. The best bass drum sound to start out with is a nice, deep (but tight) sound. However, be careful not to muffle the drum too much. A little experimentation should lead you to that deep but tight sound. (Obviously, if you're going to put a pillow or blanket in your bass drum, make sure that it's a blanket or pillow that won't be missed. Don't take it off anybody's bed. And also, never, ever take a nap inside your bass drum, even though there might be pillows and blankets in there. Once you get inside a bass drum, it can be really hard to get out again.)

You might find that your brand-new front bass drumhead has a hole in it (see Figure 2.4). It is not damaged. This is to let some air out of it while playing, giving you that nice, tight sound you want. The hole in the head also comes in very handy if you ever need to reach in and adjust the muffling material you have in there (pillow, blanket, sleeping bag, air mattress, or waterbed). If your front bass drumhead does not have a hole, you should probably make one, and I don't mean with your fist. This is a very delicate procedure, one that requires a very sharp pen knife and nerves of steel. I would suggest that you check out the setup chapter on the DVD, where you can see what the hole looks like.

Figure 2.4
Hole in the front bass drum head

I have to admit, I'm not that good at cutting a hole, and I've ruined several bass drumheads in my life. My advice to you would be to either go to the store where you bought the kit and ask whether they have any bass drumheads with holes already in them, or ask whether anyone in the drum department is an expert hole cutter. If no one is and you know someone in your family or among your friends who is exceptionally handy, have that person watch the DVD, take a look at the hole, and see whether they think they can pull off this procedure without damaging the head. (And if this person is really, really handy, send him or her to my house so he or she can build me a walk-in closet, please.)

Once you have your hole cut, you should reinforce the edges of the hole with black electrical tape. You can also check at the music store for a nifty hole protector, made for this very purpose. If you go to the music store, try your best to describe what you're trying to do (protect your hole); if they have hole protectors, they'll know exactly what you're talking about and get you one. If they have no idea what you're talking about, stop talking and slowly creep away. They probably think that you're talking about protecting the hole in your head that your brains are obviously leaking out of. That's okay, though. I know what you're talking about.

Bass Drum Pedal

THE BASS DRUM PEDAL NEEDS TO BE attached to the bass drum (see Figure 2.5). Watch the DVD to see how to do this if you can't figure it out.

Figure 2.5
Bass drum pedal

You might need your drum key to attach the beater (see Figure 2.6).

The *beater* is the thing that looks like a big felt lollipop. (Does it look like that to you, or is it just me?) You want to make sure that this is fastened on the pedal nice and tight so it doesn't come off when you're playing. The spring or springs that you'll see on the side of your pedal can be adjusted. If you're playing drums for the first time in your life, you probably won't have a preference as to the tension of the springs, but after you've been playing for a little while, you might want to experi-

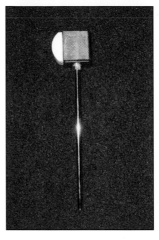

Figure 2.6
Bass drum beater

ment with spring tension. This is totally up to the individual playing the pedal. Some people like it loose, and some like it tighter. Each brand of pedal has slight differences in the way that the spring tension can be adjusted, so you'll have to figure out how yours works. Beware when messing with your springs, because your fingers can get greasy and black from the oil that lurks in the moving parts of your pedal. Check your fingers for grease before you go and scratch your face, or you'll walk around all day with a grease mark on your face.

Unless you're going for the ever-popular "grease mark on your face" look, in which case there's no need to check your fingers (see Figure 2.7).

Figure 2.7
The ever-popular "grease mark on your face" look.

Hardware

I N DRUM TALK, WE CALL all the long, shiny things *hardware*. The hardware consists of all the different kinds of stands that you use to hold up the rest of your drums and your cymbals. Depending on the kind of kit you have, you might also have legs for the floor tom in your pile of hardware.

> **Hardware can be upgraded to better quality if the hardware that comes with your starter kit is not as sturdy as you would like.**

There are three kinds of cymbal stands, the first kind being a *straight* stand (see Figure 2.8). If your kit comes with just one cymbal stand, it is most likely a straight stand.

A straight stand is self-explanatory. It's simply a straight-up-and-down stand with height adjustment. A *boom* stand, however, is a bit more complex.

The boom stand comes in handy when you've started adding more and more cymbals and stands to your kit and the bases of all your stands are getting tangled up and battling each other for floor space. The boom stand allows you to put the base of the stand farther away from your kit and use the boom to telescope the top part of the stand into a playing position.

The third type of cymbal stand is one that can be mounted on the bass drum or one that shares its base with another stand, such as a tom stand or perhaps another cymbal stand. On some bass drum hardware mounts, there will be a hole in addition to the holes for the tom mounts to add the top part of a cymbal stand. Or you could also make your own combination stand using different parts from several different stands and using brackets to hold the different parts together.

For the sake of simplicity, let's use a straight stand to illustrate a setup. It should be very easy to figure out how to set up a straight cymbal stand. When opening and adjusting the legs of your cymbal stands, there's no particular need to open them all the way. Open them wide enough so that they won't fall over, and that should be fine. We'll put the cymbals on them a little later.

Figure 2.8
A straight cymbal stand

The Floor Tom

Locate the floor tom legs and put them on the floor tom (see Figure 2.9).

Figure 2.9
A floor tom with legs on it

The *floor tom* would be the next largest drum of the bunch. Occasionally, a floor tom will not use legs, but will attach to a stand instead. If that's the case with your kit, you can skip the next few sentences. If your floor tom uses legs, figuring out how to put the legs on the drum should not be too hard for you. The height of the floor tom can be adjusted to your comfort and generally should be tilted slightly toward you when you're in your playing position. Occasionally, your largest tom might not technically be a floor tom. Sometimes the largest tom (that would be the same size as a floor tom) might have to be mounted on a stand of its own. If you look on the side of your largest tom and it has three brackets mounted on the outside

of it, it's a floor tom and the legs go into those brackets. If the drum has only one bracket that looks the same as the brackets on the sides of your mounted toms, then this drum should be placed on a stand of its own.

The Throne

Now let's set up the seat or *throne* (see Figure 2.10).

Figure 2.10
A drum throne

It's called a throne because drummers are the king of the band, I guess. Most kits that you'll buy should include a throne. If you don't have a throne in your new kit, it's not the end of the world. You could use any household stool or chair without arms to sit on while playing, but a throne is better than any regular old chair to sit in while drumming. Unlike a regular chair, you can adjust the height of a throne, which is very important to a drummer.

The top of your throne (the part of it that you sit on) is more comfortable to sit on than a regular chair, too. Find the top of your throne and fit it on top of the stand part of the throne. Then, tighten it to the stand so it doesn't slip around when you sit on it.

When you get the rest of your kit set up and you're sitting at your kit on the throne, pay attention to the height that you're sitting at and make sure you're comfortable. Sitting at just the right height for you is crucial. Lower the height of the throne if you have any difficulty reaching the pedals. The height that generally feels comfortable for you should be fine for now, but feel free to experiment with your throne height as you progress in your playing. Some players like to sit extra low, claiming that they can achieve greater speed with their footwork, while other players prefer to sit much higher and tower over their kit. There are no rules regarding throne height. Your comfort while playing is the most important thing.

There are several different types of height adjustment mechanisms, depending on the type of throne you have. Some have a long bolt and a wing nut that goes through a hole in the stand part of the throne. To adjust the height, fully remove the bolt and wing nut from the hole in the shaft and put the bolt through another hole, either higher or lower. Then, screw the wing nut onto the end of the bolt.

Another type of height mechanism that you might encounter will require you to use your drum key to unlock the height adjustment. Once it's unlocked, you can move the shaft up and down to the height of your choice, and then use your key to lock it again when you've found the height that's right for you. There are several other height adjustment types, but these two are the most common. Occasionally, you'll see a throne that can be adjusted by a lever or one that needs to be spun to adjust height.

The Snare Drum

The *snare drum* can be made of shiny chrome or wood that's the same color of the rest of the kit (see Figure 2.11).

Figure 2.11
A chrome snare drum

The snare is a shallow drum with crooked, wiggly wires attached to one of the heads. These crooked wires are called *snares*, and they are what give this drum both its name and its distinctive sound.

The head that has the snares lying against it is a special extra-thin head and should never be hit with your sticks. It should be treated as carefully as an egg (see Figure 2.12).

The snare drum uses a special stand to hold it, called (you guessed it) a *snare stand*. There are generally two different kinds of snare stands—one on top of which the drum sits flat, and another kind that has an adjustment that allows the stand to grab the snare drum tight. Whichever kind of stand you have, it is very important to pay attention to that fragile bottom head when putting the drum on the stand. It's very easy to break that head by setting the drum down on the stand and letting the little fingerlike parts of the stand accidentally poke through the head instead of resting against the outside of the drum, as they're supposed to.

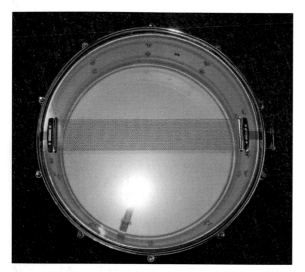

Figure 2.12
Bottom snare head with snares showing

If you're having a hard time picturing what I'm trying to explain, the DVD will demonstrate the correct way to put the snare drum on the stand. It's very important that you understand this part of setting up your snare drum.

You will find a device on the side of your snare drum called a *throw-off*. This is like a switch that can turn the sound of the snares on and off and can also control how tightly the snares hug the bottom head. Feel free to turn the snares on and off and use the fine-tuning adjuster to get an idea of how the throw-off affects the sound of the snare drum. The fine-tuning adjuster is turned like a knob, while the on/off control is more like a switch. You generally want to find a medium setting where the snares aren't rattling around too

loosely and aren't so tight against the bottom head that they sound choked. Experimentation with the throw-off will lead you to the sound that works best for you.

Once you have the snare drum on its stand, it's time to put it in the kit. When you're sitting at your bass drum on the throne, your right foot should be on the bass drum pedal with the snare drum stand between your legs. (Take a moment to make sure that the height of the snare drum is right for you; it can be adjusted. The snare drum should generally be at the same height as your stomach.)

The Hi-Hat: Stand and Cymbals

This is probably the most complex piece of hardware on your drum kit. You definitely should watch the DVD to see how to assemble the hi-hat stand and cymbals, but I will try my best to explain it in words.

The bottom part of the hi-hat stand looks like the other cymbal stands except it has a pedal as one of its parts. Set the bottom part upright and spread the legs out until the base of the pedal is sitting flat on the floor, and then tighten the legs in place.

Now look for a thin metal rod that has a threaded end. There might be an odd-looking contraption with a hand screw on the side of it attached to a long, thin rod. This contraption is called a *clutch* (see Figure 2.13).

Figure 2.13
Hi-hat stand with clutch attached

Cymbalism: What You Need to Know about Cymbals

There are many different types of cymbals to choose from. Your first drum kit might come with cymbals made by the same company as the drums. These are usually not the greatest quality. This is common with starter kits. You can always buy better cymbals later, after you've put a little more time into your drumming.

When shopping for good cymbals, keep in mind that there are basically three cymbal companies that are considered the best: Zildjian, Paiste, and Sabian. Each of these cymbal companies has several lines of cymbals, from beginner to professional. Obviously, the professional line is the best and also the most expensive, but some of the lines between beginner and professional are surprisingly quite good. You might see mid-line cymbals sold in packs (for example, hi-hats, a crash, and a ride together in one box). These can be a good bargain, but make sure you're able to try them out in the store and that they sound reasonably better than the no-name cymbals you already have.

Another option for you to check out is used cymbals. I personally think it's a better bargain to have used professional cymbals than brand-new mid-line cymbals. You can look for used cymbals in the newspaper, but if you do, you should be familiar enough with cymbal lines to determine from talking to the seller whether they are of the quality you're looking for. It wouldn't really be worth your time or money to buy used mid-line cymbals. Go for the good stuff.

Or, you could go to a music store looking for used cymbals—most stores will have some. This can also give you an opportunity to hear a bunch of cymbals, both new and used, so you can make comparisons in the sound. I always cruise the used cymbal section of any music store I go to. Sometimes you can find some real gems hidden there. Remember, just because a cymbal isn't shiny and new doesn't mean it's not good. In fact, some drummers prefer a used cymbal that is broken in and mellow. Let your ear be your guide, and with some comparing, you'll learn what a good cymbal sounds like. When checking out used cymbals, obviously feel them all over to make sure they're not cracked anywhere, although it would be highly uncommon to find a cracked cymbal for sale.

If the clutch is not attached to the long, thin rod, locate it in the pile of hardware. You don't need it right now, so unscrew it from the long rod and put it aside. Don't let it go too far, though—you'll need it very shortly. If you look down into the bottom upright half of your hi-hat stand, you'll notice a small rod the same size as the thin, threaded rod that you just found (see Figure 2.14).

Figure 2.15
Hi-hat stand part

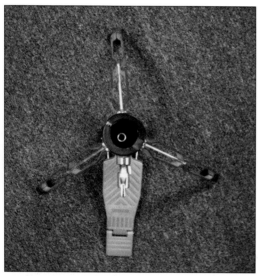

Figure 2.14
Bottom half of hi-hat stand

Thread the two rods together. Now the bottom part of the hi-hat stand should have an extra-long rod sticking out from the open end of it. Depending on the type of hi-hat stand you have, the rod might have a hinge in it, causing it to flop over while still connected, rather than being straight upright. Next, look for a thick, hollow tube with what looks like a small plate on one end with a felt disc stacked on top of it (see Figure 2.15).

Take this hollow tube with the plate side facing up and put it over the long rod, so that the long rod is inside the hollow tube. If your long rod has a

hinge, you'll need to hold it upright as you put the hollow tube over it. When the hollow tube is on the stand surrounding the long rod, tighten the hand screw on the side of it so it will stay in place.

Now it's time to look for the hi-hat cymbals. They are most likely the two smallest cymbals in your collection of cymbals that came with your kit, and they are identical to each other in size, but not always in weight. There's a good chance that you'll find stamped writing on your hi-hat cymbals, telling you which one is the top hi-hat cymbal and which is the bottom hi-hat cymbal. If your cymbals don't have stamped writing on them, then, by holding one in each hand, determine which is heavier. The heavier of the two is the bottom hi-hat cymbal. If you can't determine which is heavier, don't worry about it. They may be the same weight, depending on the kind of hi-hat cymbals you have. If that's the case, it makes no difference which is the bottom or which is the top. Pick one and, with your magical powers, declare it to be the bottom.

Now take the bottom cymbal and, holding it upside down (so that the dome on the top of the cymbal is facing down toward the floor), place it on the hi-hat stand with the thin, long rod going through the hole in the cymbal. The bottom hi-hat cymbal should now be resting on the felt stacked on top of the plate on the end of the hollow tube.

Locate your clutch and the top hi-hat cymbal. If you look at your clutch, you'll see that one end of it has a little disc that you can turn until it comes off of the end of the clutch. Take that disc off of the end of the clutch, along with one of the two small fuzzy discs (called *felts*) that you'll also see there. Now, take your top hi-hat cymbal and put the exposed end of the clutch through the hole in the cymbal and up against the felt, with the dome of the cymbal facing up. Next, take the felt and the disc that you removed from the clutch earlier and thread it onto the exposed end of the clutch that is now sticking out of the hole in the bottom of the top hi-hat cymbal. You will have to hold the cymbal and clutch upside down with the dome of the cymbal facing the floor to do this properly. Now your top hi-hat cymbal has the clutch fully attached to it. If the clutch is not holding the cymbal very tightly and it's wiggling around, tighten it by turning the disc that is now underneath the cymbal. Don't over-tighten it so that it doesn't wiggle at all; tighten it just enough so that it doesn't feel as if it might come undone.

Now, take the cymbal and clutch and insert the long rod sticking out from the top of the hi-hat stand into the hole in the clutch with the cymbal facing right-side up. Your two hi-hat cymbals will now be on top of each other on the hi-hat stand, looking like a sandwich. (If this kind of talk about sandwiches is making you hungry, take a break for lunch.) If you step on the hi-hat pedal, you'll see the rod going up and down uselessly. Step on the pedal just a little bit, and then tighten the hand

screw on the outside of the clutch. Then, when you lift up your foot and the rod goes up, it will take the clutch and the top hi-hat cymbal up along with it. The amount of space between the hi-hat cymbals when your foot is not on the pedal is determined by how much you press down on the pedal while tightening the clutch. The average distance between the two cymbals in the open position should be about an inch.

After you've been playing drums for a while, you'll develop your own idea of how open you want your hi-hats to be in the pedal-up position. Feel free to experiment. If you look on the side of the disc that's under the bottom hi-hat cymbal, you might find a small thumb screw (see Figure 2.16).

Figure 2.16
Thumb screw under the bottom hi-hat cymbal

This is used to tilt the bottom cymbal so that you'll get a solid "chick" sound when you press down on the pedal with your feet and bring the two cymbals together. If you press down on the pedal and you feel a cushion of air, and the sound of the two cymbals joining is not very loud, tilt the bottom cymbal slightly using the thumb screw. In your setup, the hi-hat goes to the left of the snare drum so that you can use your left foot to step on it while playing. By now, you should have your throne, your bass drum with the pedal on it, your snare drum and stand, and your hi-hat in your setup. Go grab your floor tom and put it over to the right, outside of your legs. Now you're ready to move on.

Tom Toms

The *tom toms*—or usually just plain *toms*—are the last drums you will set up in your kit.

You might have two toms in your kit, or you might only have one, depending on whether you have a four-piece or a five-piece kit. Both are fairly standard, although you might often see other drum kits that have a few toms or, in some rare cases, many more toms than one or two. I'm going to assume you have two toms in your kit.

If you do in fact have two toms in your kit, you will notice that one is slightly smaller than the other. We'll call this the first tom. The first tom will be mounted on the bass drum by a piece of hardware called a *rack*. (You might occasionally hear someone refer to their toms as *rack toms*; now you know why. They might also be called *mounted* toms because they are mounted on the bass drum. If you're really old-school, you might refer to them as *ride* toms, because they ride on the bass drum. You dig? I call them *rack toms*. I guess that makes me middle-aged school.)

The L-shaped piece of tubing goes into the hole on the top-left side of the bass drum (if you're sitting behind the kit), long end first. Tighten the hand screw on the mounting bracket on the bass drum to fasten it in place. Then, insert the short end of the tube into the hole in the side of the first tom.

You might have to loosen the tom mount on the bass drum in order to swing the tom around to a playing position, which should be above the snare drum at a tilt.

Once you have the first tom locked into a playing position, repeat the entire procedure for the second tom. Obviously, the second tom will be at your right, next to the first tom. You should now have the bass drum in front of you with the bass drum pedal under your right foot, the snare drum on its stand in front of you between your legs, the hi-hat cymbals on their stand to the left and somewhat higher than the snare drum, with the hi-hat pedal under your left foot. The mounted toms should be in front of you, above the snare and tilted slightly toward you, and the floor tom should be at your right, slightly tilted toward you (see Figure 2.17).

Figure 2.17
Toms set up on the bass drum

Now we set up the cymbals.

Cymbals

When it comes to cymbals, there are four basic types: *hi-hat* cymbals, *crash* cymbals, *ride* cymbals, and what we call *special effects* cymbals. You've already met your hi-hat cymbals when you were setting them up earlier, so now I'll talk about the other types.

The Crash Cymbal

If your new kit has only one cymbal, it is likely to be a crash cymbal. These can vary in size, usually from 16 to 20 inches. The cymbal in your kit that is the next size larger than your hi-hats is most likely your crash cymbal. (When you're learning how to play later on in this book, you'll get a full explanation of the different types of cymbals and their uses, but for now let's just get them set up.) Earlier, I had you set up the cymbal stands, so let's bring that crash cymbal over to one of them and take a look at that stand. You'll notice that the height of the cymbal stands can be adjusted, so bring the height of the cymbal stand high enough so you can stand up and work with it. At the top of the stand, you'll see what's called the cymbal *tilter*.

The tilter may or may not be in a folded-up position when you first go to set it up. You'll know it's in the folded-up position if you're looking at it and you can't picture a cymbal being attached to it. In this case, simply unscrew the hand screw that you'll find on the side of the tilter just enough so you can move the tilter up and down. Put the tilter in a more or less horizontal position, and use the same hand screw to tighten it in place. When the tilter is in its upright position, you should see either a metal wing nut or a plastic sleeve, two felts, and a metal disc, all stacked up on each other on the tilter.

To put the cymbal on the stand, unscrew the wing nut or sleeve all the way and put it aside (but not too far aside because you're going to need it again in a second). Next, take one of the two felts off the tilter and place the cymbal right-side up on the stand on top of the remaining felt. Then, take the first felt and put it on top of the cymbal. Now, take the wing nut or sleeve and screw it on top of the tilter. When screwing down the wing nut on top of the cymbal stand, be careful not to screw it down so tightly that the cymbal barely moves when it's on the stand. You want the cymbal to have as much movement on the stand as it can without falling off. If you put the death grip on the wing nut, you run the risk of breaking your cymbals by not allowing them free motion when they're being played.

Now that the crash cymbal is on its stand, you can put it in your setup. As a general rule, most drum kits have only one set of hi-hat cymbals and one ride cymbal, but they can have any number of crash cymbals. For example, my setup has three different crash cymbals in various places. If you have only one crash cymbal at this time, the best place to put it would be between the hi-hats and the first tom.

The crash cymbal is made to be hit on its edge, so you should put it at a more or less horizontal position. Put it at a height that's comfortable for you and the length of your arms. Be careful not to put it up so high that you need to stretch your arm all the way to hit it, and don't put it low enough to knock against the top of your hi-hat stand or your first tom when it's in free motion after being hit. Think of the height that Goldilocks would like: just right.

The Ride Cymbal

The ride cymbal is most likely the largest and heaviest cymbal in your collection. Go ahead and put it on a cymbal stand the same way that you put your crash cymbal on its stand, with one felt under the cymbal and one felt and the wing nut on top of the cymbal. You might want to tighten down the wing nut just a little bit more than you did with the crash cymbal, but again, not too much.

On a regular right-handed kit setup, the ride cymbal should be placed above the floor tom on the right side of your kit. Because the ride cymbal is made to be played on its top and not its edge, like the crash cymbal, it should not be placed up as high as the crash cymbal. Be careful not to place it low enough so that it knocks against the top of your floor tom, either. Be a little Goldilocks again, and find just the right height for you. Now it's time to go have some porridge because your kit is all set up. Your setup should look something like Figure 2.18.

Special Effect Cymbals

Special effect cymbals usually don't come with a beginner's kit, but can be added later. These include *splash* cymbals (tiny crash cymbals) or *china-type* cymbals, which can sound like either a really bad trashcan lid or a really good one. China-type cymbals have very unique upturned edges and are made to be mounted upside down on a cymbal stand so that the underside or shoulder of the cymbal is easily struck, creating a very intense barking type of sound, sending cats on the run for miles around and creating a chain reaction of dogs barking throughout your neighborhood.

Figure 2.18
A complete setup

Hey Lefty!

In drumming there is not only a right way and a wrong way, but there's also a right way and a left way to set up your kit. I've shown you the way to set up your drum kit for a right-handed (and right-footed) person. I suppose the majority of people in the world are right-handed, but maybe you're left-handed. If you *are* left-handed, then there is a good chance that you're left-footed also.

In that case, your drum setup would be identical to a right-handed setup as far as where all the parts of the kit would go in relation to each other, but completely reversed, as in a mirror. For example, in a right-handed setup, the snare drum would be between your legs, and the hi-hats would be to your left. Your left foot would be on the hi-hat pedal, your right foot would be on the bass drum pedal, and the toms would go from smallest to largest from left to right in front of you. In a left-handed setup, the snare drum would still be between your legs, but the hi-hats would be to your right, with your right foot on the hi-hat pedal, your left foot on the bass drum pedal, and the drums in descending order from right to left in front of you.

No special gear needs to be added to your kit if you're left-handed. The only possible drawback to playing on a left-handed setup is that you would have to reverse everything on someone else's kit if you wanted to play a friend's right-handed kit or if you wanted to sit in with a band whose drummer is already set up in a right-handed manner. I have a couple of students who play a left-handed setup, and it just takes a few minutes to reverse everything when it's their turn for a lesson. It's really not that big of a deal, but it is something to be aware of if you're a left-handed person.

There are some even more rare cases (like myself) in which drummers play a left-handed but right-footed setup. In that case, the drum set is set up completely for a right-handed person, but the ride cymbal is moved over to the left side of the kit instead of the right, over near the floor tom. To play drums in this way requires slightly different playing techniques than just a full right- or left-handed setup; I will demonstrate on the DVD.

If you're left-handed, you might want to check out a left-handed/right-footed setup and playing style. It might work for you—it worked for me. I don't have to reverse a right-handed kit completely, just the ride cymbal position. So actually, there is no right or wrong way to set up. Nor is there a right or left way. But if you're right-handed, you don't have to worry about any of this. See what we left-handed people have to deal with? Unfortunately, it's a right-handed world. But not for long. When I rule the world, which I'm planning on doing very soon after I finish writing this book, there are going to be some changes made. Yes, indeed. Big-time changes.

Accessories

THERE ARE SOME OTHER THINGS you should pick up that will be essential to your drumming education. I've listed these accessories in order of importance.

1. **A metronome: It's about time!** A metronome is a mechanical or electronic device that keeps perfect time. The electronic kind, preferably one with a headphone jack, is best for a drummer (see Figure 2.19).

Figure 2.19
An electronic metronome

Learning to work with a metronome is crucial for any drummer, because it allows the drummer to gauge his or her sense of time against the perfect time of the metronome. There are exercises later in this book that will require a metronome, so for that reason alone, you definitely should pick one up as soon as you can. You'll also need a decent pair of headphones or ear buds to use with your metronome.

2. **Huh? Hearing protection and you.** If you plan on having good hearing for the rest of your drumming career and your life, start thinking about hearing protection now. I know you're probably not in the mood to hear a lecture, but hear me out for a few minutes (pun intended). I never used hearing protection when I was young and starting out, so I have suffered significant hearing damage over the years. It's a real drag having to ask people to repeat themselves constantly and having to watch TV with headphones on because I can't hear from across the room.

It's very easy to imagine that your hearing is always going to be tip-top, but if you practice for hours on end (which I hope you will) without protection of any type (which I hope you won't), that type of abuse can catch up to you very quickly. Your parents are right about some things. It's not true that if you keep making that funny face, your real face will freeze that way, but it *is* true that you will lose at least some of your hearing if you play very loudly without using hearing protection of some kind. The sooner you get used to the sound of your drums with earplugs in, the better.

I'm not trying to discourage you from hitting the drums hard when you play them. A confident playing style is important, but not as important as your hearing. I actually prefer the sound of my drums with my plugs in. When I take them out, the drums sound too harsh to me. You can find suitable earplugs not only at a music store, but also at a drugstore or supermarket. You might have to try a couple of different types before you settle on the ones that will work best for you. I always keep a bag of them in my stick bag, and so should you. This concludes my lecture on protecting your hearing.

3. **A blank manuscript book.** This a notebook that has a music staff instead of the usual lines to write on that you would find in a regular notebook. You'll need this for your lessons so your teacher can write down the exercises that you'll be working on.

4. **A music stand.** This will come in very handy when you're working on exercises out of your book at home. It's true that you could simply put the book down on your floor tom to read it…until you go to play something that actually uses the floor tom. Then you'll probably try to balance it on the bass drum or on your lap while playing, but you'll end up in frustration as it falls to the floor again and again. Save yourself this aggravation by getting a music stand. There's probably no need to get a big, fancy, expensive stand. The fold-up kind should work out just fine. They're not very expensive at all. Ask for them by name—they're called "the fold-up kind."

5. **An alarm clock or a timer with a buzzer or bell.** I know what you're thinking: "What does an alarm clock have to do with drumming?" Well, most people will tell you that an alarm clock has nothing to do with drumming. But then again, I'm not most people. I will be showing you a practice technique later in this book that will use an alarm clock as a tool. The best kind would be a digital clock whose alarm you can easily figure out how to set. Or, you might find a timer on which you could set an alarm, such as a cooking timer. You might already have one in your kitchen. Just make sure that you put the cooking timer back where you found it before someone notices that it's missing. Or better yet, go buy your own alarm clock or timer.

6. **Stick + Bag = Stick bag.** A good stick bag is a wonderful thing indeed (see Figure 2.20). For one thing, you can keep your sticks in it. Also, a good stick bag will have a little pocket on the side in which you can keep your drum keys. Most stick bags have elastic straps with hooks at the end of them so you can hang your stick bag on your floor tom, keeping your sticks well within reach. (For some reason, I never seem to do this. Instead, I usually lean my stick bag up against the floor tom so I can be absolutely sure that at some point the bag will fall over, putting my sticks out of my reach. I wonder why I do this. Fear of commitment, probably.) You could spend as much money as you want on a fancy stick bag with a really cool color or design, but why bother?

You might see a deal in a music store where if you buy a certain number of sticks, you get a free stick bag. That's probably where I got my stick bag 20 years ago. When it comes to a stick bag, I say the simpler the better.

Figure 2.20
A stick bag

7. **Speed key: For those who just can't wait.**
A speed key is a drum key with a crank-type design that is much faster to use than a regular drum key. It's not absolutely necessary to have one of these, but if you ever find yourself having to change a head in a hurry, you'll be glad that you have one (see Figure 2.21).

Figure 2.21
A speed key

8. **Brush up.** Brushes are sometimes used as an alternative to sticks in a quieter playing situation or for playing certain types of jazz. The use of wire-type brushes requires special technique, while plastic or wooden bundle-type brushes can be used much like sticks. These are not absolutely essential when you're first starting out, so there's no great hurry to acquire brushes, but if you're interested in playing jazz or you want to experiment a little with different sounds and techniques, pick up a pair. I always have a pair of both wire and plastic bundle types in my stick bag. But then again, I also have five different toothbrushes, and I sometimes go weeks without using any of them. If you want to see what brushes look like, look at the picture of the stick bag and you'll see a pair tucked into the bag. They are the things that are not sticks.

9. **Cases and bags: No hurry.** There are any number of types of hard cases or soft bags available for your drums and cymbals that are great to have if you plan to take your drums out of the house and on the road a lot, but they are not necessary right away.

Now let's learn how to play drums.

In Which You'll Learn a New Language and Meet the

"Big Three"

IKNOW WHAT YOU'RE THINKING: "I thought drummers didn't read music. That's the whole reason why I wanted to play drums in the first place—so that I wouldn't have to learn how to read. None of my favorite famous drummers that I see on MTV read music." It's true that you might not see your favorite drummer with a music stand onstage with all his drum parts on it, but more drummers know how to read music than you think.

Reading Drum Music: Stop Your Whining

I PROMISE YOU THAT READING DRUM music is nowhere near as hard as you think it is. I've taught kids so young that they still had their baby teeth when they showed up for lessons on how to read music. By the time their baby teeth fell out, they were reading drum music better than they were reading words in the English language. They might have walked into the wrong public bathroom because they couldn't tell whether it said "Men" or "Women," but they were reading drum music as if it was second nature. And that's not just because I'm the world's greatest teacher. (Look it up in the *Guinness Book* if you don't believe me.) It's because reading drum music is easy.

It's Just a Language

The most important thing for you to understand about drum music before we actually dive into learning it is that it's just another language. One of the ways we can use language is to describe specific objects to each other. Let me give you an example. Suppose I wanted to describe to you something that I saw outside in the yard. I could say, "I saw this thing out in the yard. It was attached to the ground, it was brown, and it had green stuff near the top of it. What was it?" Your first answer would probably be, "That's a tree, silly. It's growing out of the ground, the brown part is the trunk, and the green stuff near the top is leaves. It's called a tree." But as it turns out, the object that I saw was a brown fence painted green near the top. If, instead of trying to describe the object using a whole bunch of words that could be easily misunderstood, I simply said the word "fence," you would have immediately known what I was talking about. Everyone knows what a fence is. That's why we use the word "fence" when we mean "fence."

In case you think I'm totally nuts for talking about trees and fences in a drumming book, let me tie it together for you. When there's something in this book that I want you to work on, I can write it out in a language that we both understand so we can be absolutely sure that we're both thinking about the same thing. Music notation is simply a language that I can use to show you how to play something without being wherever you are and playing it in front of you. It's sometimes true that the best way to learn how to play something new on the drums is to watch or hear someone play that something new in front of you enough times that you can begin to develop an understanding of how it's done. Then you can try it on your own with a pretty good idea of how to get started.

On the DVD that came with this package, you will see examples of me doing just that—playing something new for you a few times so you can get the hang of it. But in my opinion, learning by seeing and hearing can only take you so far. By using music notation, you will have a deeper and longer-lasting understanding of how something is played, because by knowing how to understand and read the notation, a concrete picture of what's being learned will form in your head.

More Reasons to Learn to Read Music

So you want more reasons to learn to read music? How about these?

Such Sweet Memories

Another benefit of using notation to learn is that you will have an easier time retaining what you've learned because you have that concrete picture in your head of how a particular exercise looks and sounds. The more concrete the picture in your head of an exercise, the easier it will be to have total recall of that exercise later.

When you are learning to play the drums, there will be many times when we will take an exercise that we've learned in the past and add something new to it, thus creating a new exercise to play. In other words, we'll constantly add new things to learn and play that build on things we've played before. Because of this, it's extremely important that you remember every exercise that you've ever learned. You don't play something correctly a few times and then consider it done and completely flush it from your memory. You'll need to call up that exercise in your memory in the future in order to build on it to create something new, so you'll need to hold on to it.

Unless you happen to possess an extraordinary memory, this will be a difficult task. When you know how to read music, you will have a better chance of recalling an exercise because you'll have not only the memory of how it's supposed to sound, but you'll also have a memory of how it looked when it was written out. Also, if you know how to read music and your teacher wants to remind you of something that you've played in the past, he needs only write it out for you to jog your memory. I do this all the time with my students. I'll write out something that I know they already know how to play, but haven't played in a while. They'll look at it for two seconds and immediately remember it and play it perfectly. I can then take the exercise as it's written out in notation and add some notes to it to create something brand new to play. It's not like the students are learning something new from the very beginning—instead, they're relearning something they already knew and adding to it.

Pick It Up

Being able to read and understand notation will greatly increase the speed at which you can pick up new things to play. If you rely on memory alone, you don't stand as good a chance of remembering everything that you've ever learned as easily as someone who reads and understands notation will. It's as simple as that.

Reading music will also help you with the homework you will get from your drum teacher. Usually, when I show one of my students something new that I think they should work on, I will play it for them over and over until they let me know that they think they have a good enough understanding of it to try it themselves. While they're working on playing it, I'll write down the exercise in their manuscript book while I'm listening. Then, I can point to the exact spot in the notation that they might be having trouble with.

This takes the guesswork out of learning. The students know by looking at the notation exactly where the danger zone is. Then, I have them work on playing it while reading the notation, which usually clears up any confusion they might have had about what they should be playing and when. If we both feel that the part could use a little more work, their homework assignment is to work on that particular exercise at home over the next week.

Now, unless they go straight home from drum lessons and start to work on that exercise, the chances are not very great of them remembering a few days later exactly what they were working on at lessons. When they're ready to work on the new exercise, all they have to do is open their book to the notation of that exercise, and it will probably take them just a few tries while reading it to get right back to the point at which they left off in their lesson. Then, the students can make real progress at learning something new, rather than wasting time trying to relearn something they already know. Without knowing how to read, the students would have to rely on their memory alone to pick up where they left off.

Knowing how to read music will also allow you to learn new routines from drum books and magazines. You'll be able to open any drum book or look at any written example in a drum magazine and instantly pick up something new to work on. This ability will allow you to greatly add to your drum vocabulary. You might see a transcription of a popular song in a drum magazine that you'd like to learn, and if you know how to read, you can get started on it right away.

School Band: Make Friends and Get an Easy Credit

If you know how to read music, you can be in your school band. Maybe you have no interest in being in the school band because you think it's uncool. That's fine, but consider this: I was in every one of my school bands, and I'm the coolest dude in the world. Just ask me.

Seriously, I'm a firm believer in pursuing every musical experience you can. Every musical experience that I've had in my educational training has contributed greatly to my overall musicality, especially working with a conductor. If you can learn to watch a conductor, look at your music, and play your parts all at the same time, playing a drum kit will be much easier.

Also, you can make friends in band. I had some great times with some really funny people in my school bands. And you might make friends of the opposite sex that become more than just friends, if you know what I mean. Having friends like that can make band trips and those Saturday afternoon football games much more interesting. (How do I know? Well now, that's a whole other book.)

If you need another good reason to be in the school band, think about the easy credit. In case you're not in high school yet, let me explain. When you get to high school, you're allowed to pick some of the classes that you take. All classes have a credit value attached to them, and you need to have a certain amount of credits each school year in order to advance to the next school year. Band is usually worth one credit, which will come in handy since you probably won't find being in the band too hard. There are usually no written exams, and if you show up to all the classes and concerts, you get a credit. If you know how to read music, this will be an easy credit. Plus, your band might go on trips to other parts of the country, which can be a lot of fun. The first time I ever went to Disneyland was with my school band, and it was one of the best times of my life.

More about That Language Thing

Knowing how to read and understand music notation will also be useful if you find yourself in a musical situation outside of school with other players who read and understand music notation. When everybody is on the same page in the way they communicate musical ideas to each other, the creative process can be much less confusing and much more productive. The band leader might ask you to play "straight eighths on the hi-hat, kick drum on one and three, and snare on two and four." If you don't know what he's talking about, you're in for an embarrassing experience as you try desperately to come up with something. As I said before, music notation is simply a language that we can use to communicate musical ideas. Being able to name things for the sake of discussing them can make the creation of music so much easier. So, now that you know why you should read music notation, let me show you how.

To Play or Not to Play: Notes and Rests

THIS IS FAIRLY SELF-EXPLANATORY but in case this is completely new to you, in musical notation a *note* is an indication to play, or in the case of drum notation, to hit something. The amount of time we wait before we play (or hit) something again after hitting it once is determined by what kind of note it is. Each kind of note has its own time value, and knowing the value of each kind of note will determine how long you wait until you play the next note.

Keeping track of the differences between the kinds of notes is easy because they all look slightly different from each other. Knowing the time value of each note and recognizing what each note looks like will give you the ability to read those notes and to play on the drums what those notes indicate. Each note (which is just an indication to play something) comes with its own indication not to play, called a *rest*. For example, there are quarter notes and quarter rests, eighth notes and eighth rests, and so on. A rest is an indication not only *not* to play, but for *how long* not to play. If this seems a little bit confusing right now, don't worry. It will make more sense to you when you see it written out if you just try to make some sense of it now. Now, we need somewhere to write these notes and rests that we're talking about.

The Framework: Staff, Key, Measures, Beats, and Time Signature

T HE MUSICAL NOTES THAT WE WILL be working with will appear on something called a *staff* (see Figure 3.1).

Figure 3.1
A staff

Your blank manuscript notebook has pages of blank staffs in which you or your teacher can write notes. The staff has five lines and four spaces that you can use to place notes where you want them. Because the drum kit as an instrument has many different parts to play (different drums and different cymbals), you can use the staff to show what to hit and when. You can assign each line or space to represent a different part, or voice, of the drum kit. You will usually find those assignments laid out at the beginning of a piece of music, and that layout is called a *key* or *legend*.

This is not to be confused with what is called the *tonal key* to a song, about which you might hear other musicians who play instruments that deal with specific pitches talk. There is no tonal key in drum music. In other words, drums are not in any specific key. The notes in drum music fall on certain spaces or lines on the staff according to their key or legend, not according to the tonal key of the song.

For an example of a key for drum music, take a look at Figure 3.2.

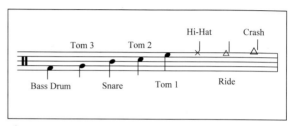

Figure 3.2
Drum music key or legend

So now you know that whenever you see a note in the top space of the staff that has an x instead of a regular note as its body, that particular note is meant to be played on the hi-hat. When you see a note or rest on the bottom line, that note is meant to be played on the bass drum, and so on for all the other voices of the kit. Sometimes, instead of a key, you might see words right near the notes at the beginning of the piece of music, indicating to you what's what. When you look at a blank manuscript page, you will see the five lines and spaces flow uninterrupted across the page. When you read or write music on those lines, however, you'll see and use other lines that will be placed vertically (straight up and down) against the horizontal (straight across) lines of the staff, as shown in Figure 3.3.

These lines are called *measure lines* or *bar lines*, and the space between any two of these vertical lines is called a *measure* or a *bar*. The notes and rests will now be seen within a measure, like words in a sentence. A drum part (or *pattern*, as you'll sometimes hear it called by drummers) is made up of a measure or a group of measures, like sentences in a paragraph.

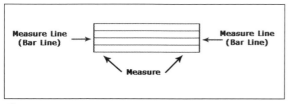

Figure 3.3
Lines in a measure

Working with measures is very important when discussing specific parts of songs. You can count measures in a pattern or song and name them according to their corresponding numbers. For example, you can now refer to "the third measure" or "measure 312," and so on.

Measures themselves vary in length according to rules that are set down at the beginning of a piece of music, called a *time signature*. A time signature looks like a fraction. (I know, I know. You hate fractions. They remind you of math class, and you hate math class. I hated math class too, but don't worry. These are friendly fractions. We only have to understand what they mean. We don't have to add them together or divide them or any of that stuff.) Let's look at a time signature—see Figure 3.4.

Figure 3.4
A time signature

This time signature is called *four-four* and is the most common for most of the styles of music that you're likely to want to play. The top number of the time signature tells you how many *beats* there are in a measure. A beat is simply the musical term for a part. All the parts of a measure are equal in length of time, kind of like how a football game has four quarters that are all of an equal time length.

You will now also be able to name the beats of a measure with numbers in order. For example, if you want to talk about the third part of a measure, you would say "beat three." The bottom number of the time signature tells you what kind of note will equal the length of one beat—the number four in this case, indicating a *quarter note* (see Figure 3.5).

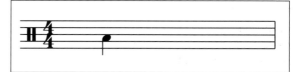

Figure 3.5
One quarter note in a measure of 4/4

So, the two important bits of information that a time signature of 4/4 tells you is that there will be four beats per measure (the top four of the fraction) and that a quarter note will equal one beat (the bottom four of the fraction). So, a measure of 4/4 with four quarter notes in it looks like Figure 3.6.

Figure 3.6
Four quarter notes in a measure of 4/4

Quarter Notes versus Eighth Notes

YOU ALREADY LEARNED ABOUT the quarter note in the last section. Now, let's meet a new note called the *eighth note* (see Figure 3.7).

Figure 3.7
Two eighth notes in a measure of 4/4

As you learned earlier, you can fit only four quarter notes in a measure of 4/4, and since two times four is eight, you can fit eight eighth notes in a measure of 4/4, as shown in Figure 3.8. That's why it's called an eighth note.

Figure 3.8
Eight eighth notes in a measure of 4/4

You can give each eighth note its own name, just like you did earlier with quarter notes. However, instead of naming each eighth note in a measure with its own number (1, 2, 3, 4, 5, 6, 7, 8), we will name them like you see in Figure 3.9, using the symbol + in between each number (1+2+3+4+).

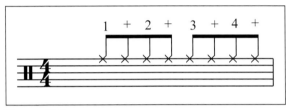

Figure 3.9
Eight eighth notes counted out in a measure of 4/4

You pronounce the + symbol as the word "and." So, if you wanted to count out the eight notes in a measure, you would say "one-and-two-and-three-and-four-and." Eighth notes are played twice as fast as quarter notes. Let's use a metronome to demonstrate this.

Take your metronome and set it at 66. (The numbers on your metronome represent *tempo*, the musical term for the speed at which you'll play something. The number 66 means that you'll play something at 66 BPM, or 66 beats per minute.) Listen to the metronome click at 66 BPM, and imagine that each click is a quarter note. Now, count along to the clicks from one to four, and then back through one to four again, and so on, like this: *One, two, three, four, one, two, three, four.*

This represents the speed at which quarter notes are played at this tempo. So, if you want to figure out how eighth notes would sound at this tempo, all you have to do is continue to count from one to four at the same speed as you did earlier, and simply add the word "and" between each number, like this: *One and two and three and four and one and two and three and four and.*

This is how eight notes will sound at this tempo, and that is what you will play on your hi-hats in a few minutes, when you learn your first beat.

Beat: A Word with Two Meanings

In drumming, you will hear the word *beat* used to mean two different things. One usage indicates specific beats of a measure (beat 2, beat 3, and so on). The other way to use the word *beat* is to indicate a pattern that you would play on the drum kit, as in, "Play that funky beat, yo." Another word to describe a pattern on the drums that you might hear is *groove*, as in "Play that funky groove, yo."

Groove #1

LET'S LOOK AT A MEASURE of 4/4 with four quarter notes in it, as shown in Figure 3.10.

Figure 3.10
Four quarter notes in a measure of 4/4

Now let's split up those quarter notes within the drum kit. Play the first quarter note on the bass drum using your right foot. Now, play the second quarter note on the snare drum with your left hand. Now, repeat those two moves for the last two beats of the measure. (See Figure 3.11.)

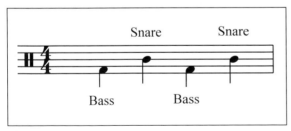

Figure 3.11
Four quarter notes in a measure of 4/4, split up between the bass drum and the snare drum

So now you have a bass drum on beats 1 and 3 and snare drum on beats 2 and 4 of the measure. Now, let's add eighth notes on the hi-hat using your right hand (see Figure 3.12).

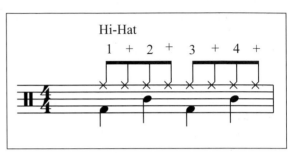

Figure 3.12
Four quarter notes in a measure of 4/4, split up between the bass drum and the snare drum with eighth notes on the hi-hats

When using your right hand to play the hi-hat, it should cross over and above your left hand, as shown in Figure 3.13. You can check out the DVD if you're having trouble picturing where your hands are supposed to be.

Figure 3.13
Groove #1 playing position

Now that you're in your main playing position, take a quick moment to make sure that you can comfortably reach the parts of your kit that you'll be using. Pay attention to the height of your throne and make sure you're not sitting too high or too low, and that you can reach both the hi-hat and bass drum pedals comfortably. Also, make sure that your hi-hats are up high enough so that when you use your right hand to play them, there's enough room under your right arm for your left arm to play the snare drum comfortably. Your left foot should be resting on the hi-hat pedal, keeping the hi-hat cymbals in the closed position. Your right foot should be on the bass drum pedal, obviously. Again, please check out the DVD if you're having trouble picturing any of this.

When you first try to play this pattern, remember that the hi-hat should be playing steady eighth notes, one after the other without stopping or slowing down. If you find yourself having to slow down the hi-hats to concentrate on playing a snare or bass drum hit, you need to work a little harder to keep those hi-hats steady. This will be true of every other pattern that you will ever learn on the drums, so the sooner you concentrate on and master the steadiness of the hi-hat , the better.

Also, when you first work on playing this groove, pay close attention to whether your hi-hat notes are lining up directly with the applicable quarter note. For example, make sure that you're playing the bass drum and the hi-hat as close to perfectly together as you can in the first and third beats of the measure. The same thing goes for the snare drum and the hi-hats together in beats 2 and 4 of the measure. You want to make sure everything that's supposed to be hit together is actually hit together as closely as you can possibly make them. This will make your grooves sound nice and tight, as they should sound.

When you can play this measure once nice and steady, try playing it twice in a row. Then try playing it as many times in a row as you can. It's very important to play every example that you learn as many times in a row as you can without making a mistake. The drummer's main job in the band is to create a solid rhythmic foundation for the rest of the band to play along with, and to a drummer, that often means playing the same patterns over and over again. And then over and over again.

By the way, this beat that you're now learning to play could be described as "straight eights on the hi-hat, kick drum on one and three, and snare drum on two and four." Does that sound familiar? It should. I used this exact description of a beat earlier in this section of the book as an example of something that a band mate might use to describe what he wants you to play on the drums. Now, you're speaking his language.

It's time to congratulate yourself. You've just learned your first beat. This is the first day of the rest of your life. Or the first 10 minutes of the rest of your hour. Or something like that.

Get a Grip

There are two different ways to hold drumsticks, called *grips*, and the most common is is called a *matched* grip (see Figure 3.14). This is called matched grip because both hands grip the stick in the same way. In other words, they match.

The other grip is called the *traditional* grip (see Figure 3.15). This grip is used mostly by drummers in a drum corps or any kind of marching type situation for the simple reason that when using this grip, both arms will be at the side of the player even though the marching drum that he or she is using may be tilted to the right as it is being worn.

If you tried to use the matched grip while playing a marching snare drum that you're wearing while it's tilted to the right, your left elbow would be sticking out at an angle. Some players feel that the traditional grip offers them more agility and control over their sticks, but this is open to debate. It is generally agreed that you can play louder using the matched grip, and in rock music you'll mostly see the matched grip used. I would suggest that you use the matched grip to get started, and then after you've been playing for a few weeks, check out the traditional grip to see whether it feels good to you. If it does, go with it. If it feels awkward to you, then go with the matched grip. I play matched grip, if that makes any difference to you.

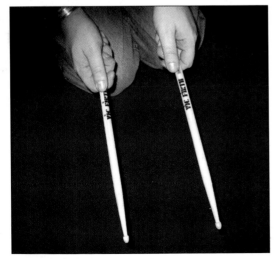

Figure 3.14
Matched grip

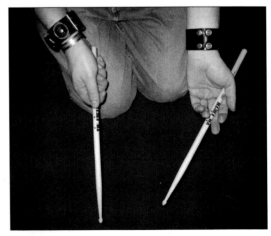

Figure 3.15
Traditional grip

Groove #2

THE SECOND BEAT THAT YOU WILL now learn is remarkably similar to the one you just learned. In fact, we're going to add only one note to the first beat to make the second beat (see Figure 3.16). This new note will be played on the bass drum, in a place called the "and of three." As I explained before, each eighth note in a measure can be named (1+2+3+4+). In this new beat, there's a bass drum note not only on the note we're calling "3," but also on the eighth note immediately after it. Because this eighth note immediately after "3" is what we're calling an "and" (+), we will call it the "and of three." Just like in the first beat you learned, you'll play steady eighth notes on the hi-hat, and snare drum on beats 2 and 4. The only note we'll add is a bass drum note on the "and of three." In Figure 3.17, I've circled the eighth notes where the bass drum will be to make it easier for you to understand this.

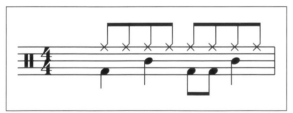

Figure 3.16
Groove #2

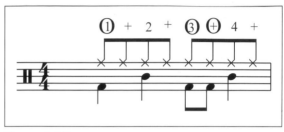

Figure 3.17
Groove #2 with circled bass-drum notes

Try it now, taking your time like you did for your first beat, and don't get discouraged if it doesn't come to you right away. Remember, just like with the first groove you learned, make sure everything that's supposed to be hit together is hit together as tightly as possible. Concentrate on making this groove as tight as you can. If it's tight, it's all right. If it's loose, try it again until it's tight.

When in Doubt, Count It Out

If you're having a hard time figuring out where the new bass drum note is supposed to be, don't be afraid to count it out. Counting out loud can sometimes be the best thing to do to fully understand where a note is supposed to be. If you always at least count out the eighth notes in your head (1+2+3+4+), you'll know right where a new note should be.

Groove #3

THIS BEAT (see Figure 3.18) is so similar to the last one that your biggest challenge will be telling the difference between the two. We're not even going to add any notes to the last beat you learned to make this new one. All we're going to do is take one bass drum note and move it to a different eighth note position. We'll still have a bass drum note on beat 3 of the measure, but we're now going to take the bass drum note that was on the "and of three" and move it to the "and of two" instead.

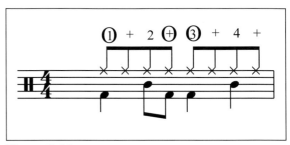

Figure 3.19
Groove #3 with circled bass-drum notes

One of these beats is not harder to play than the other; they are just different. One may come easier to you than the other. That's perfectly natural; you'll just have to work a little bit harder on whichever one gives you a little bit of trouble. Take your time and play as slow as you need to in order to get it down. Also, never be afraid to count it out if you need to. After you can play it once, try playing it twice in a row just like you did for the previous two beats you learned. Then see how many times in a row you can play it without making a mistake. If you can play it at least 10 times in a row, you're in pretty good shape. And remember, always aim for tightness.

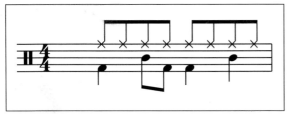

Figure 3.18
Groove #3

In Figure 3.19, I've circled the eighth notes where the bass drum will be so you can see exactly where the bass drum notes are. Compare this circled-note version with the circled-note version of the last beat to fully understand the difference between these two beats.

Review

CONGRATULATIONS! You've just mastered the first and most important beats in rock drumming history. The most important thing for you to do at this point is to make absolutely sure that you understand the difference between all three of these beats—especially the difference between the second beat and the third beat. Each of them has its own special feel that makes it quite different from another, even though they all have the exact same number of notes.

When the time comes for you to make up your own drum beat to a song that your band might be working on, having the second and third beats in your bag of tricks will be very important. Then, you can try each of these to see which one fits the best with what the rest of the band is playing. Often

you may hear a drummer on a recording playing something that sounds much more complicated than either of these two beats, but usually it's just one of these beats with some extra notes added on to it. The basic groove underneath all the extra notes will most likely be one of these beats.

To help you remember all three beats, Figure 3.20 presents an exercise for you to try. Use your metronome to help you develop steady time when switching from one groove to the next. Try a tempo setting of 70 to start with and, when you feel comfortable with that tempo, experiment with a faster tempo.

When you can play this exercise perfectly from start to finish, you're ready to move on to the next chapter. I'll see you there.

Figure 3.20
Review

In Which You'll Count to 16, Get Filled In on Fills, Crash without Getting Hurt, and Learn What Your Left

Foot Is For

MEET YOUR NEW FRIEND, the sixteenth note. You'll like your new friend because he gives you twice as much of everything as your old friend the eighth note did. But that doesn't mean you should completely forget about the old eighth note. You'll have to keep him around, even if it's just to remind yourself of how he's only half of your new friend.

Sixteenth Notes Equal Twice as Many Friends

TO UNDERSTAND HOW SIXTEENTH notes work, you'll need your metronome. This time, set it at a tempo reading of 132. Now, count the clicks of the metronome as eighth notes, like this: *1+2+3+4+1+2+3+4+....* Sixteenth notes are twice as fast as eighth notes, just as two times eight is sixteen. To review, we count eighth notes like what you see in Figure 4.1.

To count sixteenth notes, add the vowel "e" between each number and the "and" that comes after it, and then add the vowel "a" (pronounced like the "a" in the word *above*) after each "and." See Figure 4.2.

Here's an exercise to try that will get you started playing sixteenth notes. You can play this on your snare drum with your metronome set back at a tempo of 66 BPM. Each click of the metronome will equal a quarter note. Start with your right hand, and then alternate between your left and your right with each stroke. The letters "R" and "L" at the top of Figure 4.3 will help you. (If you're left-handed, start this exercise with your left hand and alternate accordingly.)

Figure 4.1
A measure of eighth notes counted out

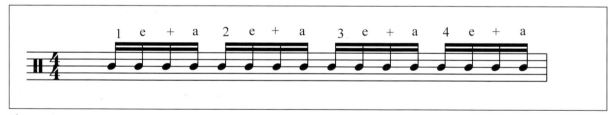

Figure 4.2
A measure of sixteenth notes counted out

Figure 4.3
Sixteenth-note exercise with sticking

Fill 'Er Up

IT'S TIME TO LEARN ABOUT DRUM *fills.* Fills are what the drummer plays when he's not playing a groove. They can be used to fill up either part of a measure or sometimes the entire measure, and they are an exciting way to send the message that a new part of the song is about to arrive. Fills can be very simple or very complex. They can use every drum in the kit, or they can use just one drum. They can be long or short. They can be the most positive attention-getting device a drummer can use, or they can be the most embarrassing moments you'll ever share with other human beings, depending on whether you pull one off correctly. Don't be too scared, though. We'll go slow. You can use your new knowledge of sixteenth notes to create many fills.

Use Your Metronome When Learning Fills

When you're working on any of the fills in this chapter, once you feel fairly comfortable with the exercise, you should practice it with your metronome as soon as you can. It's very important that the transitions from the groove to the fill and back to the groove again be as smooth as possible, and working with a metronome is the best way to develop that smoothness. When you set a tempo

at which to practice an exercise, imagine that each click of the metronome is a quarter note. The eighth notes that you'll play on your hi-hats will be twice as fast as those quarter notes. Experiment until you find a tempo that you can work with comfortably. There are no extra points for speed, so try not to be in a hurry to play a tempo that's too fast for you to play steadily. It's better to play a slower tempo more solidly than to play a faster tempo unsteadily.

Fill #1

Let's start with a very short fill that uses sixteenth notes. This particular fill will come at the very end of a measure, so the exercise that we'll use will be two measures long. When learning a new fill, there are three important questions to ask:

1. When does the fill begin?

2. What is the fill?

3. How do we get back to the groove that we were playing before we took the fill?

Let's look at the exercise (see Figure 4.4) to determine the answers to these questions.

Figure 4.4
Fill #1

When Does the Fill Begin?

As you can see, the groove itself is the same as the very first groove you learned in the last chapter, and you'll play that groove all the way up to beat 4, when you'll begin the fill on the "+ of 4."

What Is the Fill?

The fill itself consists of two sixteenth notes on the snare drum, the first note to be played with your right hand and the second with your left. To play the first note of the fill with your right hand on the snare drum, you'll have to move your right hand from the hi-hat over to the snare drum. As you can see, this snare note will be played on the "+ of 4," and because you would normally play the "+ of 4" on the hi-hats, to play this note simply move your right hand to the snare drum over and to the right of your left hand, which is already in the normal snare-drum playing position (see Figures 4.5 and 4.6).

Figure 4.6
Fill playing position

The second note of the fill, which is on the "a of 4," will be played by the left hand, which is already in the snare-drum playing position. So, the fill consists of two snare drum notes on the "+" and "a" of beat 4.

How Do We Get Back to the Groove That We Were Playing before We Took the Fill?

The most important part of playing a fill isn't necessarily playing it at all, but how smoothly you make the transition back to the groove that you were playing before you took the fill. Believe me, if your transition back to the groove isn't as smooth as silk, no one will ever remember how great the fill might have been. All they'll remember is how choppy the rhythm sounded when you were making the transition. For this reason, it's very important to pay close attention to that transition and try to make it as smooth as you possibly can.

Figure 4.5
Normal playing position

In this fill, the transition will be made by bringing your right hand back to the hi-hat from the snare drum in an eight-note rhythm to land on beat 1 of the second measure. On beat 1 of the second measure, you'll not only need that right-hand hi-hat note, but also a bass drum note to go with it to start the groove all over again. Try it whenever you're ready. Take your time and, as always, don't be afraid to count it out if it will help you.

Fill #2

Figure 4.7 shows the next fill to work on. It is called, appropriately enough, Fill #2.

This fill has four snare notes, twice as many as the first fill. Almost every fill that you'll ever play will be finished by the end of the measure in which it's being played. Because of this, the longer the fill you want to play, the sooner in the measure you'll have to start it. For example, if you wanted to try this new fill and you started it at the same place in the measure that you started the last fill, it would run over the measure line, and your groove would end up backward.

On with the questions....

When Does the Fill Begin?

This fill begins on beat 4 of the measure, one eighth note earlier than Fill #1. So, you would play the groove up to the "+ of 3" before you would begin the fill, the "+ of 3" being played on the hi-hat.

What Is the Fill?

This fill is made up of four sixteenth notes played on the snare drum. The first snare-drum note of the fill is played with the right hand, so you'll need to bring your right hand over from the hi-hat, just like you did with Fill #1. The only tricky thing about this fill is that there will still be a snare-drum note on beat 4 as if you were playing a groove, but instead of playing that snare note with your left hand, as you would normally, you'll be playing it with your right hand as the first note of the fill.

> **FLIPPY: THE NICKNAME YOU DON'T WANT**
>
> In almost every groove you'll play, the snare drum will be on beats 2 and 4 of the measure. There may be other snare notes in addition to 2 and 4, but there will almost always be snare on 2 and 4. If you play a fill that runs over the measure line, you might end up playing the snare drum on beats 1 and 3 instead. This is known as playing *backward*, or *flipping the beat*, and it is the absolute worst mistake a drummer can make, causing the band to totally fall apart before they hurl verbal and physical abuse at you, and causing audiences to run screaming from the room in tears. But on the bright side, you'll have a cute new nickname: Flippy, as in, "Let's get out of here fast! Here comes Flippy."

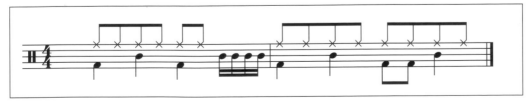

Figure 4.7
Fill #2

Then, finish the fill with the three remaining sixteenth notes.

If you'll notice, your right hand is continually playing eighth notes in this exercise. It just moves over to the snare drum while playing them to make up half of the notes in the fill. Your left hand plays the other sixteenth notes to make up the other half of the notes in the fill. Pretty cool, huh?

How Do We Get Back to the Groove?

Just like in Fill #1, your right hand is playing eighth notes throughout the entire exercise, and to play the fill it simply moves the eighth notes over to the snare drum. To get back to the groove, just move your right hand back to the hi-hat to continue the eighth notes that run through this whole exercise. Again, use the sticking indicators (L,R) to clear up any confusion you might have, and when in doubt, count it out.

Fill #3

Figure 4.8 shows a third fill for you to work on.

This fill will take up half of the measure, on beats 3 + 4, making it the longest fill that you've learned so far.

When Does the Fill Begin?

This fill takes up half of the measure that it's in, starting right on beat 3 of the measure. For this reason, rather than play a groove for just two beats of a measure before launching right into the fill, this exercise has a measure of the groove before the measure that will include the fill, giving you a run up to the fill. Using eighth notes, the count of this exercise is *1+2+3+4+ 1+2+*, with beats 3 and 4 of the measure taken up by the fill. So, you would keep continuous eighth notes on the hi-hat all the way up to the "+ of 2" before you move your right hand over to the snare drum to begin the fill.

What Is the Fill?

This fill consists of eight sixteenth notes on the snare drum, starting with your right hand. Just like the previous fills, the eighth notes that you're already playing on the hi-hat simply need to be moved over to the snare drum while the left hand plays the other half of the sixteenth notes that make up the fill.

How Do We Get Back to the Groove?

Just like Fill #2, move your right hand back to the hi-hat to continue the steady stream of eighth notes. As you've probably noticed by now, the right hand is the key to making the smooth transition from grooves to fills and back to grooves again. (You are developing what is known as a *right-hand lead*, and understanding the concept of the right-hand lead will help you later, when you want to start creating fills of your own.)

Figure 4.8
Fill #3

Fill #4

Now on to the next fill (see Figure 4.9). This fill is exactly like Fill #3 with one important difference. It's the first fill in which you'll be using a tom. The fill will begin in the same place as Fill #3, on beat 3 of the second measure. The fill also consists of eight sixteenth notes, just like Fill #3. The only difference is that you will play the four sixteenth notes that make up the second half of the fill on the first tom, instead of playing all of the sixteenth notes on the snare drum. Your right hand will travel from the hi-hats to the snare drum to the first tom and back to the hi-hats, playing eighth notes the whole time, developing your right-hand lead further. Your left hand will do some traveling for the first time too, moving to the first tom to play the rest of the sixteenth notes that make up the fill.

You might find that you have some difficulty getting your left hand to play sixteenth notes at the same speed as your right hand, but this is perfectly natural for any right-handed person. As long as you keep the eighth notes steady with your right hand, your left hand will be forced to keep up. And it will.

If you're having any problems with this fill, remember to ask yourself the three questions that will help you determine exactly how to play the exercise.

Fill #5

Now another fill (see Figure 4.10). This fill will use sixteenth notes on the snare drum and two toms. It is a good fill to learn if you have a four-piece kit (one mounted tom and one floor tom). Because this fill takes up three beats of a measure, you will once again play one measure of a straight groove as a run-up to the measure that will contain the fill.

The fill itself will occur on beat 2 of the second measure of the exercise. There will be a snare-drum note on beat 2 of the measure, just like there should be if you are playing a straight groove, but you will play that snare note on beat 2 with your right hand, as the first sixteenth note of the fill, instead of with your left hand in the regular snare-playing position.

The fill consists of three groups of four sixteenth notes—the first group on the snare, the second group on the first tom, and the third and last group on the floor tom. Of course, you could still use this fill on a five-piece kit with three mounted toms. You'd just have to skip over your second mounted tom as you make your way around the kit.

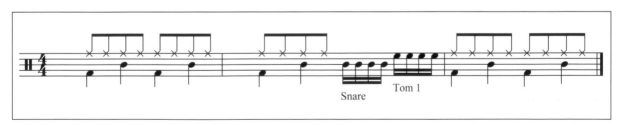

Figure 4.9
Fill #4

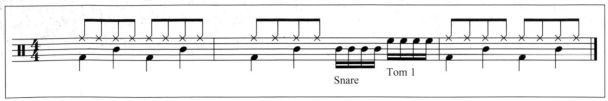

Figure 4.10
Fill #5

One thing to be aware of when trying this fill is that your hands will have to travel from the floor tom back to the groove position, which is your left hand on the snare and your right hand on the hi-hats, ready to continue the groove. This is the longest reach you will ever have to make on your kit—from one side of the kit to the other—and it will be quite a challenge to make that long reach and keep the transition from the fill back to the groove silky–smooth, as it should be.

Keep in mind that this is a tricky move for anyone, no matter how experienced, and you shouldn't feel frustrated if it takes you more than a few tries to make it. If you keep your cool and keep at it, you'll get the hang of it. Just relax and take your time. And remember, this is the longest reach you'll ever have to make, so when you can pull it off comfortably, you will really have accomplished something. Be proud and walk tall.

Fill #6

Now for the last fill of the chapter (see Figure 4.11). Now it's time to use all the drums in a five-piece kit in a full-measure fill. In this three-measure exercise, the fill will occupy the entire second measure. The fill consists of a group of four sixteenth notes on each drum (except the bass drum) on each beat of the measure. The transition from the fill back to the groove requires that same long reach from the floor tom back to the hi-hat and snare, but if you spent enough time on this move in the last fill, this should give you no trouble at all.

In this fill, as in all the others before it, your right hand will play straight quarter notes all around the kit, regardless of what it's hitting. If you're aware of this, it should help you keep your time flow consistent as you work your way around the kit. When you feel comfortable with the fill itself, pay attention to the bass drum note that goes along with the hi-hat on beat 1 of the measure after the fill, and make sure you're playing it nice and strong. You'll want that note extra strong for the next trick you'll be working on.

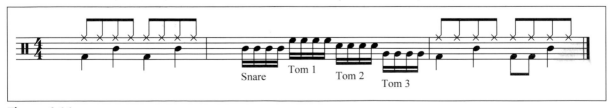

Figure 4.11
Fill #6

A Crash Course in Crashing on a Crash

IF YOU CAN IMAGINE A DRUM FILL as a sentence, then a crash at the end is like an exclamation point. We usually crash on (you guessed it) a crash cymbal. If you followed the kit setup that I showed you in Chapter 2, your crash cymbal should be between your hi-hats and your first mounted tom, up high enough so that it doesn't knock against anything else after it has been hit. Let's go back to Fill #1 to illustrate the use of the crash cymbal (see Figure 4.12).

As you can see from the exercise, when you add a crash cymbal to the end of the fill, you're not actually adding any notes. You'll simply take the first note of the first measure after the fill that was previously played on the hi-hat and play it on the crash cymbal instead. Because you're replacing a hi-hat note that would normally be played with your right hand, use your right hand to play the crash cymbal. (Crash cymbals are made to be struck on their edge, so the cymbal should be sitting in a more or less horizontal position on its stand. You might need to adjust the tilter on the cymbal stand to get the right position.)

After you play the crash cymbal, you'll need to bring your right hand back down to the hi-hat to continue playing the groove. When you play that note on the crash cymbal, don't forget the bass-drum note that goes along with it. Whenever you play a crash cymbal, you'll almost always play a bass drum with it. The two sounds together (the low thud of the bass drum and the explosive high-end sizzle of the crash cymbal) create a new sound, one that ends any fill perfectly. A crash cymbal at the end of a fill without a bass drum is like brownies with no milk. It's possible to have a crash with no bass drum, but it's way better to have them together.

Once you get the hang of playing the crash at the end of the fill, move on and try the same thing with the other fills that you learned. Figures 4.13 through 4.15 are all the fills you learned in this chapter with crashes at the end of them. Take it slow.

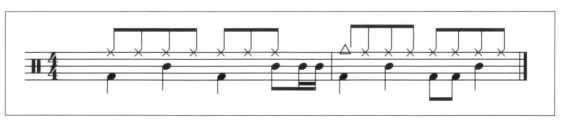

Figure 4.12
Fill #1 with crash

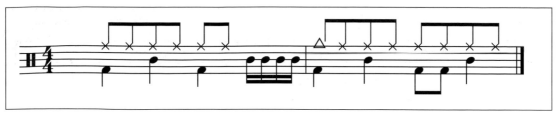

Figure 4.13
Fill #2 with crash

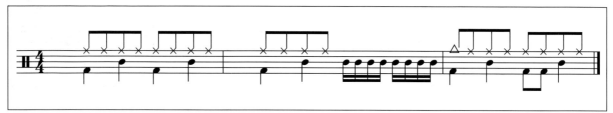

Figure 4.14
Fill #3 with crash

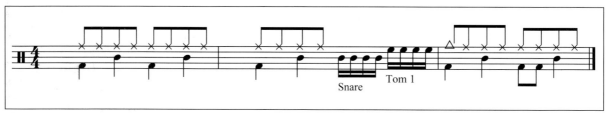

Figure 4.15
Fill #4 with crash

No matter where the fill ends on the kit, you'll need to get your right hand over to the crash cymbal to play a crash on the first beat of the measure after the fill. When you play fills #5 and #6, the long reach from the floor tom back to the hi-hat and snare will be just a little bit longer in order to play the crash cymbal that ends the fill. For this reason, you will eventually want to add some more crash cymbals to your kit. If you put another crash cymbal over by the floor tom, for example, you can use that crash to end your fills that end on the floor tom, rather than making the long reach back to the crash over by your hi-hats.

Obviously, this is not the only reason to add another crash to your setup. Another reason is to add a different sound to your kit. Crash cymbals vary in size, weight, and sound characteristics, giving you a wide choice of sounds to add to your kit, and you may see some kits with many more crash cymbals than just one or two. There are no rules when it comes to adding crash cymbals. Obviously, cost will limit the number of cymbals you could add, but adding at least one additional crash is something to consider in the future.

Figures 4.16 and 4.17 show the last two fills you learned earlier in this chapter with crashes added to them.

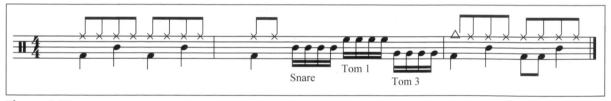

Figure 4.16
Fill #5 with crash

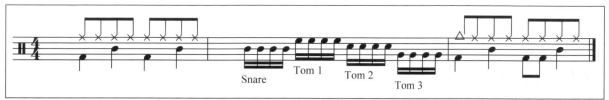

Figure 4.17
Fill #6 with crash

HEEL DOWN OR HEEL UP?

Now that you've been playing drums for long enough to learn a few beats and a few fills, let's discuss bass drum technique. When it comes to bass drum technique, there are basically two ways to play—*heel down* or *heel up.* If you've been playing without paying any particular attention to your right foot on the bass-drum pedal, you're probably playing *heel down.* Heel down looks just like it sounds, with your entire foot lying on the bass drum pedal. To play a bass-drum note using the heel-down technique, you only need to lift your toes up and down, keeping your heel down the whole time. This technique can't really offer you much volume from your bass drum because you'll only be using the muscles in your calf to work the bass-drum pedal.

There's nothing wrong with this technique when you're first starting. You'll probably be playing alone, and power and volume won't be an issue. However, the first time you need some real volume from your bass drum (when you're jamming with a loud band for the first time), you might come up short volume-wise using the heel-down technique.

Playing with the heel-up technique is much like playing on your tiptoes. To play a note, bring your entire leg up and down. This will give you more volume and power because you'll be using all the muscles in your leg, including your thigh. However, if you ever find yourself having to play at a lower volume, you might need to switch back to heel down, so it's a good idea to practice each of the exercises in this book using both techniques. I've found that it can sometimes be more challenging to play at a lower volume than you're used to, than to play louder. For this reason, it's a good idea to have a decent heel-down technique on tap in case you need it. Better to have it and not need it than not to have it and...blah blah blah....

Your Left Foot: The Last to Join the Party

UP UNTIL NOW, YOUR LEFT FOOT has been just lying there on the hi-hat pedal like a dead carp, but it doesn't always have to be that way. Actually, it's not like your left foot was serving no purpose just sitting there. It was keeping your hi-hats in the closed position for all of the grooves that we learned in this chapter, and for this it deserves some respect. But now your left foot can make you proud by taking all of those grooves to another level simply by moving a little. Suddenly, your left foot goes from being a lazy slob to being a superhero. Nice work if you can get it. To begin these heroics, let's go back to Groove #1 and add some left-foot action (see Figure 4.18).

The circle above the last hi-hat note of the first measure is a signal to you to lift up your left foot while still playing with your right hand, so that note will have an open hi-hat sound. The plus sign above the next hi-hat note indicates that your hi-hats will be back to the closed position for that note, which will simply require you to put your left foot back down to its normal playing position.

There are just a few things to keep in mind as you try this move. If you want the hi-hats to be open for the indicated note, you'll need to lift up your foot just a split second before you play the note. This might take you a few tries to get the timing right, but when you do, you'll know it right away. When you get to the first beat of the second measure, when your hi-hats are supposed to be closed again, don't forget to bring your right foot down at the same time in order to play the bass-drum note that's on beat 1. In other words, you'll need to bring both feet down on beat 1 of the second measure. (Basically, every other time that you play a note with your right foot on the bass drum, you'll also bring your left foot down to close the hi-hat. The only exception would be the very first bass-drum note of the exercise, when your left foot will just be holding the hi-hats in the closed position.)

When using your left foot to play the hi-hats, you really only need to lift up your toes to get an open hi-hat sound. There's no need to lift your entire foot all the way off the pedal. Actually, if you happen to be playing your bass drum in the

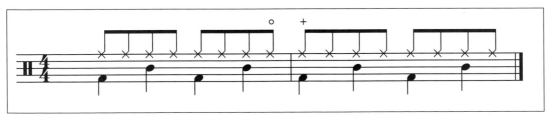

Figure 4.18
Groove #1 with open and closed hi-hats

heels-up fashion and you lift your entire foot off of the hi-hat pedal to play an open note, you'll end up with both feet in the air at the same time, possibly causing you to lose your balance and fall off of your throne and die. It's very unlikely that a fall like that would actually kill you, but better safe than sorry.

Seriously, though, you do need to pay attention to your balance when using both feet to play something. It can be very easy to greatly exaggerate your movements when you are learning something new because you're concentrating so hard. You don't need to be that aware of your movements when you're first learning something, but after you feel relatively comfortable playing something new, take a few minutes to observe your body movements and make sure you're as relaxed as you can be. You might find that fewer movements than you're making are required to play something.

The open and closed hi-hat move that you just learned can be played just as easily in any of the other beats that you learned in Chapter 3, so go ahead and try to add it to those other beats. Once you've done that, you've graduated to using all four of your limbs to play drums. Take a moment to congratulate yourself, and don't forget to tell all your family, friends, and neighbors about your new skills. In the next chapter, you'll learn how to juggle three flaming bowling balls using only your face, while using all four limbs to play drums. You know I'm kidding, right?

Where You'll Learn What to Leave Out and How to Slice and Dice, and You'll Meet Four Guys Named

5

Steve

I N THIS CHAPTER, you'll take your knowledge of sixteenth notes to another level. Up until now, the only time you've encountered sixteenth notes was in groups of two or four notes for each beat of the measure. Now you'll learn about some three-note sixteenth-note phrases and a different kind of two-note sixteenth-note phrase. We'll call these new phrases *sixteenth-note variations* because they will all be slightly different versions of the basic sixteenth-note phrase. The way these sixteenth-note variations will differ from each other is that we will take certain notes out of the regular four-note sixteenth-note phrase to create each variation. There are four sixteenth-note variations in this chapter. Let's look at them one at a time.

Sixteenth-Note Variation #1 and Groove #4

To UNDERSTAND HOW TO take notes out of a four-note sixteenth-note phrase, you'll need to remember how to count that phrase. As you recall, you count a four-note sixteenth-note phrase like what you see in Figure 5.1.

Figure 5.1
Four sixteenth notes in a measure of 4/4 counted out.

To create the first variation, we'll take out the middle two sixteenth notes of the phrase. So, instead of having all four notes in the phrase (1 e + a), we'll end up with just the first and last note of the phrase (see Figure 5.2).

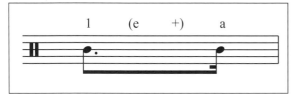

Figure 5.2
Sixteenth-Note Variation #1

Now we're going to use this particular sixteenth-note variation to create a brand-new groove (see Figure 5.3). We'll take the second groove that you learned a few chapters ago and combine it with the sixteenth-note variation, so let's review the basic version of the groove.

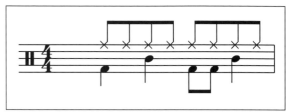

Figure 5.3
Groove #2

Now, we'll take that basic groove, remove the single snare note on beat 2 of the measure, and put the sixteenth-note variation in its place. We'll call this new exercise Groove #4 (see Figure 5.4).

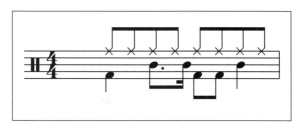

Figure 5.4
Groove #4

Understanding "In Between" Notes

When the sixteenth-note variation is placed on the snare drum underneath the steady eighth notes and the hi-hat, an interesting thing occurs. You'll notice that the second note of the sixteenth-note variation (the "a" of 2) will be played *in between* two hi-hat notes. In other words, it will be played all alone on the snare drum, unlike the first note of the phrase, which was played along with your right hand on the hi-hat note. If sixteenth notes are placed underneath eighth notes, there will end up being a sixteenth note between every eighth note. In this case, we're not playing full sixteenth notes on the snare drum underneath the straight eighth notes on the hi-hat. We're using a variation that has only the first and last notes of the sixteenth note present, but the second of those notes falls in a space between two eighth notes of the hi-hat pattern. This concept of the "in between" note is an important one to understand because all of the variations that you'll learn in this chapter and beyond will have some "in between" notes.

Back to the Groove

Now that you understand the concept of the "in between" note, try to play the groove. The second note of the sixteenth-note variation that will be played on the snare drum (the "in between" note) will lead you right into beat 3, where the hi-hat and bass drum will play together. As you learn to play this groove, remember to concentrate on keeping the eighth notes on the hi-hat as steady as you possibly can. When you keep those eighth notes rocking steady, you'll be more able to fully understand how that "in between" note on the snare drum is supposed to sound. If you slow down the eighth notes to fit that snare note between them, your groove will end up having a variation in tempo...and that's a bad thing.

Of course, if you need to slow down the entire exercise to play it correctly, please do so. Just keep in mind that once you start the groove at a certain tempo, you want to maintain that tempo as well as you possibly can.

Déjà Vu

You've played this before...kinda. If you find yourself having trouble playing this groove, check this out: You've actually played this before. In Fill #1, which was in the last chapter, you did the exact same order of hands to play that fill as you need to do to play this groove. The only difference is that when you played the two sixteenth notes that make up the fill (L,R), you played them on the snare drum. This time, your hands will be doing exactly the same thing, but your right hand will stay on the hi-hats to play the first sixteenth note, and your left hand will play the second sixteenth note on the snare. It's as if you're playing Fill #1 without moving your hands from the normal groove-playing position of your right hand on the hi-hat and your left hand on the snare drum. Take a look at Figure 5.5.

If you have trouble playing this exercise, this next section is for you.

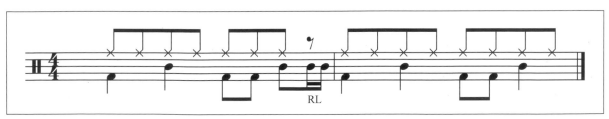

Figure 5.5
Fill #1

Learning by Repetition. Learning by Repetition. Learning by Repetition...

Remember when I told you to get a timer or an alarm clock to use as a practicing device, and you thought I was nuts? Well, I am, but go get one now if you didn't already because now I'll show you what we're going to use it for. But first, I'd like to discuss the use of memory.

You've probably had to memorize things in your life, such as your name or your address. Those are easy things to remember because they are short bits of information that don't take very much effort to retain in your memory. I'm sure you've had to memorize much longer and more complicated bits of information in school, such as the Pledge of Allegiance or maybe the Gettysburg Address. The easiest way to memorize something like that is to say it over and over again, either out loud or in your mind. This is known as learning by the use of *repetition*. When you're working on something new in drumming, you can use the same approach. The only difference is that you won't be trying to memorize the Gettysburg Address. Instead you'll be memorizing movements of your limbs.

Your limbs are perfectly capable of making the movements required to play something on the drums; it's just that when you're working on something, your brain can't always remember quite what it's supposed to do next. Should the right foot press down on the bass drum pedal before or after the left hand hits the snare drum? The only way to train your brain to remember the order of actions that you want it to take is through the use of repetition. That means you just have to keep trying to play something over and over until you get the result you're looking for. But what if you get so frustrated that you want to quit playing drums forever just because you can't get past a certain point? It's time to fire your brain.

Hey, Brain—You're Fired!

The brain is a pain. It always has to know everything. It won't even let your arms and legs move when you want them to just because it can't memorize a series of actions quickly enough. And then, when it can't memorize quickly enough, it creates little voices inside your head that say things like, "This is stupid. I can't do this. I'm stupid. This is too hard. I hate this book. I'm hungry. Maybe I'll go eat something right now instead of practicing. Maybe I'll go outside. Maybe I'll play a video game instead. I'll never become a good drummer. It takes too long. If I can't even get this thing I'm working on now, imagine how long some other things are going to take that are even harder than this. Maybe I'll just play something that I already know how to play instead of this new thing. I think I'm getting a pimple."

How do I know what you're thinking? Well, I don't really; I'm just guessing. But I do know that I've thought all of those things myself when I was working on something new and having problems. And do you know what I did about it? I got rid of the very thing that was creating those thoughts. I fired my brain. You can fire your brain, too. But you're not going to fire your brain forever; you're only going to fire it for ten minutes. Then you're going to rehire it so it can do something useful, such as tell your lungs to work so that you can continue to live or something like that.

Using the Timer: Ten Minutes to Change Your Life

Set the timer to go off 10 minutes from now, and then begin to practice. But before you do, I want you to make a promise to yourself that you will do nothing else for the next 10 minutes but try to play the exercise that you're working on over and over. You won't answer the phone. You won't get a drink. You won't play anything else on the drums except the exercise on which you're currently working. And most important, you won't think.

Each time you begin the exercise and you make a mistake, just start over right away, before your brain starts working and telling you how hard this is. You're simply going to memorize a series of movements by repetition. Actually, technically you *do* need your brain to practice because it's the brain that tells your arms and legs to actually move when you want them to. I just want you to ignore the messages that come into your brain that tell you that you can't play something. There's no hurry, so take it as slowly as you need to while concentrating.

If you do this for 10 minutes, and the buzzer goes off and you haven't quite mastered the exercise you're working on, walk away from the drums or stay and play something else. There's no need to keep trying anymore. Then you can listen to your brain tell you that it knew all along that you'd never be able to play that exercise. You have a chance to prove your brain wrong tomorrow. All you need to do is repeat this whole 10-minute routine the next time you sit down at the drums to practice.

If you find that 10 minutes is just way too long for you to try to play the same thing over and over, then cut it back to 5 minutes. The length of time that you concentrate is not as important as how much you focus your concentration. If you spend 10 minutes on something and you can't get it, when you start over the next time you practice, you're not really starting from scratch. You've already put some time in at your last practice session, and it will probably come to you before that 10 minute session is up.

When you're working toward something, every minute counts. I use this method with my students. Each lesson is usually half an hour long, and I'll use 10 minutes to coach them through repetitions of a certain exercise. Sometimes, if they're feeling particularly discouraged, I'll make a deal with them. I'll bet them a dollar that they can master the exercise before 10 minutes is up. They usually lose because it often takes even less than 10 minutes to master something new, as long as you concentrate and focus as hard as you can for those 10 minutes.

I'm not telling you that if you want to be a good drummer and learn new things you have to practice for hours and hours until your eyes bleed. I'm telling you that all you have to do is practice for 10 solid minutes at a time. Let's do some quick math. Suppose you spent 10 minutes a day for 4 days a week working on something. That adds up to 40 minutes a week, just over half an hour. Now, imagine if you learned something brand-new every week of your life, using just 40 minutes a week, or a miracle occurred and you learned more than one new thing a week. Within a few years you could learn how to play enough things on the drums to conquer the whole world. Okay, maybe I'm exaggerating. There might be some things that take you two weeks to learn. That means in few years, you could conquer only half of the world. Then your brain will probably take all the credit, because that's what brains do. But please don't blame your poor brain too much. It just doesn't know any better.

Sixteenth-Note Variation #2 and Groove #5

I N THE LAST SECTION, we took out the middle two notes of a sixteenth note to create the first variation. This time, we'll take out just one note to create the second variation (see Figure 5.6).

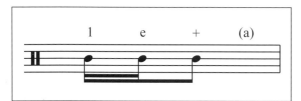

Figure 5.6
Sixteenth-Note Variation #2

In this variation, we'll take out the very last of the four sixteenth notes, so we're left with three sixteenth notes in a row. We can use this particular variation to create a groove by splitting up the different sixteenth notes in the variation between the bass drum and the snare drum. We'll call this exercise Groove #5 (see Figure 5.7).

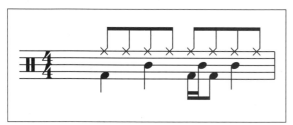

Figure 5.7
Groove #5

As you can see, the sixteenth-note variation can be found in beat 3 of the measure. This new groove is very similar to Groove #2 that you learned back in

Chapter 3. In Groove #2, there are two eighth notes on the bass drum on beat 3 of the measure (3 +). In this brand-new groove you're learning, those eighth notes on the bass drum are still there, but there's a snare note between them. Each of the bass drum notes has a hi-hat note that goes with it, but the snare drum note that falls between them is played alone.

Alone at Last: Isolating the Trouble Spot

To fully understand the third beat of the measure where all the action is, let's just take that beat and look at it outside of the measure itself (see Figure 5.8).

Figure 5.8
Isolated part of Groove #5

Try playing just this part of the measure. You'll play two notes of hi-hat and bass drum together with a snare note alone in between them. Take your time and run through this piece of the measure over and over until it's nice and smooth. When you can play just this part of the measure smoothly, putting it in place with the rest of the measure will be a piece of cake.

You've played everything else in this measure before in all of the other grooves you've already learned, so if you can work out the new challenging piece of the measure and then just slot it in its place in the measure, you should be good to go. As with all the exercises you're learning, play the entire exercise as many times in a row as you possibly can until you either bore yourself to death with your excellence or you make a mistake—whichever comes first. If you happen to make a mistake before you bore yourself to death, start all over again and continue until you bore yourself to death. Okay, maybe not actually to death, but as near to death as you can. I certainly wouldn't want your death on my hands. And besides, you'll need to be fully alive to play this next groove.

Groove #6: A Funky Combination, a Groove Sensation That Will Cause Elation All across the Nation

In this section, you'll be combining the two sixteenth-note variations that you learned in this chapter into one measure. Each of the exercises that you learned still works perfectly well on its own. The new groove that you'll learn is not meant to be a replacement for them, but is instead another addition to your rapidly expanding bag of tricks. To create this new groove, we'll take the front end of Groove #4 and stick it onto the back end of Groove #5 to create Groove #6 (see Figure 5.9).

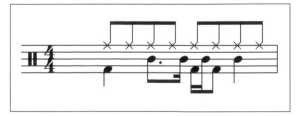

Figure 5.9
Groove #6

If you want to isolate the tricky spot in order to try it outside of the measure, go right ahead (see Figure 5.10).

Figure 5.10
Isolated part of Groove #6

Isolating the tricky spot can be a good way for you to tackle the part of the measure that requires the most concentration, but be careful not to spend too much time playing just this part of the measure, because the phrase will only make sense musically when it's in place in the measure.

Once you have a decent flow going with the isolated phrase, try to put it into the measure as soon as you can so you can see how it fits it in. When you put this phrase into the measure, run the entire measure until you see how both parts fit together. Then, just as with all the previous exercises, try playing it over and over as many times as you can. Take your time and congratulate yourself when you finally get it nice and smooth. This is by far the most complicated groove you've tried so far, but it can stand as a really cool groove on its own, and it's a groove that we'll be returning to repeatedly in this book to add other pieces to it to create more and different funky grooves. Make sure that you play this groove as smoothly as you possibly can before you move on to the next section. You will be tested later.

Oh, by the way, "elation" means the feeling of being very, very happy or elated—as in, "Gee, when I first started playing Groove #6 smoothly, I was just filled with elation." Just so you know.

Using Sixteenth-Note Variation #2 in a Fill

Sixteenth-Note Variation #2 can also be used to create fills or parts of fills. Up until now, anytime we've used sixteenth notes in a fill, they've been in groups of two or four. As you'll remember, Sixteenth-Note Variation #2 has just three sixteenth notes, leaving out the very last note of a group of four sixteenth notes (see Figure 5.11).

We've already used this particular variation in Groove #5 and Groove #6, but in those grooves the variation was split up between two different drums—the bass drum and the snare drum. Now you'll be playing each note of the variation on one drum at a time to create several new fills. In each of these fills, you'll be using a right-hand lead, which means that you'll start each fill with your right hand and continue to play straight eighth notes with your right hand while using your left hand to play the other notes of the fill. These new fills using this sixteenth-note variation are very similar to the group of fills that you learned in the last chapter. Let me use what we call Fill #2 to show you what I mean (see Figure 5.12).

As you can see, we have a group of four sixteenth notes on the snare drum on beat 4 of the measure. We can take out that group of four sixteenth notes and replace it with Sixteenth-Note Variation #2 to create a fill that's slightly different but every bit as effective (see Figure 5.13).

Figure 5.11
Sixteenth-Note Variation #2

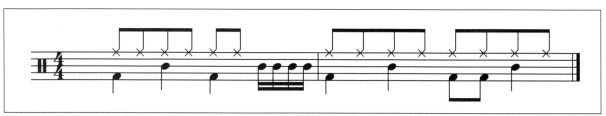

Figure 5.12
Fill #2

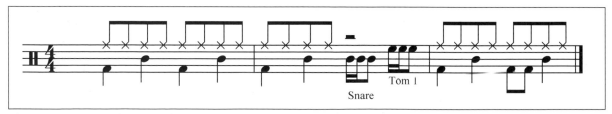

Figure 5.13
Fill Exercise #1

Basically, all you'll do is leave out the very last sixteenth note that would have been played by your left hand on the snare drum, leaving a space the length of a single sixteenth note at the very end of the measure. When practicing this exercise, pay attention to how smoothly you're making the transition back to the groove from the fill. Make sure that you don't rush into the first beat of the third measure, where you'll be going back into the groove. You want to make sure that you give that sixteenth note's worth of space its full value, so don't be afraid to use a metronome while working on this particular exercise.

What you'll learn as you work on this exercise is that it can be sometimes just as difficult to leave a note out of a fill as it is to leave it in. You might find yourself in a situation, either learning a song that you heard somewhere or creating a new song with a band, in which a small space such as the one in this exercise is just the right thing to be playing. For example, you might want to play something on the drums that locks in note for note with a guitar part, and the guitar part might

be this exact sixteenth-note variation. Or maybe you just want to break up the monotony of always playing fills that are made up of groups of four sixteenth notes. Knowing this slight variation on the standard formula will increase the number of fills you have at your disposal, which is nice. You've gained something new by leaving something out. Sometimes it just works out like that.

More Fills Using Sixteenth-Note Variation #2

To create more fills using this particular sixteenth-note variation, simply take the fills you learned earlier, which used groups of four sixteenth notes, and replace those with this variation (see Figures 5.14 and 5.15).

All of these fills use a right-hand lead, so they have the same basic feel about them. You'll just be leaving out that last sixteenth note of the group of four. Once you get a feel for that, try it with the other fills you learned.

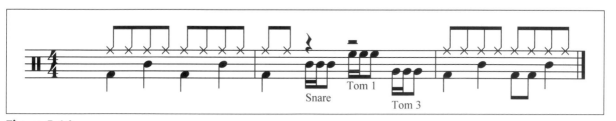

Figure 5.14
Fill Exercise #2

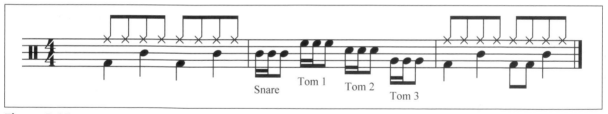

Figure 5.15
Fill Exercise #3

Just by leaving one note out of the groups of sixteenth notes, you've instantly doubled the number of fills you can play.

Slicing and Dicing

Here's an easy way to instantly create a bunch of new fills by using the sixteenth-note variations you already know and shuffling them around a little bit. Take a look at these two fills that you know and have already played (see Figures 5.16 and 5.17).

Now I'm going to create a brand-new fill out of these two fills by taking the first half of one and sticking the second half of the other one on the end of it (see Figure 5.18).

Now, I'll reverse the order of the pieces of the fills to create another fill (see Figure 5.19).

You can use this same slicing and dicing technique on any of the fills you've learned so far to create new fills. Let's use Fill #6 (the fill that takes up an entire measure and goes all the way around the kit) to get into some serious slicing and dicing. Figure 5.20 shows Fill #6.

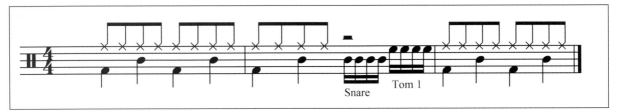

Figure 5.16
You remember this fill...

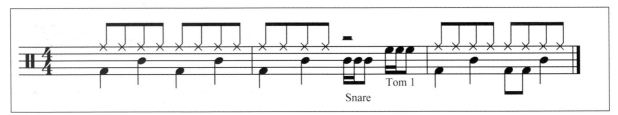

Figure 5.17
And this one too!

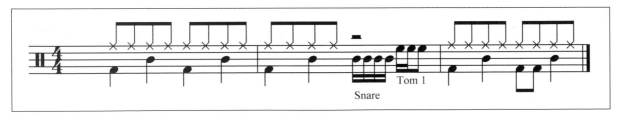

Figure 5.18
Fill Exercise #4

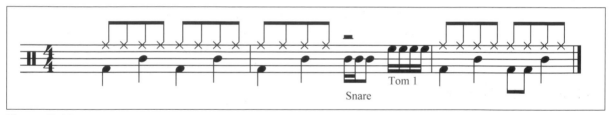

Figure 5.19
Fill Exercise #5

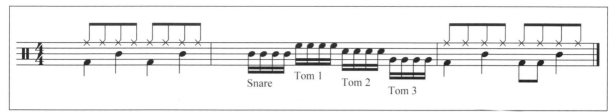

Figure 5.20
Fill #6

Figures 5.21 and 5.22 show a couple of variations
to get you started.

Figure 5.21
Fill Exercise #6

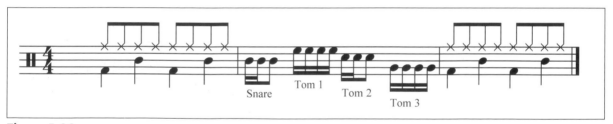

Figure 5.22
Fill Exercise #7

And Figures 5.23 and 5.24 show you some more variations.

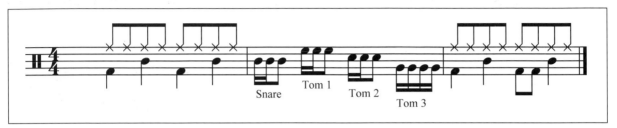

Figure 5.23
Fill Exercise #8

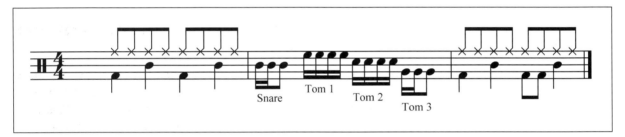

Figure 5.24
Fill Exercise #9

We'll take the slice-and-dice concept a little deeper after you learn the remaining two sixteenth-note variations.

Sixteenth-Note Variation #3

AS YOU'VE SEEN FROM the earlier sixteenth-note variations, it's all about leaving particular notes out of a group of four sixteenth notes, and this new variation is no different. We'll just leave out a different note to create the new variation. Figure 5.25 shows a four-note grouping of sixteenth notes.

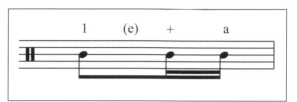

Figure 5.26
Sixteenth-Note Variation #3

Using Sixteenth-Note Variation #3 in Fills

Just like for the fills using Sixteenth-Note Variation #2, you'll use a right-hand lead to string groups of the new variation together to create fills. Figure 5.27 shows a two-beat fill using this variation.

Once you get the hang of that, try a full measure fill using that variation, as shown in Figure 5.28.

Figure 5.25
A four-note grouping of sixteenth notes counted out

In this new variation, you'll leave out the second note in the group (see Figure 5.26). Let's use it in a fill.

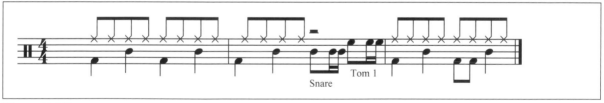

Figure 5.27
Fill Exercise # 10

Figure 5.28
Fill Exercise #11

Sixteenth-Note Variation #4

FIGURE 5.29 SHOWS THE LAST sixteenth-note variation you'll learn, and it can also be the trickiest one because it's the first variation you'll work on that does not use a right-hand-lead technique when you're stringing groups of them together. This time you'll leave out the third note of a group of four sixteenth notes.

Try two measures' worth of this variation strung together (see Figure 5.30). Pay attention to the sticking notation (L,R). This will help you figure out how to string together a bunch of these variations. In this particular variation, your left hand will be more active than your right, which might make this variation seem more difficult to play, but your left hand will not be playing notes any faster than in any of the previous variations.

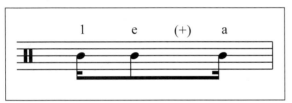

Figure 5.29
Sixteenth-Note Variation #4

Figure 5.30
Measures using Sixteenth-Note Variation #4

Using Sixteenth-Note Variation #4 in Fills

After you've done the work to make yourself comfortable with stringing together two measures' worth of this variation, using it to create fills should come pretty easily. The best way to approach the creation of fills using this variation is the same way you've created fills using all the previous variations. Start off with a string of two, one group on the snare and the second group on the first tom (see Figure 5.31).

Then move on to one measure's worth all the way around the kit (see Figure 5.32).

Figure 5.31
Fill Exercise #12

Figure 5.32
Fill Exercise #13

Review: Four Similar-Looking Friends All Named Steve

NOW THAT YOU'VE LEARNED ALL four of the sixteenth-note variations, the biggest challenge that faces you is remembering the difference between them. They are all so similar to each other that it would be easy to forget about one or two of them. It's kind of like having four friends all named Steve who all look pretty much alike, but each is a slightly different height or has slightly different-colored hair. If you saw only one or two of them at a time somewhere, you'd probably forget that the other ones even existed. But imagine that you had a party and all four of your friends named Steve who all looked almost exactly alike showed up. When you saw them all in the same place, you'd remember them. That's what this review exercise in Figure 5.33 will do for you. It will help you to keep track of the differences of all the sixteenth-note variations by putting them all in the same place. Try it. Get to know all the Steves.

Figure 5.33
Sixteenth-note variations review

More Slicing and Dicing

NOW THAT YOU KNOW ALL four of the sixteenth-note variations, you can take the slice-and-dice concept of creating fills and go even further with it. Now you have twice as many combinations than before available to you.

Figure 5.34 shows an exercise with some combinations to help you take your slicing and dicing skills to the next level.

Figure 5.34
Sixteenth-note variations fill review

Making Up Your Own Fills: It's All in Your Mind

THE KEY TO SUCCESSFULLY slicing and dicing to make up fills is all in the way that you think about fills and the pieces that fit together to create those fills. Think about fills as sentences. Sentences are just a bunch of words put together in a certain order to make a particular point. You can use the same words that make up any particular sentence to make different sentences that have entirely different meanings. You can shuffle the order of the words already in the sentence to create a new meaning or you can take certain words out of that sentence and bring in different words to change the meaning of the sentence. Words are interchangeable in any sentence; it just depends on what you're trying to say in the sentence you're creating.

Drum fills can be seen in the same way. Think of each part of the fill as one word in a sentence that can be changed or even removed completely, as opposed to thinking of the fill as one big object that cannot be changed in any way. As long as the fill you create doesn't run over the measure line at the end of its measure, you can play almost any kind of fill that you can possibly imagine.

Thinking of fills in this way can unlock your creativity and help you to create fills of your own that I (or any other drummer in the world) have never thought of before. The way you create fills of your own will be a part of what gives you your very own style of drumming, unlike that of any other drummer. This concept of interchanging parts to create custom fills will also come into play later, when we get into more complex grooves. So get creative. Slice and dice some fills and see what you can come up with.

Adding Spice to Your Life and Crashes to Your Fills

NOW THAT YOU'VE BECOME a slicing and dicing fill monster, it's time to start adding some crashes to the end of some of those fills. Almost any fill that you hear in any song ends with a crash, and so should almost all of your fills. Remember, when adding a crash to the end of a fill, you're not actually adding anything; you're just replacing the first hi-hat note at the very beginning of the measure that comes after the fill with a crash cymbal instead. Then, after you play the crash cymbal, move directly to the hi-hats to play the second eighth note in the measure. Hopefully, this explanation sounds familiar to you from the section on crash cymbals in Chapter 4. Figure 5.35 presents a quick exercise you can work on to help remind you how to add a crash cymbal to the end of a fill.

As always when playing a fill, making the transition back to the groove after laying a fill is just as important as playing the fill in the first place.

Actually, the transition is more important than the fill itself. You could invent and play the most original and exciting fill in the world, but if you blow the transition back into the groove, no one will ever remember what the fill was—they'll only remember how you blew the transition and threw the whole band off.

Adding a crash cymbal to the end of a fill can make the transition back to the groove even trickier, so it's a good idea to go back over all of the fills in this chapter, as well as those you might have created in your slicing and dicing, to make sure you have no problem making that transition from the fill back to the groove while adding a crash cymbal. Once you feel comfortable adding a crash cymbal to the end of any fill you might play, you'll be able to punctuate the end of your fills with a nice exclamation point that a solid crash represents. Do you know what I mean? Of course you do!

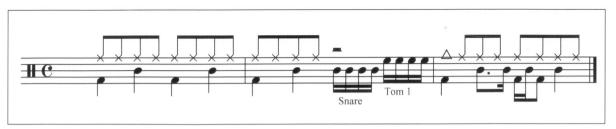

Figure 5.35
Adding a crash

6

The Triumphant Return of Your

Left Foot

IT'S BEEN AWHILE SINCE you did anything with your left foot other than using it to make sure your hi-hats didn't fly away, so now let's give that left foot a little piece of the action. But before you involve your left foot, try the groove in Figure 6.1 first.

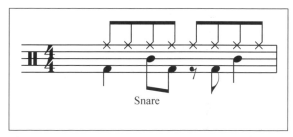

Figure 6.1
Exercise #1

A Slightly Different Groove

THIS GROOVE IS A LITTLE BIT different than any of the others you've worked on before. The hi-hats have straight eighth notes through the whole measure, which you've done in all the grooves you've played before, and there are snare notes on beats 2 and 4 of the measure, just like in most of the other grooves. In other words, your hands will be doing exactly the same things that they did in the first three grooves you learned back in Chapter 3. But the bass drum will be playing something you've never played before.

The easiest way for you to determine what the bass drum pattern is supposed to be is to look at the hi-hat notes and look below at the bass drum notes to find out which of those hi-hat notes will have a bass drum played along with it. Once you figure out for yourself what the groove is, try to play it as many times in a row as you can, and make sure you're comfortable with it because we're going to add some open and closed hi-hats to this groove.

Figures 6.3 through 6.6 show four open and closed hi-hat exercises:

REPEATS

When you're working on a new exercise and you can play it through at least once, your next step should be an attempt to play it twice in a row. After that, you should try to play it over and over as many times as you possibly can. Rather than remind you of this in every chapter, I'm going to use a musical notation device that was designed for the exact purpose of instructing you to play a particular piece over and over. This device is called a *repeat sign*, and it can be found at the beginning and the end of the measure that is to be repeated. For example, take a look at Figure 6.2.

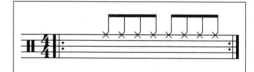

Figure 6.2
Measure with repeats

So now you'll know to look at the beginning and the end of each measure or group of measures in an exercise for the repeat signs.

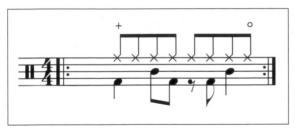

Figure 6.3
Exercise #1: Example #1

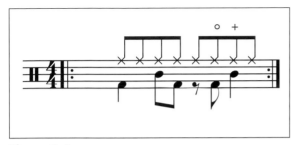

Figure 6.4
Exercise #1: Example #2

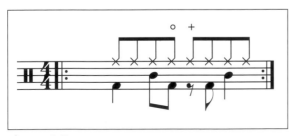

Figure 6.5
Exercise #1: Example #3

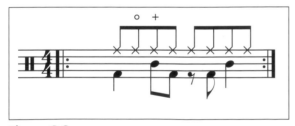

Figure 6.6
Exercise #1: Example #4

Each of these exercises uses the same groove, but has open and closed hi-hats in different spots. The first exercise should not give you too much trouble because the open and closed hi-hat move comes at the very end of the measure. You've already used the open and closed hi-hat move in this same part of the measure in the first exercise that had open and closed hi-hats in it. The open and closed hi-hats in this part of a measure act as sort of a link back to the beginning of the measure when you repeat this exercise. (You may have noticed that there are repeat signs bracketing this measure, indicating that you should repeat this measure over and over as an exercise.)

The remaining three exercises have the hi-hat opening and closing at various places in the measure. Take your time with each exercise and repeat them as many times as you can before continuing.

The Declaration of Independence

THESE EXERCISES ARE DESIGNED to give you a handful of new grooves to play, but they will also help you to develop greater independence. When your limbs can do four different things that don't depend on each other, they are independent of each other.

Let me give you a quick history lesson to illustrate my point. The United States once belonged to England. All the laws under which England lived, the United States lived under, too. Then one day (July 4, 1776, actually) the United States decided that it no longer wanted to belong to England. It wanted to split off from England and become its own country and do its own thing. The U.S. declared its independence.

When you play the first exercise with open and closed hi-hats in this chapter, both of your feet will be coming down at the same time on the first beat of the measure. Both of your feet are dependant on each other since they are both doing the same thing at the same time. But when you move on to the other exercises in this chapter, your feet will be moving independently of each other in order to play the open and closed hi-hat moves where they're supposed to be.

In the last chapter you developed some independence between your hands when you played Sixteenth-Note Variation #1 in a groove. The only difference between independence in drumming and independence between countries is that in drumming, your limbs are only going to be independent of each other for a very short time within a measure before they join back together to move dependently again. This very short history lesson was brought to you by me. Class dismissed.

Groove #6 with Open and Closed Hi-Hat

HOPEFULLY, YOU REMEMBER Groove #6 from Chapter 5. It's the groove sensation that's sweeping the nation with a funky vibration. If you take that groove as it was and add some open and closed hi-hat moves to it, you'll create an even more intense groove sensation that will rock all nations, bringing funk infestations to all your friends and relations.

These open and closed hi-hat moves you'll add to Groove #6 should not be much more difficult than the last series of exercises, in which you took a groove and added open and closed hi-hat moves. If you need to refresh your memory as to how Groove #6 goes before you start to add the open and closed hi-hat moves, please do so. Just ignore the open and closed indictors above the hi-hat notes. Then, when you feel comfortable with the groove itself, try to add the open and closed hi-hat moves (see Figures 6.7 through 6.10).

Just like the last open and closed hi-hat exercises in this chapter, the first exercise should be the easiest. You'll be using the open and closed hi-hats to link the very end of the measure to the beginning of the repeat of that same measure. Remember to try to play each example over and over as many times as you can, observing the repeat signs you will see at the beginning and end of the measure.

Once you can play the exercise you're working on several times in a row, it's time to try it with your metronome. Pick a tempo at which you can rock steady. Use the timer technique if you want. Set it for 10 minutes for each exercise, and go for it.

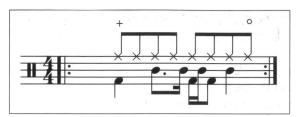

Figure 6.7
Groove #6: Example #1

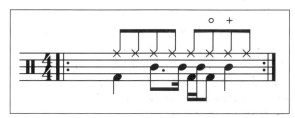

Figure 6.8
Groove #6: Example #2

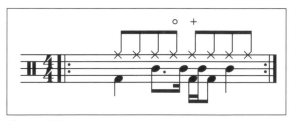

Figure 6.9
Groove #6: Example #3

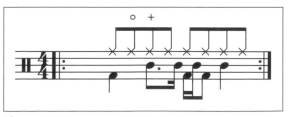

Figure 6.10
Groove #6: Example #4

Sixteenth-Note Variations Using the Bass Drum: The Big Four

NOW LET'S TAKE YOUR developing independence to yet another level. When you take some of the sixteenth-note variations that you already know and move them to your right foot on the bass drum, you not only have an opportunity to develop independence between your limbs even further, but you will also gain access to a bunch of new grooves to play.

The Big #1: Sixteenth-Note Variation #1 Using the Bass Drum

To review, Sixteenth-Note Variation #1 has only the first and last notes present in a group of four possible sixteenth notes (see Figure 6.11).

We can take the two notes that make up this particular sixteenth-note variation and split them up between the snare drum and the bass drum to create a new groove (see Figure 6.12).

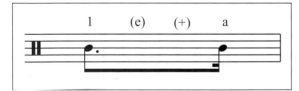

Figure 6.11
Sixteenth-Note Variation #1

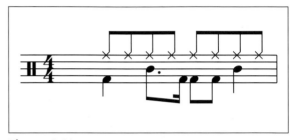

Figure 6.12
The Big #1

As you may remember, the second of the two notes in this particular variation will end up falling in place between two eighth notes, which you'll be playing on the hi-hat in this particular groove. Also, when you play this groove correctly, your bass drum foot will be playing two notes that are placed closer together than any two notes you've ever played on the bass drum before. This can be a little tricky at first, so let's isolate this tricky part of the measure so you can work on just that part before you try the whole measure (see Figure 6.13).

Figure 6.13
Isolated part of the Big #1

To play just this part of the measure, play two bass drum notes close together, like a heartbeat. Then try to play a hi-hat note just with the second of those two bass drum notes, not the first note. It might seem a little easier than it actually is. You may find yourself playing both notes on the hi-hats along with the bass drum. This is because your right hand and your right foot are still fairly dependent on each other. Work on this piece of the measure until you can make your foot play that one note without your hand.

Use the timer technique to practice this part of the measure if you're having trouble. Keep in mind that as challenging as this might seem at first, all you're doing as you practice this part over and over is giving your arms and legs an opportunity to memorize a certain order of actions. When you make a mistake, just start over and try it again without too much thought. The more times you try to play it, the closer you'll get to playing it right. Then, when you finally get it right, play it over a few times to make sure you've got the hang of it. When you feel comfortable with that particular piece, it's time to put it inside the measure to create a brand-new groove.

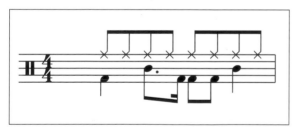

Figure 6.14
The Big #1 again

When you go to put the pieces of the measure together to form the groove, take some time to determine and understand exactly where that "in between" note on the bass drum is going to land. The "in between" note on the bass drum that begins the phrase will land after the "+" of beat 2 that you'll be playing on the hi-hats. After you play

that "in between" note on the bass drum, add two more bass drum notes along with the eighth notes that you'll be playing on the hi-hats throughout the entire measure. So, you will be playing three bass-drum notes in row in that part of the measure. Just remember that the distance between the first and second bass-drum notes in the phrase is smaller than the distance between the second and third notes of the phrase.

Take your time, and use the timer technique. Remember, you'll be getting closer and closer to playing this exercise correctly each time you try it. Give your limbs enough chances to memorize the order of actions that you want them to do, and suddenly you'll find yourself playing this exercise correctly. When you feel comfortable playing it through at least once, try to play it twice through. Then, just like you did with all the previous exercises, try to play it as many times in a row as you can. Try playing it to your metronome at a tempo setting that's comfortable to you. When you master this particular exercise, you've taken a major step forward in the development of your independence skills. Everything beyond this big step will be easier because you've developed some major coordination skills that are essential to progress toward your goal of becoming a good drummer.

After you've mastered this exercise, you might want to take a moment and go look at yourself in a nearby mirror. See whether you notice any difference since the last time you checked a mirror. You should notice a difference. As you look into the mirror, you'll see a super-coordinated human being instead of the uncoordinated slob that you were before you mastered this exercise. Take a moment to bask in your newfound glory. But wait—before you step away from the mirror, check your teeth. I think you've got something stuck between your two front ones.

EVERY DAY IN EVERY WAY, YOU'RE GETTING BETTER AND BETTER

It might seem as if the exercises that I'm giving you to work on are getting harder and harder. It's true that the exercises are becoming more challenging, but please don't despair. If you take your time and practice each exercise until you can play it as close to perfectly as you possibly can, you are doing more than just learning how to play that particular exercise.

I've put all the exercises in this book in a certain order designed to increase your skills as you move forward through the book. Each exercise uses and builds on skills that you've developed in the previous exercises. You're becoming a more skilled and coordinated drummer as you go, so when you're faced with a new and challenging exercise, it's not like you're starting at the beginning every time. You have the skills that you've developed up to that point to draw on.

As you become more coordinated, you'll have to spend less time perfecting something new to play. That's because you're getting better as you go. When you look at a new and challenging exercise, your brain might try to discourage you by trying to tell you that the new exercise is too hard and that you'll never be able to figure it out and play it. Don't listen to your brain. Give the exercise you're working on a try without listening to your brain too much, and you might find that it's easier than you thought.

It will just take your brain a little bit of time to catch up to the reality that the rest of your body already knows. You're more coordinated than you ever were before you started to play drums and you're becoming more and more coordinated with every new exercise that you play correctly. You'd think your brain would know better, but sometimes your brain is the last to know.

The Big #2: Sixteenth-Note Variation #3 on the Bass Drum

In this exercise you'll be playing all three notes of Sixteenth-Note Variation #3 on the bass drum in the third beat of the measure. To refresh your memory, Figure 6.15 shows what Sixteenth-Note Variation #3 looks like.

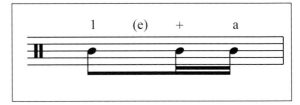

Figure 6.15
Sixteenth-Note Variation #3

When Sixteenth-Note Variation #3 is put in place in the measure you'll be working on in this exercise, you'll find that you'll be playing two quick bass-drum notes in a row, just like in Sixteenth-Note Variation #2. But when you add the eighth notes on the hi-hat that the full measure will include, an interesting difference between the two exercises will reveal itself. When you isolated the two quick bass-drum notes together with the hi-hat in the last exercise, you were playing a hi-hat note with the second of the two bass-drum notes. In this exercise, if you were to isolate those bass drum notes and play the hi-hat along with them, you should be playing the hi-hat on the first of the two notes instead. Figures 6.16 and 6.17 show a comparison of the isolated parts of both measures.

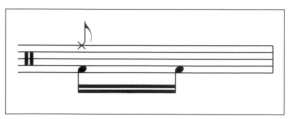

Figure 6.18
Isolated part of the Big #2

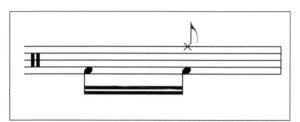

Figure 6.16
Isolated part of the Big #1

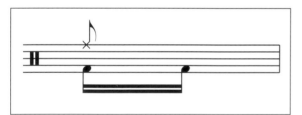

Figure 6.17
Isolated part of the Big #2

Before you decide to tackle the entire measure, take a few minutes to play just this isolated part of the measure. To do this, play two bass-drum notes (like a heartbeat) and play a hi-hat note with your left hand, along with just the first bass-drum note and not the second (see Figure 6.18).

When you've got a feel for that part of the measure, putting it in place within the measure should be easy for you. Figure 6.19 shows the measure in its entirety.

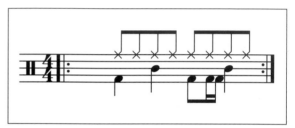

Figure 6.19
The Big #2

Remember that just like the last exercise, in which you played Sixteenth-Note Variation #1 between the snare drum and the bass drum, you'll be playing a total of three bass-drum notes in the third beat of the measure to make this new phrase, not just the two notes that you played in the isolated piece of the measure. Actually, both this exercise and the last one you learned contain the same number of notes, so technically this particular exercise should be no more difficult for you to play than the last one. The bass-drum notes in the third beat of the measure are simply in different places than they were in that previous exercise.

Keep this in mind if you run into any difficulties while trying to play this. You're simply giving your limbs a new order of actions that you want them to remember and, as with anything that you're trying to memorize, repetition is key. Play it once, play it twice, play it as many times as you can. Use the timer technique if you have to; play it to your metronome. You know the drill.

HEY—WHATEVER HAPPENED TO SIXTEENTH-NOTE VARIATION #2?

As you've hopefully noticed, I showed you how to incorporate Sixteenth-Note Variations #1 and #3 into groove exercises and skipped right over Sixteenth-Note Variation #2. No, this was not a mistake. Sixteenth-Note Variation #2 didn't die in a tragic gardening accident or anything like that. It's just not practical in this particular application.

As you remember, Sixteenth-Note Variation #2 contains only the first three notes of the four notes that would be in a group of four sixteenth notes (see Figure 6.20).

Figure 6.20
Sixteenth-Note Variation #2

This particular variation is not as easily adapted to a groove as the others that you'll be learning in this chapter. In the first two exercises in this chapter, and in the next two, there are only two quick bass-drum notes in a row, followed by a note at a greater distance from those other two in its phrase. If we were to use Sixteenth-Note Variation #2 in a groove in the same way that we're using the other variations, you'd have to be able to play three quick bass-drum notes in a row, which would be difficult and unlikely for any drummer, no matter what his or her level of expertise might be.

This can be done with one foot with great effort and would be easier to play with two feet on a double pedal or two bass drums. If you're feeling very daring, please feel free to try it (see Figure 6.21). You may be one of the few blessed with a super-fast bass-drum foot, in which case you'll have no problem playing three sixteenth notes in a row on one bass drum. Or maybe you already have a double pedal. If you have the guts to attempt this exercise, go for it. Consider it extra credit. Go ahead, I double-dog-dare you.

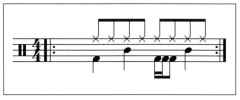

Figure 6.21
Extra credit

The Big #3: Using Four Sixteenth Notes to Create a Groove

In this exercise you'll be playing four quarter notes split up between the snare drum and the bass drum in the third beat of the measure to create a groove. Just like we did with all the previous exercises in this chapter, let's start by isolating the third beat of the measure so we can get a good look at all the action (see Figure 6.22).

Figure 6.22
Isolated part of the Big #3

This group of four sixteenth notes is very similar to the last exercise that you worked on in this chapter, your old pal Sixteenth-Note Variation #3. Let's compare them (see Figures 6.23 and 6.24).

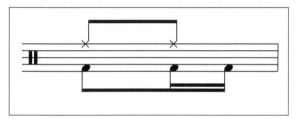

Figure 6.23
Isolated part of the Big #2

Figure 6.24
Isolated part of the Big #3

As you can see, we will be adding one note to Sixteenth-Note Variation #3 to create this new piece of a groove, which has all four possible sixteenth notes in a group present. Sixteenth-Note Variation #3 is a group of three notes. The distance between the second two notes of the group is smaller than the space between the first two notes. You play all three of the notes in the group on the bass drum to create the groove that you learned earlier.

To create the brand-new groove that you'll work on right now, you'll be fitting a snare-drum note into the space between the first and second of the three bass-drum notes. You've actually done this before when you learned Groove #6 in the last chapter. (Groove #6 is the groove sensation that's rocking the nation, etc. You also played it earlier in this chapter and added some open and closed hi-hat moves to it. Now you remember it, don't you?) In the third beat of the measure that makes up Groove #6, you played two eighth notes on both the bass drum and the hi-hats on the "3+" of the measure, and you played a snare-drum note between those two notes.

I'm pointing this out so you don't become too intimidated when you first try this piece of the measure. This piece of the measure that we'll use to create a new groove is actually a combination of two different things that you've played before. The only thing that might be challenging to you in this particular piece is that those two different things that you've played before are going to be combined in this particular exercise. The best way to begin to get a handle on this complete exercise is to isolate the piece of the measure where all the action is and work on that piece alone (see Figure 6.25).

Figure 6.25
Isolated part of the Big #3

As you can see, you'll be playing a total of three hi-hat notes. The best way to determine for yourself where the snare-drum and bass-drum notes will land in this piece is to line them up with the hi-hat notes so you can clearly see where the "in between" notes are supposed to be. Then, when you're ready, give this piece of the measure a try.

Remember, you've already played everything in this exercise, just not all at the same time. As with all the other exercises that you've worked on up to this point, repetition will be the key to memorizing the particular order of actions that you want your limbs to take to play this exercise. Take your time, ignore your brain, and allow the memorization to take place. When you're ready, put this piece into place to create a full-measure groove that you can be proud of (see Figure 6.26).

Figure 6.26
The Big #3

Just as with all the other exercises earlier in this chapter, it should be pretty easy for you to play the rest of the measure because you took the time to isolate and practice the most difficult part of the measure already. In this exercise, all the heavy action will begin right on beat 3 of the measure.

Follow the same practice drill for this exercise as you did with all the previous exercises you've learned so far. Play it once, play it twice, and play it as many times in a row as you can. Use the timer practice technique if you think it will help. It's very

important not to become frustrated if you find yourself having a hard time with this particular exercise. Remember, you're simply allowing your limbs to memorize a certain order of actions that you want them to take by playing this exercise over and over. With every try you make, you're getting one step closer to playing the exercise correctly. One of those tries will be the special try, when it will all fall together magically and you'll play the exercise perfectly. And that will bring you one step closer to being cool enough to hang out with me.

The Big #4: Sixteenth-Note Variation #4 on the Bass Drum

Remember this bit shown in Figure 6.27?

Figure 6.27
Sixteenth-Note Variation #4

Sure you do. It's Sixteenth-Note Variation #4, which you used to create some fills back in the last chapter. Now you'll be using this particular variation on the bass drum in the third beat of the measure to create a new groove. Just like we did with the earlier exercises in this chapter, let's isolate the part of the measure where all the action is (see Figure 6.28).

To get started, it's important that you determine and understand where each bass drum note in the phrase is supposed to land. Look at the hi-hat notes and figure out which bass-drum notes are going to line up directly with a hi-hat note and which bass-drum notes will end up being placed

Figure 6.28
Isolated part of the Big #4

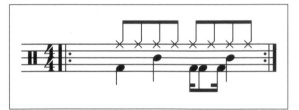

Figure 6.29
The Big #4

between two hi-hat notes. As you can see, the first bass-drum note in the group of three that makes up this phrase is lined up directly with the first hi-hat note in the phrase.

The next bass-drum note you'll be playing in the phrase comes immediately after that first bass-drum note. This note will be played all alone, without a hi-hat note accompanying it. You've already played two quick bass-drum notes while playing a hi-hat along with just the first bass-drum note, back when you were practicing the isolated part of the measure that makes up the Big #2 groove earlier in this chapter, so this little move shouldn't give you too much trouble.

After you play two quick bass-drum notes with a hi-hat note along with the first note, the next note in the phrase is simply a hi-hat note played all alone, with nothing accompanying it. Then, play a bass-drum note all alone immediately after the last hi-hat note you played. To finish the phrase, use both hands to play your snare drum and your hi-hats together. Getting the feel of the two "in between" notes that you'll be playing on the bass drum might take some work, but all you need to do is take it slow and give yourself enough chances to memorize the order of actions that you're trying to execute. Once you get this piece of the measure down, it's time to put it into place within a measure to create a new groove (see Figure 6.29).

Everything that makes up the rest of the measure (apart from the isolated piece you just worked on) should be very easy for you to play because you've played it all before in all the previous exercises in this chapter. The only challenge you'll face in playing the entire measure is in fully understanding how the pieces fit together to complete the entire measure.

In this exercise, you'll be inserting the isolated piece that you worked on earlier right at beat 3 of the measure. Don't forget to play the hi-hat note on the "+" of beat 2 that comes right before you begin to play the phrase that was isolated earlier. Then, after you play that previously isolated phrase, you'll need to play one more hi-hat note alone to end the measure, just like you did with all the other exercises in this chapter. Try the entire measure whenever you're ready, following the same drill that you did with all the other exercises in this chapter. Play it once, play it twice, play it as many times as you can. Use the timer practice technique if it will help you. Then, play this exercise along with your metronome at a tempo that's comfortable for you. Something tells me you've heard all this before. And you'll hear it many times again before you're through with this book. Sorry, that's just the way it goes.

The Extra-Special "Congratulations, You've Reached the Middle of the Book" Review That I Hope You're Happy About

YOU'VE LEARNED A GREAT MANY important things in this chapter, so it's a good idea to have a review from the DVD right about now. At this point in your drumming career, your biggest challenge will be remembering all the different things that you know how to play by now. Not only that, but by the time you reach the end of this chapter, you've reached the halfway point of this book. If that's not a good enough reason for a review, I don't what is.

This review will start off easy enough, covering what I call the "Big Four" that you learned in this chapter. Then you'll be mixing it up with the fabulous Groove #6, both with and without open and closed hi-hat moves. Then, an exciting finish contains a thrilling mix of some of the grooves you learned earlier in this book (see Figure 6.30).

Keep your eyes peeled for open and closed hi-hat moves that may or may not be sprinkled throughout the entire review exercise. Take this review exercise slowly at first to make sure you understand everything in the review, although I promise you that there is nothing in this review exercise that you haven't played before. Play each measure one at a time if you have to in order to get a handle on all the information contained in the exercise, but when you're ready to try to play the entire exercise in one shot, it's very important that you go back and start from the beginning, no matter how far along you get before making a mistake. The reason for this is because if you always start from the beginning, you'll be going over and over the same parts leading up to the part with which you're having problems. As you go over and over those parts, you're improving your coordination so that by the time you reach the part you're having trouble with, you'll be even more coordinated than you were earlier.

Although it's more time consuming to practice this review exercise in this way, it will pay off in the end. The key to being a good drummer is being able to play something over and over again as many times as it takes to play an entire song. It does you no good to be able to play something once, twice, or even 10 times in a row without making a mistake. It would not be out of the question to find yourself playing the same pattern more than 16 times in a row before making a change, such as adding a fill or beginning a different pattern. It takes a lot of patience to be a good drummer on whom the rest of the band can rely to build that solid rhythmic foundation for them to play along to. But I'm sure you have a lot of patience. After all, you've read six chapters so far, haven't you?

When you can play the whole exercise all the way through without making a mistake, next try playing it to a metronome setting that's comfortable for you so you can make sure you're flowing smoothly through the entire exercise without slowing down or speeding up.

You could consider this review exercise to be a drum solo, so don't be afraid to play it for people who will appreciate the effort you've shown so far in learning how to play drums. Be as proud of yourself as they will be of you when they hear it. You've come a long way. Congratulations. Now, turn the page.

Figure 6.30
Review

In Which You'll Learn Why Over and Over, Become Sharp, Get Lectured, Enter a Brave New World, and Learn How to Smoke

and Throw

NOW THAT YOU'VE reached the halfway point in this book, you've digested a lot of information and picked up a lot of things to play on the drums. In fact, you've picked up so many things to play that you might find yourself forgetting some of the things that you already know how to play. This is a good problem to have—a worse problem would be not having enough things to play.

Practice Routines and Learning by Repetition, Learning by Repetition, Learning by Repetition: Does This Sound Familiar?

A S YOU'VE PROBABLY FIGURED OUT by now (and as I pointed out earlier in this book), the easiest way for me to introduce you to something new to play is to take something that you already know and add something to it. However, if you're having trouble remembering the original piece that we'll be adding something to, then it will be as if you're starting over from scratch, and that can make your learning process twice as long as it needs to be. I wouldn't want you to lose your patience when trying to learn something new just because you've let something you already learned slip from your memory, so you need to work on your memory skills. But how, you ask? You need to set up a practice routine.

As you learned earlier in this book, the best way to memorize something is to repeat it over and over, giving it a chance to burn its way into your memory. So, what you need to do is set up a routine for yourself in which you'll be spending a certain amount of time going over certain grooves or fills you have already learned. You don't need to practice them over and over again so much that you become sick of them; you just need to go back over all the things you've learned so far and touch on them enough so that when you need to return to them to add things to create something brand-new, they'll immediately spring back to life in your memory.

Reviews: Keeping It Sharp

Y OU'LL FIND MORE REVIEWS in other chapters of this book. This will help you not only reinforce the material that you've learned in the chapter in which you're working, but will also touch on some things you've already learned in the past. Think of all the things that you've already learned how to play on the drums as a set of knives that all have slightly different uses and sizes. Some knives are used to cut small things, some are used to cut large things, and so on.

Now, you may find yourself mainly using one particular knife more often than the other ones, so you spend a lot of time sharpening that particular knife so it will always be nice and sharp every time you use it. But sometimes the main knife you've been using might be too large or too small for a particular job that you're faced with, and you have to reach into your knife case for a different knife—one that you don't use that often. Now, you would want that rarely used knife to be just as sharp as the one that you use more often, wouldn't you? Well, all those other knives that you've gone to the trouble of buying and adding to your knife collection aren't going to sharpen themselves as they sit there in the knife case. You need to sharpen all of the knives in your collection so they will always be ready to use.

I realize it's weird and maybe a little creepy to be talking so much about knives and knife collections in a drum book. I don't have a knife collection myself, nor am I particularly obsessed with knives or anything. It's just a comparison that makes sense. I don't recommend that you start a knife collection. Unless, you know, you were going to anyway even before you read this book.

When you work on a review, you're keeping some of those grooves and fills that you've learned in the past nice and sharp. For this reason, it's important for you to take the time to work on a review when you come across one in the rest of this book. Keep in mind that you won't find anything in any review that you haven't played before; you just might not have played it lately. It shouldn't take you more than a few tries for something that you've played before to immediately fall in line for you in a review.

How to Set Up a Practice Routine

THE BEST WAY TO SET UP a practice routine that will ensure that you'll use your practice time to its best advantage is to apply a little bit of organization to your practice sessions. Now, I must admit that I have a harder time getting organized in any way, shape, or form than most people I know. I don't even particularly like the word "organization." But I've learned that at least a little bit of organization in your practice sessions is a good thing.

It's very easy to let time slip away when you're practicing. Ultimately, drumming is a creative activity, and letting your mind wander for the sake of creativity is just as important as being at least a little bit organized while practicing. If you were only organized but not particularly creative, you'd probably be more interested in becoming an accountant or a math teacher than becoming a drummer. (Not that we don't need accountants or math teachers in this world, but picture your math teacher for a minute. Kinda boring, huh?)

Let's organize a typical 40-minute practice routine into four parts, 10 minutes each, as an example of how you might possibly organize your practice routine for maximum effectiveness. Make sure you keep your metronome handy so you can work on playing all of the exercises you'll be working on in time and as steadily as you possibly can. You can also use your timer to keep track of when 10 minutes is up and it's time to move on to the next 10-minute chunk of time in your practice session.

▶ **First 10 minutes.** Work on the last exercise you were taught in the latest chapter. Use the timer technique as you have been to make sure that you're devoting 10 full minutes to the latest exercise.

▶ **Second 10 minutes.** Work on the review that was included in the chapter you are currently working on. The reviews will be placed at the end of each chapter, but you don't have to wait until you get to the end of the chapter before you start to practice the review. When you begin a new chapter, include the review in your practice routine right away. If you're spending 10 minutes of every practice session working on the review in that chapter, those fills and grooves in that review are going to remain sharp enough to cut glass.

▶ **Third 10 minutes.** Go back to the first review you practiced in this book and spend 10 minutes running through it. Then, go to the next review in the book and run through that for 10 minutes in your next practice session. When you've caught up to the review that you're currently working on, go back to the very first review and start the process all over again. I know this sounds a little crazy, as if I might be asking you to overdo it a little, but the sharper you keep those past exercises, the easier it will be to learn new exercises because they all build on each other. And you'll be improving your ability to remember all the things you already know how to play.

▶ **Fourth 10 minutes.** Use these 10 minutes to have fun and be creative. Make up some grooves and fills of your very own using all the things you've learned and reviewed in this practice session. Take out your frustrations with this book and this silly practice routine by trying to play as fast as you can. Experiment and find new sounds by hitting your cymbals in different places. Cut loose for as long as you feel like it, not just 10 minutes. Reward yourself for working hard for 30 minutes on your drumming skills and rock out. Just don't hurt yourself. Or if you do, don't blame me.

A Short Lecture

LOOK, I KNOW THAT BREAKING a practice routine down to the minute seems totally unrealistic and strict. I must admit that if I were starting out on drums and the dude who wrote the book I was using was trying to tell me exactly what to do and for how long, I'd think he was a jerk and he needed to lighten up. Well, I am a jerk sometimes, but not for this particular reason. If I was your actual drum teacher and I met with you every week, I would be able to decide how much practicing I thought you should be doing and exactly what you should be practicing. But because I'm not your teacher and I can't hear you play in order to decide a practice routine that will work for you alone, I can only set up a practice routine in this book that I know for sure will work for anyone.

Of course, you can decide for yourself how to practice, but sometimes we're not always the best judge of our own abilities. You might think that you're good enough at something in particular, or maybe you need to work on something but you're avoiding it because you think it's too hard. I understand laziness and avoidance of things that might take more work to perfect than you're comfortable with. I understand these things because I was not always the best student in the world when I was first learning to play drums. I was disorganized and lazy and I didn't know how to practice properly to get the results I could from my practice time. Because of this, it took me much longer to learn certain things than it might have taken other students who had their acts together.

I'm not saying that you should be in a great hurry to become the world's best drummer and that you need to follow this practice routine or you'll never be any good. What I'm saying is that if you're serious enough to buy this book because you want to become a good drummer, you might as well try to be as serious as you can about following the lessons. I can almost guarantee that following the exercises and practice routines exactly as they are in this book will help you become the good drummer you want to be. If you don't follow the program I'm laying out for you, you might end up a far worse drummer than someone who follows my program.

There are no guarantees, so I hope you'll try your best to follow my program and, with the benefit of private lessons, go on to become a truly great drummer. Then, someday, when someone asks you how you got to be such a great drummer, you can look that person right in the eye and say, "I don't know. I'm just lucky, I guess." You can go ahead and fib a little. You and I know the real truth.

Triplets: A Brave New World

IN THIS SECTION OF THE BOOK you'll learn about a new note called the *triplet*. Actually, you'll learn about three new notes called *triplets* because triplets always come in packs of (you guessed it) threes. However, you can sometimes see notes hanging around together in groups of three that are not triplets. For example, Figure 7.1 is not a triplet.

Figure 7.1
Sixteenth-Note Variation #2

Of course you recognize this as your old pal Sixteenth-Note Variation #2, which you learned about in Chapter 5. Figure 7.2 presents another example of a group of three notes that's not a triplet.

Figure 7.2
Sixteenth-Note Variation #3

That's Sixteenth-Note Variation #3, also from Chapter 5. Sixteenth-Note Variation #4 from Chapter 5 is not a triplet either (see Figure 7.3).

Figure 7.3
Sixteenth-Note Variation #4

So, now that you know what a triplet isn't, let's find out what the heck it is.

What Is a Triplet?

Put in the simplest terms, a triplet is a group of three notes that take up the same space or note value as a group of two notes. The word *triplet* can be thought of as a last name, the first name being the kind of triplet it is. For example, if you were to use the word "triplets" alone as an instruction or an indication of something that you wanted someone to play, that would not be enough information to accurately make your point. But if you were to instruct someone to play "eighth-note triplets," then they would have all the information that they need to play what you're instructing them to.

The words "eighth note" are like someone's first name, while the word "triplet" is like the person's last name. It's just like how my first name is "Jon" and my last name is "Peckman: The World's Greatest Teacher of Drums." (Okay, that's not really my last name. I had the word "Peckman" legally added to my birth name. It means "The World's Greatest Teacher of Drums" in an ancient and forgotten language.) When you see triplets in a measure of notation, they usually have a small number 3 and a little arch conveniently above each group of three notes. Figure 7.4 presents an exercise to get you started on eighth-note triplets.

As you can see, you'll be playing quarter notes on the bass drum in both measures of the exercise. This will help you get a feel for the difference between eighth notes and eighth-note triplets. Each quarter note on the bass drum represents one beat of the measure, and when you play eighth notes on the snare drum in the first measure of the exercise, you will be playing two notes on the snare drum for every one note that you play on the bass drum. However, when you get to the second measure and the eighth-note triplets, you'll play three snare drum notes to every one bass-drum note.

When you play the eighth-note triplets on the snare drum, make sure that all three notes are evenly spaced. Don't mistake Sixteenth-Note Variation #2 for eighth-note triplets. Remember that Sixteenth-Note Variation #2 is actually three sixteenth notes in a row, with one sixteenth note's worth of a rest at the end of the group. The eighth-note triplets that you're shooting for consist of three evenly spaced notes with no rests between them.

Watch Your Sticking

When you start the exercise by playing the first note on the snare drum with your right hand, simply alternate hands from right to left as you continue to play eighth notes on the snare drum all the way through the measure. You'll be using your right hand to play a snare-drum note on each beat of the measure. When you get to the second measure of the exercise, where you'll begin to play triplets, pay attention to your sticking. If you're playing the triplets while still playing in an alternating style of sticking (from your right hand to your left and so on), you'll end up using the opposite hand from one beat of the measure to the other. This can be very tricky at first and may take a little bit of extra concentration to get the hang of, so take it slow. Figure 7.5 shows the exercise again, with sticking notation to help you out.

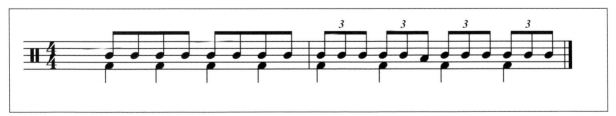

Figure 7.4
Eighth notes versus eighth-note triplets

Figure 7.5

Eighth notes versus eighth-note triplets with sticking

Eighth-Note Triplets: Not Quite This and Not Quite That

Mathematically speaking, eighth-note triplets occupy a place between eighth notes and sixteenth notes. (Please don't let this math stuff scare you off. As I revealed to you earlier in this book, I'm no math genius—far from it. Just try to bear with me and a little bit of math for a few minutes in this section.) As you remember from the multiplication tables, 2 times 8 is 16. Understanding this simple fact of mathematics can allow you to understand and play eighth notes and sixteenth notes.

Eighth-note triplets fall between eighth notes and sixteenth notes. Knowledge of how triplets work can afford you opportunities to create pieces of grooves and fills in which eighth notes would seem a little too slow and sixteenth notes would seem a little too fast. For this reason, triplets deserve our undying devotion and eternal gratitude.

Sixteenth-Note Triplets: Not Quite That and Not Quite the Other Thing

Now we'll move on to sixteenth-note triplets. But first, back to the multiplication tables. In case you forgot or you weren't in school that day, 2 times 16 is 32. You'll just have to take my word for it. Now, you've played plenty of fills earlier in this book using sixteenth notes to create them. Figure 7.6 shows one from Chapter 4 that we called Fill #6. This is the fill that uses sixteenth notes all the way around the kit using the snare drum and all three of the toms. Please travel back in time with me to the good old days of Fill #6.

Figure 7.6

Fill #6

Now, suppose you were perfectly happy with Fill #6, but you wanted to learn another fill similar to Fill #6 except that it was more exciting or had more notes to it. Using a mathematical approach, you could simply multiply the number of notes in the fill by two, or double the number of notes to create a new and exciting fill. Using your advanced mathematical skills (or counting on your fingers, which is what I do), determine the value of 2 times 16. That's right: The magic number in this case is 32. So, one way to create a fill of the same length but with more notes than sixteenth notes is to play a one-measure fill with thirty-second notes all the way around the kit. Instead of playing four sixteenth notes on each drum as you make your way around the kit to play the fill, you would instead be playing eight thirty-second notes on each drum (see Figure 7.7). The fill will still take up only one measure, but you'll have to fit twice as many notes in the measure. Go ahead and try it. I dare you.

Hopefully, you've figured out that it is very difficult to try to jam all those thirty-second notes into the space of one measure at any tempo, even a slower one. Does this mean you're always going to be stuck having to make a choice between sixteenth notes that are perfectly doable but not always very exciting and next-to-impossible-to-execute thirty-second notes? You would be stuck if you didn't know about sixteenth-note triplets. But lucky for you, you're about to get unstuck.

I NEED SOME SPACE

Sorry, I can't stop myself from interjecting what I feel is an important concept in drumming. Adding more notes to a fill does not necessarily or automatically generate more excitement. Often, it's the notes that you leave out or don't play that can add to the excitement of a groove or a fill. The concept of leaving out notes to create space in your playing is something we'll get into a little later in this book.

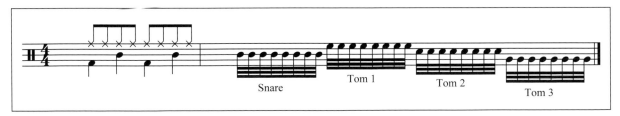

Figure 7.7
Extra credit

Sixteenth-Note Triplets: The Happy Medium

SIXTEENTH-NOTE TRIPLETS are the perfect choice to make a fill when sixteenth notes are not enough and thirty-second notes are too much. Figure 7.8 presents a fill that goes all the way around the kit using sixteenth-note triplets instead of just sixteenth notes.

You'll notice when looking at this fill that the sixteenth-note triplets are in groups of six on each drum, instead of groups of four, as they would be in sixteenth-note groups, or groups of eight, as they would be in thirty-second-note groups. If there are six notes on each drum (and six is an even number just like four or eight), this means you will be using a right-hand lead to get all the way around the kit. In other words, your right hand will be the first hand to reach each drum as you go around the kit. For this reason, it should feel fairly natural to you as you make the transition from drum to drum because the transition is very similar to every other transition you've made in all the other fills in which you traveled all the way around the kit.

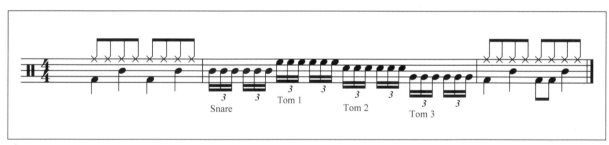

Figure 7.8
A fill using sixteenth-note triplets

Speed Kills

BECAUSE SIXTEENTH-NOTE TRIPLETS have more notes in their groupings than regular sixteenth notes do, it's important to be aware that you might have to practice a fill full of sixteenth-note triplets at a slower tempo than you would if you were just playing sixteenth notes. You want the fill to be in the same tempo as any groove you would play, whether made up of sixteenth-note triplets, eighth notes, or even ten-thousandth notes.

It's important that you maintain a rock-steady tempo when coming in and out of fills, so it might be a good idea to play the entire exercise—from groove to fill and back to groove again—at a tempo that you can easily manage when first trying to tackle sixteenth-note triplets. If you play the fill at one tempo and then slow down the groove to fit in all the notes of the fill, you are in violation of the first law of drumming, which is to keep all tempos as steady as possible so the rest of the band can play along to you. I've said this before but I'll say it again: You could play what you think is the greatest fill known to mankind, but if you slow down or speed up at any point before, during, or after the fill, all that will be remembered is that you blew the tempo, and your so-called awesome fill will be long forgotten before you're even chased out of the room by the band and any audience member who was unfortunate enough to hear your bumbling mess of a fill.

I'm overstating this point because I've been there, and it's a lousy place to be. Don't get me wrong—anyone can make a mistake occasionally (even me), but let the mistake be a dropped stick, ripped pants, or uncontrollable nervous vomiting, and not a bungled attempt to fit more notes into a fill than you are capable of realistically fitting. There are exercises that will help you build your speed if more speed is your goal. I'll show you those exercises soon, but until then, try this fill using sixteenth-note triplets at a tempo that is not too fast for you to handle.

Another thing to keep in mind when working with sixteenth-note triplets is that they can actually be most effective and generate the most excitement when played in a song with a slower tempo in the first place. You can be cruising along playing a slow groove during a song, and then break into sixteenth-note triplets during a fill, making the fill seem much faster and more exciting than regular sixteenth notes would be in the same fill. You'll be an instant hero for rocking the sixteenth-note triplets.

Depending on the tempo at which you play them, you might find that your hands may not move any faster than they would if you were playing regular sixteenth notes at a faster tempo. The sixteenth-note triplets will seem faster when played during a song with a slower tempo because they are technically faster than any other groups of notes in the song, but they might not necessarily be the fastest notes you've ever played in your life. So don't feel discouraged if you can't immediately burn these as fast as you can regular sixteenth notes. The longer you play drums and the more comfortable you feel with sticks in your hands, the easier pure speed will be for you.

Slicing and Dicing with Sixteenth Notes and Sixteenth-Note Triplets

N OW THAT YOU'VE GOT A HANDLE on sixteenth-note triplets, it's time to mix them up with straight sixteenth notes to create some interesting fills. In the fills you'll learn in this section, I want you to try something new that you've haven't done in any fill you've worked on up to this point. You will notice that I've added quarter notes on the bass drum to the fills that you'll learn in this section. Playing quarter notes on the bass drum underneath whatever your hands might be playing during a fill can be very useful in helping you understand how the shift from straight sixteenth notes to sixteenth-note triplets will feel to you as you play the fill.

Remember that sixteenth-note triplets will actually be played faster than straight sixteenth notes because there are more notes in a group of sixteenth-note triplets than there are in a group of straight sixteenth notes. (You will find that there are four notes in a group of sixteenth notes taking up one beat in a measure, whereas there are six notes in a group of sixteenth-note triplets occupying that same space of one beat in a measure.) As I mentioned earlier, you will be using a right-hand lead as you make your way around the kit on all of these fills, which means that your right hand will be the first hand to get to the next drum as you go around the kit.

Figures 7.9 and 7.10 show a couple of fills in which you'll switch back and forth between sixteenth notes and sixteenth-note triplets. You'll start off with a couple of half-measure fills that switch between straight sixteenth notes and sixteenth-note triplets so you can work on making the transitions as smooth as you can before you move on to full-measure fills.

> If you find that trying to add the quarter notes on the bass drum in these fills is more than you can handle at this point, you can try the fills without the bass drum at first. But, do your best to add those quarter notes as soon as you can because they will really help you understand how the switch between those sixteenth notes and sixteenth-note triplets is supposed to feel.

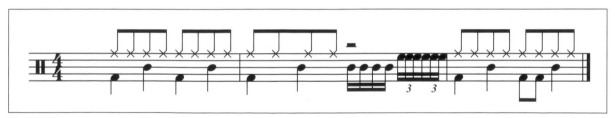

Figure 7.9
Exercise #2

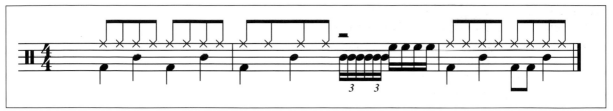

Figure 7.10
Exercise #3

When you feel comfortable with these fills, try
to add a crash cymbal to the end of the fill.
Remember that when you add a crash cymbal to
the end of a fill, you're not actually adding any
new notes. You're simply replacing the first hi-hat
note at the beginning of the measure, after the fill
with a crash cymbal. Then you'll move quickly from
the crash cymbal to the hi-hat to finish off the rest
of the eighth notes you'll play for the rest of the
measure after the crash. Figures 7.11 and 7.12 show
the last two exercises you worked on with crashes
at the end of them.

Figure 7.11
Exercise #2 with crash

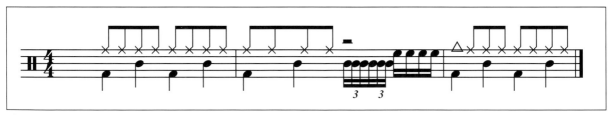

Figure 7.12
Exercise #3 with crash

When you've mastered the half-measure fills that switch between sixteenth notes and sixteenth-note triplets, it's time to do some full-measure slicing and dicing. Figures 7.13 and 7.14 present two exercises that include full-measure fills that switch between sixteenth notes and sixteenth-note triplets.

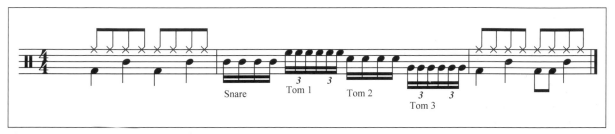

Figure 7.13
Exercise #4

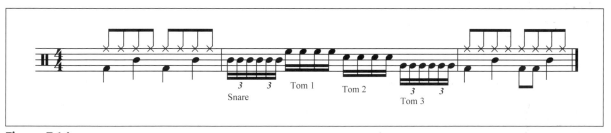

Figure 7.14
Exercise #5

Smoke and Throw

YOU'LL FIND YOURSELF HAVING to make the longest reach you'll ever have to make on your drum kit as you move from the floor tom that ends each fill back to the hi-hat way over on the other side of the kit. This reach can pose a particular challenge if the fill ends with a group of sixteenth-note triplets on the floor tom. This is when you can use a little technique that I call the old "smoke and throw." I call it the "smoke and throw" because you create a little bit of smoke to hide your movements. You create a distraction so you can make a certain move that no one will ever notice, but that will allow you to make a difficult transition more easily.

In this case, the "smoke" consists of the crash cymbal you play to end the fill. As I've pointed out before, that reach from the floor tom at the end of the fill over to the crash cymbal can be quite challenging, especially when you need to go immediately to the hi-hats to continue the eighth-note hi-hats that make up an important part of the groove you play both before and after the fill. Figure 7.15 shows an exercise in which you'll play a groove, go to a fill, end the fill with a crash, and then move back to the groove. After you play the crash cymbal on

beat 1 of the measure following the fill, you'll start eighth notes on the hi-hats on the "+ of 1," or the second eighth note of the measure. On beat 2 of the measure, you'll play the hi-hats and the snare drum together, and then continue the groove to the end of the measure.

A crash, if played confidently, creates quite a loud noise. And a big, loud, confident noise is a great way to end a fill. You can use the volume of the crash to cover up your move to the hi-hats that you'll be making to get back to the groove. This will buy you a split-second of rest for your right hand, which is doing all of the hard work in making the long reach from the floor tom on one side of the kit to the hi-hats way over on the other side.

As you saw in the last exercise, you would normally move to the hi-hats on the "+ of 1," but you can take advantage of the crash cymbal and move over to the hi-hat for beat 2 of the measure instead. No one will ever really notice if you leave out that one eighth note of the "+ of 1" of the measure with the crash cymbal ringing out nice and loudly like it should when you play it with confidence.

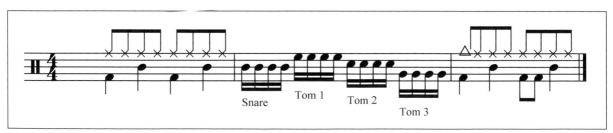

Figure 7.15
Play a groove, go to a fill, end the fill with a crash, and go back to the groove.

The first time you play the hi-hats in the measure following the fill will be on beat 2, along with the snare drum. Even though you will not be playing the hi-hat on the "+ of 1" of the measure right after the fill, make sure you don't rush into beat 2 of the measure, when you'll play the hi-hats and the snare together. Give the eighth rest that now occupies the place where the hi-hat would be its full value. Beat 2 of the measure will end up in the same place rhythmically whether there's a hi-hat note or a rest on the "+ of 1" of the measure. Give it a try.

If you find yourself having trouble working with that rest, you should definitely try this exercise along to your metronome. If you set your metronome to a tempo at which each click represents a quarter note, you'll find that you should be playing the crash cymbal along with the bass drum during one click, which is beat 1 of the measure after the fill, and then you'll play the hi-hats along with the snare drum during the next click, which will be beat 2 of the measure (Figure 7.16).

Learning how to leave out just one eighth note on the hi-hats might seem like a lot of trouble to go through for what seems like nothing, but once you try it enough times to get the hang of it, you will find that the one split-second you gain by not having to go to the hi-hats right away may be the exact split-second you need to make sure the all-important transition back to the groove after the fill is as smooth as it can possibly be. And smoothness is what it's all about. You're sacrificing an actual note in the name of smoothness. That note should be honored to be sacrificed in the honor of something so much bigger than itself. Hats off to that note. May we all aspire to be as brave and strong as that note. I'll respect and miss that note for the rest of my life. Or not.

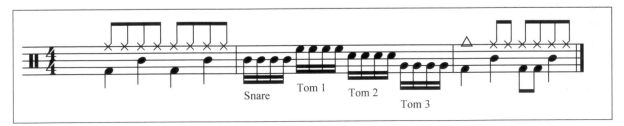

Figure 7.16
Smoke and throw

Review

NOW THAT YOU'VE REACHED THE END of Chapter 7, Figure 7.17 presents a big, juicy review for you to work on that contains some things you learned in the last few chapters as well as some things you learned in this chapter. You should definitely practice this review to your metronome to make sure you're making everything as smooth as it can possibly be.

Take it slow, have fun, and I'll see you in the next chapter.

Figure 7.17
Review

Where You'll Meet Your Two New Best Friends (the Quadruplet and the Flam), Join the Secret Brother and Sisterhood of the Flopping Fish, Slam Doors in Your House, and Say Inappropriate Things at the Dinner Table— All in the Name of

Drumming

A QUADRUPLET IS A GROUP OF (you guessed it) four notes. However, unlike a group of four sixteenth notes, quadruplets are special. In notation, a quadruplet is actually one group of three sixteenth-note triplets with an extra note added on to the end and taking up the space of one beat in a measure of 4/4. You can tell the difference between a group of four sixteenth notes and a quadruplet very easily because a quadruplet will have a number 3 above it, just like any form of a triplet will.

The Quadruplet

IN THE PARTICULAR VERSION of the quadruplet that I'm about to show you, you'll take the four notes that make up a quadruplet and play them each on a different drum of your drum kit to create a fill (or a piece of a fill) that is very exciting and can be used in many different ways. Learning a quadruplet in which each note is played on a different drum can be very challenging at first, so I'd like you to take a look at the quadruplet alone before you attempt to insert it into a fill. Figure 8.1 shows what the particular version of the quadruplet looks like all alone.

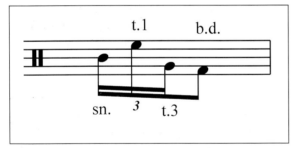

Figure 8.1
The quadruplet

How to Play the Quadruplet: The Secret of the Flopping Fish

To play this particular version of the quadruplet, you'll play each note of the quadruplet on a different drum. To do this, which hand you use on which drum is extremely important. Let me break it down for you. Figure 8.2 shows the quadruplet with sticking indications.

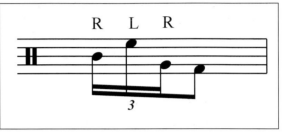

Figure 8.2
A quadruplet with sticking indications

The first note of the quadruplet is played on the snare drum with your right hand. The second note of the quadruplet is played on the first of your mounted toms with your left hand. Then your right hand will move from the snare drum, where it just played the first note, over to the floor tom to play the third note of the quadruplet. Then, you will play the fourth and last note of the quadruplet with your right foot on the bass drum. If you have a four-piece kit, this particular version of a quadruplet can be seen as hitting each drum in the kit only once. (If you have a five-piece kit with two mounted toms, you'll skip over the second mounted tom, which is over to the right of your kit.)

Now that you have a basic idea of how the quadruplet is played, give it a try. The first thing you'll have to do is get both of your hands in the correct starting positions. Put your right hand above the snare drum, ready to strike it, and put your left hand up near your first mounted tom.

When you play the first note of the quadruplet with your right hand on the snare drum, you'll need to get your right hand over to the floor tom, ready to play the third note of the quadruplet. The easiest way to do this is to use a technique that I've named the "Flopping Fish." Instead of moving your entire right arm to switch from the snare drum over to the floor tom, after you've played the first note of the quadruplet on the snare drum, simply flip your hand over with your arm loosely at your side while holding the stick. Just flip your hand over as if it's a fish out of water, flipping over onto the floor. (I admit that the imagery of a fish flipping over and gasping for air is kind of harsh. For a happier image, picture yourself flipping over a pancake as you prepare breakfast for your loved ones. Isn't that a much nicer picture? Everybody loves breakfast. But whatever you do, try not to picture yourself flipping over a fish pancake. That's really harsh.)

Using this quick and simple flick of the wrist, you will find the move from the snare a lot quicker and easier than you might think. The less you have to think about moving from the snare over to the floor tom, the better chance you'll have at playing this particular version of the quadruplet as smoothly as you should. Because all four notes

of the quadruplet should be evenly spaced, pay attention to the bass-drum note that ends the quadruplet and make sure that it is spaced apart enough from the floor-tom note right before it. If you're having problems getting the timing of that bass-drum note that ends the quadruplet just right, just try to do your best for now. I'll give you an exercise a little later on in this section that will help you to fully understand where that bass-drum note should land. For now, let's concentrate on what your hands will be doing in the quadruplet.

The Quadruplet with the Focus on Your Hands: A Lane, a Circle, and a Flopping Fish

When played correctly, this particular version of a quadruplet can either be an entire fill all by itself or can serve as a piece of a fill. But whichever way you use it, you'll definitely have to learn how to move from a groove into a quadruplet. Figure 8.3 shows an exercise using the quadruplet as a one-beat fill.

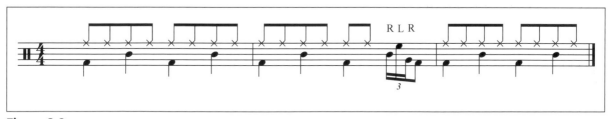

Figure 8.3
Quadruplet Exercise #1

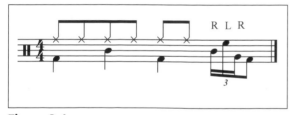

Figure 8.4
The measure in the exercise containing the quadruplet

To get you started on moving from the groove to the quadruplet, let's closely examine the particular measure in this exercise where the quadruplet will take place (see Figure 8.4).

All of the grooves you've learned so far in this book have snare-drum notes on both beat 2 and beat 4 of the measure. (Some grooves that you've learned have more snare-drum notes in them than that, but they still all have snare notes on beats 2 and 4 of the measure.) The measure that has the quadruplet also has snare-drum notes on beats 2 and 4 of the measure. Because the quadruplet itself starts with a snare-drum note, and the quadruplet is in beat 4 of the measure, we can say that this measure also has a snare-drum note on both beat 2 and beat 4 of the measure.

If you can picture the first note of the quadruplet on the snare drum as simply the snare note that would normally be on beat 4 of any groove you might play, you'll have a very good chance of fully understanding when you should begin to play the quadruplet in the measure. (You'll begin the quadruplet on beat 3 of the measure.) There is, however, one big difference between a regular snare note that you would normally find on beat 4 of a measure and the snare-drum note that starts off a quadruplet in beat 4 of a measure. Normally, if you were to play a snare note on beat 4 of a measure as part of a groove, you would use your left hand to play that snare note in a normal groove-playing position, with your right hand on the hi-hat and your left hand on the snare drum. However, because this particular version of a quadruplet starts with a snare note played by your right hand, you'll have to make a shift from playing the snare drum with your left hand during the groove to playing the snare drum with your right hand to play that first note of the quadruplet. If you want to practice just this move before you attempt the entire quadruplet, Figure 8.5 presents an exercise for you to try.

In this exercise, you'll start off in a normal groove-playing position, with your right hand on the hi-hats and your left hand on the snare drum.

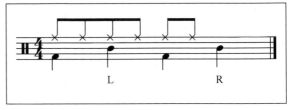

Figure 8.5
Practice this move before you try the entire quadruplet.

You'll play a snare note with your left hand on beat 2 of the measure, just like in any groove you're likely to play, but when you reach beat 4, instead of playing the snare note that you'll find there with your left hand, play that particular note with your right hand. You won't need to play anything on the hi-hat on beat 4. In other words, stop playing completely. Your playing is all finished for that measure.

This exercise will give you a head start on figuring out how to play the rest of the quadruplet by showing you what move you'll have to make to play the first note of the quadruplet. The second note of the quadruplet will be played by your left hand on the first mounted tom. So, while your right hand is moving over from your hi-hats to play the first note of the quadruplet on the snare drum, your left hand moves up to the first tom from its normal groove-playing position at the snare drum.

To move your left hand up to the first tom from the snare, it might help to picture your hand moving along a straight lane that exists from the snare to the tom. That's the extent of the traveling that your left hand does while playing its part of the quadruplet. It will simply move in a straight line up a lane from the snare drum to the first tom. It's the right hand that does most of the traveling in those big moves from the hi-hats while it's playing the groove—over to the snare drum to play the first note of the quadruplet, winding up way over on the floor tom to play the third note of the quadruplet, and then moving all the way back to the hi-hat to continue the groove.

If you want to end a quadruplet with a cymbal crash, then your right hand will have one more move to make. It will travel from the floor tom over to the crash cymbal and then back to the hi-hat, either on the very next eighth note of the measure or maybe on beat 2 if you use the old "smoke and throw" technique I showed you before. Whether or not you end the quadruplet with a crash, you'll find that your right hand will be doing most of the work and most of the traveling when playing a quadruplet in an exercise in which you'll be moving from a groove to a quadruplet and back into the groove again.

It might help to picture your right hand moving in a circle all around the kit from the hi-hat to the floor tom, over to the crash cymbal, and back to the hi-hats. Picturing a circle may help you to achieve the smoothness of motion you'll need to make all of the required moves. If you picture the journey that your right hand will make around the kit with all of its stops as random disconnected motions, then you might find yourself becoming confused as to what you're supposed to be hitting next at any given time, and your execution of the exercise will probably sound very jerky and uneven, if you can get through the exercise at all. Picturing

the same journey as a smooth circle with no interruption of motion will keep your right hand moving smoothly around the kit, laying waste and destruction to all who are foolish enough to cross its majestic, circular path. (Of course, within that magic circle you'll use the "Flopping Fish" technique when you're moving from the snare over to the floor tom in the quadruplet. And then you'll use a "Reverse Extended Flopping Fish" to move from the floor tom over to the crash cymbal or the hi-hat, depending on whether you end the quadruplet with a crash. Sounds easy enough, right?)

The Quadruplet with the Focus on Your Right Foot

The last note of the quadruplet is played with your right foot on the bass drum, and it's crucial that you get the timing of that foot move just right in order to make the quadruplet as smooth as it can be. The key to getting the timing of that bass drum note just right is to fully understand exactly where it is supposed to land. Take a look at the exercise in Figure 8.6.

As you can see, there's a bass drum note at the very end of the first measure on the "+ of 4." After that, there's a bass-drum note on the first beat of the second measure. So, in this exercise you'll play two eighth notes on the bass drum in a row, with hi-hat notes right along with them as the hi-hat plays straight eighth notes throughout the entire exercise. Now, the last note of the quadruplet on

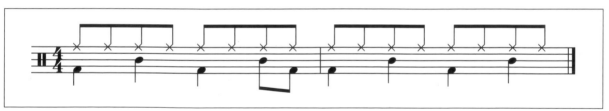

Figure 8.6
The last note of the quadruplet is played with your right foot on the bass drum.

the bass drum will land in the same place in the measure, the "+ of 4." And you'll play a bass-drum note on the first beat of the second measure after the quadruplet, just like in the previous exercise. The only difference between the bass-drum note that ends the quadruplet and the bass-drum note that you'll find on the "+ of 4" of the first measure in the previous exercise is that you won't play a hi-hat along with the bass-drum note that ends the quadruplet.

If you can fully understand the exact placement of that last note of the quadruplet by using the exercise in Figure 8.6, you'll have a much better chance of putting that bass-drum note that ends the quadruplet right where it belongs, resulting in a nice, smooth quadruplet. Remember that after you play the very last note of the quadruplet with your bass drum, you'll need to play another bass-drum note one eighth note later, on beat 1 of the measure after the quadruplet measure. By focusing on your foot while playing the whole exercise that contains the quadruplet surrounded by a groove, you should be able to put that bass-drum note that ends the quadruplet right where it belongs. Make sure you don't rush into the bass-drum note that begins the second measure of the exercise. You have the same amount of time between bass-drum notes as you did in the example in Figure 8.6, in which you played two eighth notes on the bass drum while going from the end of the first measure into the beginning of the second measure.

The Quadruplet: Putting It All Together

Now that you know all the moves and understand when and where they're supposed to take place, it's time to try putting it all together. Figure 8.7 shows an exercise you saw earlier in this section, but I'd like you to take a look at it again with the benefit of all the detail that I went into in the last section about playing the quadruplet as a one-beat fill. After you give this exercise a few tries, try to play it along with your metronome at a tempo that is comfortable for you. This will help you fully understand how the quadruplet and the first beat of the measure that follows it are supposed to feel.

In this exercise, you'll play one entire measure's worth of a groove before you reach the second measure of the exercise that contains the quadruplet itself in beat 4 of the measure. This will give you a chance to play a groove for a short while before you have to even think about playing the quadruplet. When you practice this exercise to a metronome (as you should), make sure that beat 1 of the measure following the quadruplet lands squarely on a click of the metronome that will mark the quarter note you'll play on your bass drum to start that third measure of the exercise. Take it nice and slow and don't be afraid to use your timer technique to make sure you're giving yourself enough time of solid work on this exercise. Don't be discouraged if you have a hard time trying to play this exercise at first. Remember that each time you try it, you'll be closer and closer to getting it right. Good luck.

Figure 8.7
Quadruplet Exercise #1

Why Play Just One Quadruplet When You Can Play Two?

Now that you've used a quadruplet to play a one-beat fill, the next step is to use a quadruplet to make a two-beat fill. (Well, actually, you'll learn how to use two quadruplets to create a two-beat fill.) Figure 8.8 shows an exercise containing two quadruplets to make a fill.

This exercise starts off with a full measure of straight groove, while the second measure contains the two-beat fill made up of two quadruplets in a row. When you play the two quadruplets in a row, make sure you don't rush into the second quadruplet of the two. When played correctly, each quadruplet will take up the space of one beat of the measure. The snare-drum notes that begin each quadruplet should land squarely on beats 3 and 4 of the measure that they're in.

Once you work on this exercise long enough to get a fairly decent handle on the moves required to play two quadruplets in a row, try the exercise to your metronome. As usual, pick a tempo at which you can work comfortably, and make sure that whatever notes are supposed to be lining up with a click of the metronome that marks the quarter notes line up as closely as you can possibly make them. Try not to rush into the third measure, which returns you to the groove after the fill. Once you practice the fill enough and concentrate on making that magic circle with your right hand as it travels around the kit, you'll understand that you have enough time to let your right hand flow smoothly around the kit to play all the notes that it's supposed to.

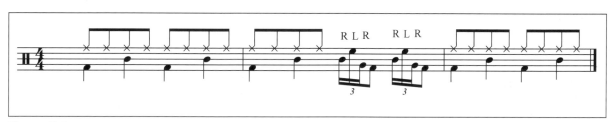

Figure 8.8
Quadruplet Exercise #2

The Great and Mighty Flam

NOW I'D LIKE TO INTRODUCE YOU to a little something called the "flam." The flam is a very simple move (or at least it seems simple until you try it), but it can make a huge difference in sound and feel to any groove or fill. It can have as many uses as you can possibly imagine, and once you learn how to use it in a couple of ways (which I'll show you), you'll wonder how you ever got this far without it. Simply put, a flam consists of both sticks coming down at almost the same time on any one drum. Figure 8.9 shows what it looks like as written.

Figure 8.9
The flam

The flam takes up one beat of a measure and is equal to the value of one quarter note in a measure of 4/4. The flam can be used to emphasize any specific note in a groove, simply by using both sticks to play one note. The flam can also be played with each stick on a different drum—one hand playing the snare drum and the other hand playing the floor tom, for example. It can also be used in a fill in many ways.

As simple as it seems, however, the flam can be quite tricky on your first attempt. When played correctly, it sounds like two notes being played so closely together that they are almost, but not quite, being played at the same time. If both notes of the flam were played at exactly the same time, you'd never be able to tell that there were actually two notes being played, defeating the whole point of playing a flam in the first place.

A Flam Experiment: Go Slam a Door

Playing a flam correctly requires expert timing. When played correctly, a flam sounds like a door slamming. If you've ever listened very carefully to a door slamming, you will notice that there are actually two different sounds that make up what most people hear as one sound. There's the quiet sound of the doorknob mechanism slipping into the slot in the doorframe, quickly followed by the louder sound of the actual door itself slamming into the door frame. Go slam a door in your house if you want to hear what I'm talking about. The best door to slam would probably be a door to a room in your house, rather than the front door or a storm door. When someone in your house wants to know why in the world you're slamming a door over and over, tell that person you're doing research, you're not to be questioned or disturbed, and that this is required of you in your drumming book. And then listen very carefully as that person grabs the book away from you and slams it shut. Notice how the slamming of the book was made up of only one sound instead of two? That's not a flam.

Follow the Leader to Flamsville

To play the flam correctly, you need to decide which one of your hands will be the leader and which one will be the follower. Because a flam is basically both hands playing the same thing on the same drum at almost the same time, you can't just bring both sticks down at almost the same time and hope that they'll be slightly spaced apart, randomly creating the sound of a flam. They will not create the sound of the flam as many times as they will if you leave it up to chance.

Because a flam is the sound of one stick striking a drum a split second before the other stick, you'll have to decide which stick will strike the head first and which stick will strike the head second. One stick will be the leader and the other stick will be the follower, and you will have to make the choice of which is which.

Obviously, to determine which hand will lead in a flam, you will have to give each hand a shot at the leader position, and the one that feels the most natural to you as the leader will be the winner. However, leader is not quite the correct word to describe which hand you will focus on as you try a flam each way in this experiment. When played correctly, the second note of the flam is usually the note that's more emphasized than the first note of the flam. In other words, the first note of the flam should be slightly quieter than the second note. Not only should it be quieter, it should arrive first just before the second and louder note in the flam.

Think of the first note as reaching the drumhead first in order to clear the way for the louder and more important second note of the flam. If you're right-handed, you'll use your left hand to play the snare more often than your right. Your right hand is usually busy playing the hi-hats, so your left hand is much more comfortable playing the snare drum than your right hand is. For this reason, try a flam with your left hand as the hand on which you're focusing. As you bring both sticks down and they're about to strike the drum at the same time, slow your left hand down just a little bit so that your right hand reaches the drumhead first. Then let your left hand strike the drum second, just after your right hand. Remember that you're trying to imitate the sound of a door slamming, one slightly quieter slamming sound just before a louder slamming sound that completes the entire sound of a door slamming. Figure 8.10 demonstrates a flam with the left hand making the second, louder hit of the two.

Figure 8.10
The flam with a dominant left hand

Give this version of the flam a few tries before you try the opposite version. The opposite version is a flam in which your left hand reaches the drumhead first and your right hand quickly follows it with a slightly louder stroke (see Figure 8.11).

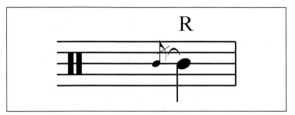

Figure 8.11

The flam with a dominant right hand

After you give each of these versions of the flam a few tries, hopefully one version will present itself as the one that comes more naturally for you to play. There's really no way for me or you to accurately predict which of the two versions will win the distinctive honor of being your preferred flam, nor does it really matter which hand you lead with. What *does* matter is that you are aware of which hand you're leading with when you play a flam from now on. If you don't decide which hand you'll lead with in a flam, you might have a momentary brain freeze mid-flam as you try to determine in a split second which hand should get to the drumhead first.

If you play a flam without absolute certainty as to which hand you're leading with, you might experience some confusion when you need to move out of the flam and onto something else, whether it's onto another piece of a fill or back to the groove position. This is why I suggest you try the flam both ways, with each hand leading, to determine which way feels right to you. Then, you can flam on to your heart's content.

Figure 8.12
Flam Exercise #1

Using the Flam as a Fill

The flam has the same note value as a quarter note, which means that it takes up one beat of a measure, allowing you to use it in many ways as a fill or as part of one. The first flam exercise I'd like to show you is very simple, but it can make a big difference to any part of a song in which it might be played. By simply playing a flam in beat 4 of a measure instead of the combination of snare drum and hi-hat that you usually would play in a groove, you can really make that fourth beat of the measure stand out in a good way.

When you play the flam in beat 4 of the second measure, make sure that you give the flam its full value of one beat of the measure before you move into beat 1 of the next measure. It might feel strange at first to leave the last eighth note of the measure after the flam alone, but the whole point of using a flam in the fourth beat of a measure is to accent or draw attention to that specific beat of the measure. The best way to accent that specific beat of the measure using a flam is to leave a little bit of space after it so that the full importance of that fourth beat is felt.

Using a metronome while practicing this exercise will definitely help you hear exactly how long you'll wait after the flam before you launch into the first beat of the measure following it. You will play the flam at the same time as one click of the metronome and play the first beat of the following measure with the very next click. It's as if the flam itself said something inappropriate at the dinner table. So inappropriate, in fact, that a stunned silence follows it for a second before anyone can answer or continue with their meal. (I was always the one who said the inappropriate thing at my family's dinner table.)

As an experiment, say something inappropriate at your family's dinner table tonight, and observe the stunned silence that follows your comment, quickly followed by shouted threats of punishments, such as grounding or banishment to one's room without the health benefits of completing the meal. The split second of stunned silence quickly followed by the barrage of threats is similar to the eighth note's worth of rest that you leave at the very end of the measure right after the flam and the first beat of the measure following the flam. (Obviously, I'm just kidding. I really don't think it's a good idea for you to mouth off at the dinner table. Or if you do, don't tell them that I told you to do it. The last thing I need is your parents mad at me. Slamming doors, mouthing off at the dinner table; I bet you didn't think drumming would be this much fun, did you?)

Review

FOR THIS CHAPTER'S REVIEW, I'd like you to try playing a crash cymbal after the various fills that you learned in this chapter. Then you'll be comfortable ending each fill with or without a crash cymbal, depending on your desire. Remember, when adding a crash cymbal to the end of a fill, you won't actually be adding any more notes. You'll simply be replacing the hi-hat note that usually starts off the measure after a fill with a crash cymbal instead.

Don't forget to play the bass-drum note that goes along with the crash. A crash cymbal without a bass drum is like cookies with no milk. You can also try the "smoke and throw" technique if you're uncomfortable with moving to the hi-hat right away after the crash cymbal. Take your time with this review, and when you feel that you can play your way through it fairly smoothly, try playing along with your metronome to make absolutely sure that it's as smooth as you can possibly make it. Then go back and play the review section of the last chapter so you won't let anything you learned in the past slip out of your memory. Make sure that you can play your quadruplets and flams nice and strong before moving on to the next chapter, because in the next chapter, you'll be combining them both in the same fill. I'll bet you can hardly wait. Figure 8.13 shows the review.

Figure 8.13
Review

Where You'll Meet the Flam Tap, Make Combinations and Reverse Them, Learn How to Change Your Voice, Cross Over to the Dark Side, Receive Permission to Bail, and Find Out What a **Paradiddle Is**

NOW THAT YOU'VE LEARNED how to play a flam, let's take it a step further with something called the *flam tap*. A flam tap is simply a flam tap followed by one note on the bass drum, phrased as a pair of eighth notes. Figure 9.1 shows what a flam tap looks like

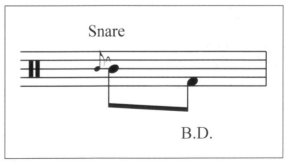

Figure 9.1
Flam tap

Let's go back to the last fill that you learned using a flam. (This would be the fill that I compared to an inappropriate remark at the dinner table.) In that fill, you played a flam on beat 4 of the measure and left an eighth note's worth of rest to finish off the measure before you launched into the first beat of the next measure. In this exercise using the flam tap, you'll take that eighth note's worth of rest and fill it with one eighth note on the bass drum. In other words, in the first version of the fill, the flam was played on beat 4.

The flam has the same note value as a quarter note, which means that you played the flam and let it ring out for one whole beat of the measure before you moved on to the next measure. That means that on the "+ and 4" of the measure with the flam at the end of it, nothing was played. In this exercise, there will be a flam tap on beat 4 instead of just a flam. So, the "+ of 4" that had no notes in it in the first exercise will now have a bass-drum note in it. Figure 9.2 shows a new exercise with a flam tap used as a fill on beat 4 of the measure.

You'll notice from looking closely at this exercise that you'll play two eighth notes in a row on the bass drum as you move from the flam tap to the beginning of the second measure. The second note of the flam tap will be played on the "+ of 4," followed one eighth note later by the quarter note on the bass drum on the first beat of the next measure.

Don't forget that you'll be playing a hi-hat note along with the bass-drum note that begins the second measure of the exercise. You can replace this hi-hat note with a crash cymbal if you want to, once you get the hang of playing the fill as it is written in this exercise. As usual, try playing this exercise to your metronome if you're having any trouble figuring out exactly where all the notes are supposed to land. Take your time and make sure you've got it down, because now we're going to move on and add to it to create new fills.

Figure 9.2
Flam Tap Exercise #1

More Fills Using the Flam Tap

IF YOU CAN PLAY ONE FLAM TAP to create a fill, the next step is to play two flam taps in a row to create a new fill. Because a fill that consists of two flam taps in a row would take up two beats of a measure, this exercise will contain a measure of a groove before the second measure, which will contain the two-beat fill made up of two flam taps in a row. So, you will begin the fill on beat 3 of the second measure of the exercise.

As I told you earlier, the flam tap is phrased as two eighth notes, so when you play two flam taps in a row as you would in this exercise, they will be played in the same rhythm as the eighth notes that you'll play on the hi-hats during the rest of the exercise that doesn't contain the fill. Then, just like in the first flam tap fill that you learned earlier in this section, you'll play two eighth notes on the bass drum as you go from the end of the flam tap to the first beat of the measure following the fill.

Practice this exercise to a metronome if you're having any trouble with the phrasing. Actually, practice this exercise to a metronome anyway, regardless of whether you're having trouble with the phrasing. Any practicing that you do to a metronome is practice time well spent because it helps you develop the steady time and smoothness that you'll need to be a truly great drummer. Go for it. Figure 9.3 shows the next exercise using the flam tap.

Now that you know how to play two flam taps in a row to create a fill, I'd like to show you a way that you can take your flam taps to a new level, which will greatly increase the number of fills you can play. Even though a flam is made up of two notes played at almost the same time, both notes don't necessarily have to be played on the same drum. You could play a flam with one stick on the first mounted tom and the other stick on the floor tom, for example. As a matter of fact, that's exactly what you'll be playing in the next fill I'll show you. Check it out in Figure 9.4.

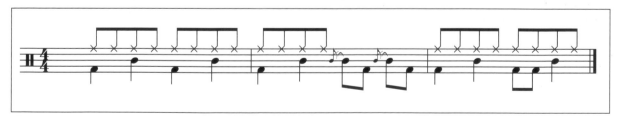

Figure 9.3
Flam Tap Exercise #2

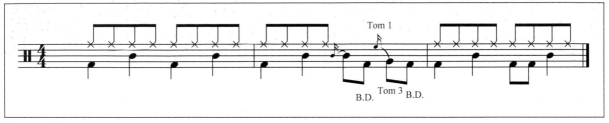

Figure 9.4
Flam Tap Exercise #3

This fill is almost identical to the last fill that you worked on, which had two flam taps in a row. There are no more notes in this new fill than there are in the earlier fill. The only difference between the two fills is that in the new fill you'll play the second of the two flam taps on your first mounted tom and your floor tom, instead of both notes of the flams being played on the snare drum only. The phrasing of both exercises is exactly the same, meaning that you'll still need to play two eighth notes as you move from the end of the first measure of the exercise to the beginning of the second measure. You'll make that long reach with your right hand from the floor tom at the end of the fill back over to the hi-hats to continue the groove, but that's a move you mastered earlier, during much more difficult fills than this one, so you really shouldn't have much trouble with this exercise at all.

Once you learn how to play this fill, you can immediately pick up a new fill simply by reversing the order of the flam taps. In the previous fill, you played two flam taps in a row—the first flam tap on the snare drum and the bass drum, and the second flam tap on the first mounted tom, the floor tom, and the bass drum. In the next exercise, you'll be playing two flam taps again, only this time you'll play the first flam tap on the first mounted tom, floor tom, and bass drum and the second flam tap on the snare drum and the bass drum. Figure 9.5 shows what it looks like.

By simply flipping or reversing the order of the two flam taps, you've learned a brand-new fill.

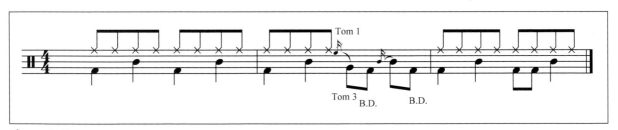

Figure 9.5
Flam Tap Exercise #4

Flam Taps and Quadruplets: A Killer Combination

FLAM TAPS AND QUADRUPLETS can be combined in several different ways to create some really interesting fills. Because both the quadruplet and the flam tap share the same note value (taking up one beat of a measure), they are easily interchangeable when creating new fills. Both the quadruplet and the flam tap end with a bass drum note on the "+" of the beat on which they started, so you should not have too much trouble stringing them together as long as you keep the rhythm of a bass-drum note on the "+" of the last two beats of the measure. Then you'll play one more bass-drum note on the first beat of the measure that follows the fill, just like you did earlier with the fills that consisted of either two quadruplets in a row or two flam taps in a row. Figure 9.6 shows an exercise that contains a fill consisting of a half-measure fill made up of a flam tap followed by a quadruplet.

As you can see, this exercise will start off with one measure of straight groove before moving on to the second measure, where the two-beat fill will occur. As with all the previous exercises, practice this exercise to your metronome at a tempo that you're comfortable with in order to make sure you're phrasing the fill correctly and also that you're making the transitions from the groove into the fill and back to the groove again as smooth as you possibly can. When you can play this exercise smoothly, try ending the fill with a crash cymbal instead of moving immediately to the hi-hat after the fill.

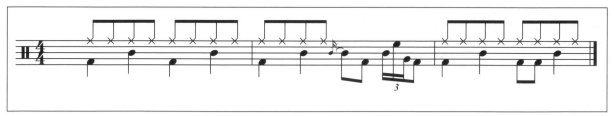

Figure 9.6
Flam Tap Quadruplet Exercise

Quadruplets and Flam Taps: Flip It

T O CREATE A NEW FILL out of the flam tap and quadruplet combination you just learned, simply reverse the order. You can create a new fill that takes up the same amount of space in a measure by playing the quadruplet first and the flam tap second. Figure 9.7 shows what that looks like.

The phrasing of the bass drum in either this reversed version of the earlier fill or the original earlier fill itself is identical. You will play a bass drum on the "+" of beats 3 and 4, whether you happen to be playing a flam tap or a quadruplet. This is what makes the flam tap and the quadruplet so easily interchangeable. Only the hand moves are different. Pretty cool, huh?

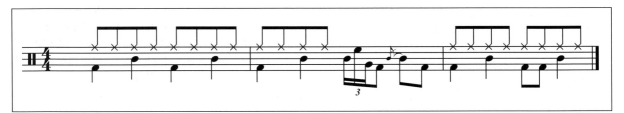

Figure 9.7
Quadruplet Flam Tap Exercise

Re-Voicing: A Word I Made Up

I LIKE TO THINK OF THE DRUM KIT as a collection of voices. Each drum and cymbal has its own unique voice. Sometimes only one voice is speaking, and other times more than one voice may be speaking at the same time. Sometimes one voice may speak only one word, or sometimes that same voice may speak a whole sentence, either along with one or more of the other voices of the drum kit or all alone. Sometimes the words of a sentence can be moved around in various different orders to create different sentences. Thinking of drumming and the creation of grooves and fills in this way can help you unlock your creativity to make up fills of your very own.

For example, let's look at the flam. When I first introduced you to the flam, you played both notes of the flam on the snare drum in order to play a simple fill. You could just as easily play a flam with one stick on one drum and the other stick on any other drum in your kit, depending on the kind of sound you want to make. Playing both notes of a flam on the snare drum will produce a very bright and cracking type of sound, while playing a flam with one stick on the first mounted tom and the other stick on the floor tom will produce a more dark and woody type of sound, for example. Or you could play a flam with one stick on the snare drum and the other stick on any of the toms.

You're playing the same thing in all of these examples as far as the actual note values, but you're playing the notes on different voices of the drum kit in each example. I refer to this as *re-voicing* a fill or a piece of a fill, and it's a very easy way to greatly increase the number of fills you can create. Because a flam tap is made up of a flam and an eighth note on the bass drum following it, you can very easily re-voice any flam tap by simply re-voicing the flam itself on different voices on the kit. Re-voicing a quadruplet, however, is more challenging, but can also help to add some very interesting and exciting versions of the quadruplet to your growing arsenal of fills.

Crossing Over to the Dark Side: A Dark Version of the Quadruplet

THE VERSION OF THE QUADRUPLET that I started you off with is the one that makes the most sense when you are first learning to play the quadruplet, but that version of the quadruplet can be re-voiced to create different versions. The first version of the quadruplet that you learned consisted of four notes in a specific order as far as the voicing on the kit. The order of voicings in this version of the quadruplet is as follows: the first note on the snare drum, the second note on the first mounted tom, the third note on the floor tom, and the last note on the bass drum. A re-voicing of this version of the quadruplet will follow the same sticking order as the original version. The sticking order is as follows: R, L, R, Right Foot. Figure 9.8 shows a regular quadruplet.

Figure 9.8
Regular quadruplet

Now try playing a quadruplet using the exact same sticking order, but change the order of voices. For example, try playing the quadruplet without using the snare drum at all. You could still start the quadruplet with your right hand, but instead of playing the snare drum with your right hand as the first note of the quadruplet, play the floor tom with your right hand instead. Now the order of voices with sticking will be: first note on the floor tom with your right hand, second note on the first mounted tom with your left hand, third note on the floor tom with your right hand, and fourth note on the bass drum. Figure 9.9 shows what I call the dark version of the quadruplet.

Figure 9.9
Quadruplet: dark version

This re-voicing of the quadruplet is much darker-sounding than the original version you learned because it's played on the toms and bass drum with no snare drum. Also, it's slightly easier to play than the original version because your right hand, which traveled from the snare drum over to the floor tom in the original version, will now stay over on the floor tom for the entire quadruplet. The bass-drum note that ends this version of the quadruplet is in exactly the same place as the earlier version that you know.

It might take a few tries to get your right hand all the way over to the floor tom to start the quadruplet from its usual groove-playing position on the hi-hat. Figure 9.10 shows an exercise using this particular version of the quadruplet for you to work on.

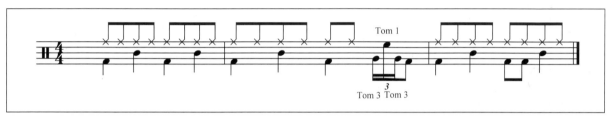

Figure 9.10
Quadruplet: Dark Version Exercise

Telpurdauq Esrever: Reverse Quadruplet

NO, IT'S NOT A MISPRINT or a foreign language. Telpurdauq esrever is the words "reverse quadruplet" spelled backward. Now you'll learn how to play a new version of the quadruplet that will take the original version you know and reverse the voicings that you'll play with your hands. If you get confused, remember that when you re-voice a quadruplet, you won't be changing the sticking at all. The order of sticking will still be R, L, R, Right Foot. You'll play the same voices on the kit in both versions, but in different orders. In the case of the reverse quadruplet, you'll reverse the voicings that you play with your hands in the first version of the quadruplet that you know.

In the first version of the quadruplet that you know, you start off with a note on the snare drum, move to the second note on the first mounted tom with your left hand, play the third note of the quadruplet on the floor tom with your right hand, and play the last note of the quadruplet on the bass drum. In the reverse quadruplet, you'll play the first note of the quadruplet on the floor tom with your right hand instead of the snare drum, play the second note on the first mounted tom with your left hand just like in the first version of the quadruplet, and play the third note of the quadruplet on the snare drum with your right hand.

The reverse quadruplet ends with a note on the bass drum, just like all the other versions of the quadruplet you learned so far. So, you're not actually reversing everything in a regular quadruplet to play the reverse quadruplet; you're just reversing the voices that you play with your hands. The middle of the three notes you play with your hands will be the same in either the normal or the reverse version of the quadruplet—the first mounted tom, which you'll play with your left hand. Try the reverse quadruplet alone a few times before you move on to the exercise that contains it as a fill. Figure 9.11 shows the reverse quadruplet.

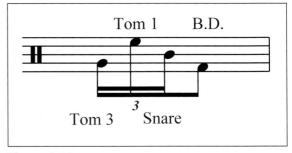

Figure 9.11
Reverse quadruplet

It might seem a little awkward at first to play the reverse quadruplet, especially playing the snare drum in the third position of the quadruplet, but give it enough tries before you give up on it. Your right hand will still do the same traveling between the snare drum and the floor tom in the reverse quadruplet that it did in the regular version of the quadruplet, just in the opposite direction. In other words, your right hand will move from the floor tom and over to the snare drum instead of the other way around, as it did in the original version.

The Reverse Quadruplet as a Fill

W HEN YOU'VE GIVEN THE REVERSE quadruplet enough tries that you're somewhat comfortable with it, try the exercise in Figure 9.12 that uses it as a fill.

As you can see, you'll play the reverse quadruplet as a one-measure fill in the last beat of the measure. Remember, your right hand will go from the hi-hats all the way over to the floor tom in order to play the first note of the reverse quadruplet. Then, as your left hand lays the second note of the quadruplet on the first mounted tom, you right hand will move over to the snare drum to play the third note of the quadruplet. As your right foot plays the last note of the quadruplet, your right hand will move to the hi-hats to continue the groove that you were playing before you launched into the reverse quadruplet as a fill.

The move your right hand makes from the snare drum at the end of the quadruplet to the hi-hat is a tricky one, as your left hand moves from the first mounted tom back down to the snare drum at the same time to continue the groove. This might take you more than a few tries to get the hang of it, but don't give up. Give your limbs enough tries to memorize the order of actions you want them to take, and eventually they will remember exactly what it is you want them to do.

Permission to Bail

If you absolutely, positively cannot play the reverse quadruplet as a fill, no matter how hard you try, don't worry about it too much. The reverse quadruplet is not necessarily the next thing you absolutely have to learn how to play before you can move on in your drumming career. There are plenty of other things to do as you move on in this book, and few of them use the reverse quadruplet as their basis.

If the reverse quadruplet comes to you fairly easily after a few tries, then consider yourself very fortunate. If, in attempting the reverse quadruplet, you get so frustrated that you want to quit drumming forever and go play soccer or something, just stop trying. You can always return to the reverse quadruplet later on in your drumming development, when you have more confidence in your abilities. Or you can never return to it if you really don't want to. It's your choice.

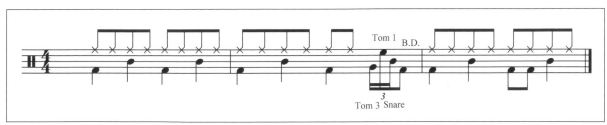

Figure 9.12
Reverse Quadruplet Exercise

Forward and Reverse Quadruplets as Fills

IF YOU *can* PLAY THE REVERSE quadruplet, then you can use it in the new fill you'll work on in this section. The new fill is a two-beat fill, which means that it will take up half of a measure. In the exercise containing the fill, you'll play one measure of a groove before you move on to the second measure of the exercise that contains the fill, and then you'll return to the groove in the third measure of the exercise, just as you've done before in all of the other two-beat fill exercises you've encountered in this book so far. This two-beat fill consists of two quadruplets in a row—a regular quadruplet followed by a reverse quadruplet. Check it out in Figure 9.13.

As you can see, this fill is very interesting and exciting. When played correctly, it is an excellent addition to your arsenal of fills. When you are fairly comfortable playing this fill, try ending the fill with a crash cymbal. Adding a crash cymbal to the end of this particular fill will pose an extra challenge because your right hand will have to move from the floor tom over to the crash cymbal, while avoiding your left hand as it makes its way from the first mounted tom (where it played the second note of the quadruplet) back to the snare drum to continue the groove that the fill interrupted.

This move will probably take you a few tries until your limbs memorize the order of actions required to play this fill correctly, so don't get discouraged and give up right away. Remember that the only way your limbs have a chance to learn a series of actions—especially such a challenging series of actions as this fill contains—is to try it over and over again. Use the timer technique if it will help you get the results you're looking for. Spend 10 minutes trying the exercise over and over without letting your brain enter the process and start to discourage you. If, at the end of 10 minutes, you still are far away from getting this exercise down, quit trying for now and promise yourself that you'll devote 10 minutes of your next practice routine to trying it again. Remember, every try brings you closer to success, so don't be afraid to try often.

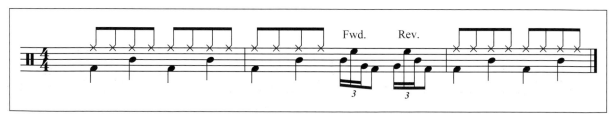

Figure 9.13
Forward and Reverse Quadruplet Exercise

A Flam Tap and Reverse Quadruplet Fill

BECAUSE YOU TOOK THE TIME to learn the reverse quadruplet, why not get as many uses out of it as you possibly can? You've already learned how to create a two-beat fill using the flam tap and the regular version of the quadruplet. You can just as easily create a fill using a flam tap and a reverse quadruplet. Why not? Figure 9.14 shows what that would look like.

This fill should be no more difficult for you to play than the last fill you learned that had two quadruplets in a row (the first one forward and the second one reversed). Getting from the end of the reverse triplet back to the hi-hats in order to continue the groove is the most difficult part of using the reverse quadruplet as the end of a fill, and because you already spent time on this move in the last fill you worked on, you really shouldn't have much of a problem with this fill.

The next fill you can create using the same parts as this fill would be reversing the position of the flam tap and the reverse quadruplet, playing the reverse quadruplet on beat 3 of the measure and the flam tap on beat 4. Figure 9.15 shows the fill.

When you've spent enough time on these two fills to feel comfortable, try ending them with crash cymbals. You'll find crash cymbals at the end of some fills in the review at the end of this chapter, but if you spend some time now learning how to add crash cymbals at the end of these fills, you'll be more than ready for the review by the time you get to it. I just want you to be prepared. Is that so wrong?

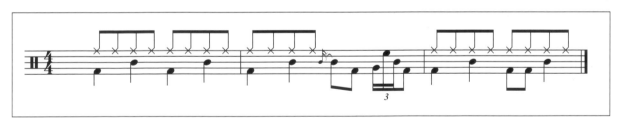

Figure 9.14
Flam Tap and Reverse Quadruplet Exercise

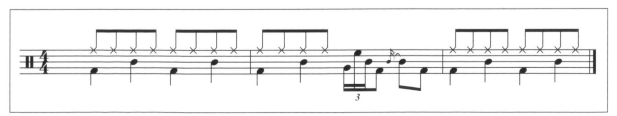

Figure 9.15
Reverse Quadruplet and Flam Tap Exercise

Introduction to the Paradiddle

WHAT IN THE WORLD IS A PARADIDDLE? Is it some kind of weird new snack food or a breed of dog or something? I'll give you a hint: It has something to do with playing the drums. In drumming, a paradiddle is what is called a *rudiment*. Rudiments are certain exercises that are usually meant to be played on the snare drum only and are meant to build up coordination and independence between the hands. They can be especially useful to a drummer who specializes in the snare drum only, such as in a drum corps, a marching band, a concert band, or a symphony.

There are 26 different rudiments in existence, and they can be useful in a warm-up routine before you move on to playing the drum kit in a practice session. Or, you could use them to create a practice routine for yourself, perhaps on a drum pad, if your drum set isn't available to you for some reason. The reason I didn't suggest that you get a drum pad right away is because I wanted you to move to the drum set immediately, since I figured that you would be more interested in playing the drum set than playing a bunch of things just on the pad for weeks or months.

Although some drum teachers would insist that before you move on to the drum set, you should have the stick control that working extensively with rudiments will grant you, I disagree. I feel it's important that you get as much experience on the drum set as quickly as you can so you can decide as soon as possible whether drumming is for you. I'm assuming that you hope to eventually play drums in a band with your friends or other musicians you know, so I've made that the goal of this book.

I don't mean to downplay the importance of rudiments or suggest that they are unnecessary to be a good drummer. When you get through with this book and start lessons with a private instructor, you can use your knowledge of rudiments to add to the drum-set skills you've already gained from this book.

Your drum set skills will definitely increase when you gain some knowledge of rudiments, and for this reason I'd like to introduce you to the paradiddle. A *paradiddle* is a group of four notes usually phrased as sixteenth notes. Up until now, you've played any sixteenth notes you've encountered as a fill or part of a fill with alternate sticking. *Alternate sticking* means that you simply went hand to hand as you played groups of sixteenth notes: L, R, L, R, L, R, and so on. When playing a paradiddle, you will play that same sixteenth-note phrasing, but with a different and unique sticking pattern. Figure 9.16 presents an exercise for you to try containing two paradiddles.

Figure 9.16
Two paradiddles

Figure 9.17 shows a full measure of sixteenth notes as paradiddles with sticking notation above them.

As you can see, the paraddidle starts with three alternating strokes, but you will play the fourth note of the paradiddle with the same hand you used to play the third note of the paradiddle. Then, when you play the next paradiddle that makes up the second beat of the measure, you'll start it with the opposite hand with which you started the previous paradiddle. If you were to play a full measure of sixteenth notes in a straight non-paradiddle type of phrasing, you would start each new grouping of four sixteenth notes with the same hand. Figure 9.18 shows a full measure of non-paradiddle sixteenth notes with sticking notation above it to demonstrate what I mean.

In this example, you would use your right hand to play the first note of each group of sixteenth notes. If you compare this to the earlier example of the sixteenth notes in a paradiddle-type sticking pattern, you'll notice that the first note of the paradiddle in the first beat of the measure will be played by your right hand, the first note of the paradiddle in the second beat of the measure will be played by your left hand, the third paradiddle will start with your right hand, and the last paradiddle will start with your left.

To play a full measure or more of paradiddles, you'll need to play what is called a *double* with either hand. In other words, to play the paradiddle correctly, you'll need to play two strokes with the same hand at the same speed that you play two strokes using alternating sticking. Learning to do this will not only increase your speed and dexterity, but can also increase your flexibility when you are ending fills and returning to the groove that the fill interrupted. I'll explain what I mean more fully a little later, but first I'd like you to try the exercise in Figure 9.19 to help you become more familiar with the paradiddle in general before you learn to use it in a fill.

Figure 9.17
Full measure of paradiddles

Figure 9.18
A measure of regular sixteenth notes

Figure 9.19
Paradiddle Exercise

This exercise is simply a four-measure string of paradiddles phrased as sixteenth notes on the snare drum with quarter notes on the bass drum throughout the entire exercise. You also might have noticed some strange never-before-seen markings above the notes and under the sticking notation. These are called *accents*, and they are simply an indication to play that particular note louder than the other notes.

Accenting each beginning note of a quadruplet while playing a string of them can help you keep track of where exactly the first note of each paradiddle is supposed to be. I suggest that you try to simply play the string of paradiddles without worrying about the accents at first. Then, when you feel somewhat comfortable playing the string of paradiddles, try to add the accents. Learning to start each beat of the measure with an alternating accent will increase your independence and also help you keep track of each beat of the measure while playing a string of paradiddles.

It might seem as if learning to play paradiddles with accents in this way is more trouble than it's worth for now, but if you devote enough time to this exercise, you can expect a big payoff in the next chapter, when I show you how to use the paradiddle in a fill. Take this exercise nice and slow at first, and don't hesitate to use the timer technique to make sure you're giving your confused limbs enough chances to fully memorize the series of actions that you want them to take to play this exercise correctly.

When you're comfortable enough playing this exercise, you should definitely try to play it to your metronome as soon as possible, so you can be sure you're playing it as steadily and smoothly as you can. Pick a tempo that you're comfortable with to start. There are no extra points for speed in this particular exercise because it's very unlikely that you would ever use this exercise as a fill as it is. In the next chapter, when you learn how to use a paradiddle in a fill, you'll only play a paradiddle once in that fill, so don't worry too much if you don't feel totally comfortable with this exercise. Just give it your best shot and move on when you're ready.

Review

W E'VE COVERED A LOT OF GROUND
in this chapter, and what better way to
make sure that this ground stays covered
than having a review? Actually, there's no better
way. As always, practice the review in Figure 9.20
to a metronome setting that you're comfortable
with, and don't rush through it. Pay particular
attention to the voicings of the flam taps and the
quadruplets you'll find sprinkled throughout the
review. You might find some surprises—but not if
you surprise them first. Good luck.

Figure 9.20
Review

Where You'll Break the
Magic Circle, Learn a
Bunch of Combinations,
Eat a Bunch of Deluxe
Cheeseburgers, Learn to
Look Where You're Going,
and Eat Some Broccoli

with Style

NOW THAT YOU'VE TAKEN THE TIME to learn about the paradiddle and how to play it, let me show you how it can be used in a fill and why you would do so. As you learned in the last chapter, the paradiddle is usually phrased as a group of four sixteenth notes. This means any fill that uses sixteenth notes in a normal alternating-sticking type of pattern can also use the paradiddle in the same fill instead.

Using the Paradiddle in a Fill: The Magic Circle Is Broken

I F YOU'RE PERFECTLY HAPPY playing sixteenth notes in the regular alternating sticking style, you might be wondering why in the world you would want to replace something that is relatively easy to play with paradiddles, which seem much more confusing and difficult to play. The good news is that you won't be replacing all the sixteenth notes in a fill with paradiddles—only one grouping of sixteenth notes. By replacing the last group of sixteenth notes in a full-measure fill made up of sixteenth notes with a paradiddle, you will be able to make the difficult transition from the end of a fill that uses all the drums in the drum kit back to the hi-hat to continue the groove.

As in some of the fills you've already worked on earlier in this book, you might find yourself ending the fill way over on the floor tom and having to make that long reach either over to the crash cymbal if you want to end the fill with a crash, or back over to the hi-hat to immediately continue the groove that the fill interrupted. If you have absolutely no problem making that reach and you're totally comfortable with making it every single time that you end a fill on the floor tom, then continue to do that. However, being able to

play at least one paradiddle within a full-measure fill of sixteenth notes can make that reach a little easier and will also give you an extra split-second of time to wind up for a crash cymbal with which you might want to end the fill.

If you *do* decide to end a fill with a crash cymbal, it's important that you hit the crash cymbal with as much confidence as you can. Having an extra split-second of wind-up time that using the paradiddle gives you will definitely help you gain that confidence. Figure 10.1 shows an exercise using the paradiddle to demonstrate what I mean.

As you study this exercise, play close attention to the sticking notation below the sixteenth notes in the fill. The first three groupings of sixteenth notes in the fill are of a normal alternating-sticking type of pattern. It is in the fourth and last group of sixteenth notes that you will find the only paradiddle in the bunch. About the crash cymbal on the first beat of the measure after the fill: You'll play that crash cymbal with your left hand instead of your right, as you did in all other similar fills that you learned before.

Figure 10.1
Paradiddle in a fill

The hi-hat note that comes right after the crash cymbal you play on beat 1 of the third measure of the exercise is optional. If you choose to leave this note out, you're using the technique I call the "Smoke and Throw," which I revealed to you in the last chapter. This will break up the "Magic Circle" that your right hand would travel in if it were to play the crash instead of your left, as it does in this particular exercise.

This doesn't mean that the "Magic Circle" wasn't useful before or that you will never use it again. We owe much eternal respect to the "Magic Circle" for serving us well at a certain time in our lives, but it's time to send it on its way for now. Let's observe a moment of silence and perhaps even weep a little as we wave goodbye to our friend, the good old "Magic Circle."

Anyway, by using a paradiddle in the fourth beat of a four-measure fill, your right hand will play the last two notes of the paradiddle, giving your left hand the wind-up time it could use to play a nice, solid crash cymbal to end the fill. Also, learning to play a crash cymbal with your left hand just as easily as with your right hand (which is the only hand you've been using up until now to play all your crashes) is a very important step in developing greater independence and flexibility in your playing. You may not fully realize it now, but when you play a bass-drum note and a crash at the same time using your left hand, you're making a giant step in your coordination, so please don't give up until you've given this exercise enough tries.

I can imagine you wondering why I would want you to stick a confusing paradiddle onto the end of a fill that you were perfectly able to play before. You'll just have to take my word for it that learning to play this exercise will actually make a full-measure fill made up of sixteenth notes easier in the long run. With this exercise, you are developing freedom of choice as to the hand with which you feel more comfortable playing a crash cymbal to end a fill. When you practice this exercise enough to make it second nature, you'll never get tangled up or confused when you want to end a fill with a crash by always having to use the same hand to play the crash. You'll be able to use whichever hand you want at any time.

It's like having twin cobras dripping with poisonous venom, out for revenge and ready to sink their fangs into any crash cymbal that would be foolish enough to be in their path. Or maybe that's just how I like to picture it. Remember that when you work on a new exercise, you're only memorizing a series of physical motions, and the key to memorization is the use of repetition. Use the timer technique if you have to, and make sure that you practice this exercise to a metronome to ensure that you're playing it as smoothly as you possibly can.

Sixteenth-Note Combination Combinations

NO, I DIDN'T STUTTER. In this section of the book, you'll take all the sixteenth-note combinations you learned earlier and combine them to create a whole bunch of new grooves that will push your powers of independence to the max. Figure 10.2 shows the sixteenth-note variations that you'll work on in this section of the book.

Figure 10.2
Sixteenth-note variations

You'll play those sixteenth-note variations either on the bass drum alone or on both the bass drum and the snare drum as a bunch of different grooves, so if you've forgotten how to play any of the sixteenth-note variations in groove form, go back to Chapter 6 and refresh your memory. It also wouldn't be a bad idea for you to play the review at the end of that chapter.

Before you begin this section, it's important for you to understand it contains nothing that you haven't played before. You'll simply take two or three things you've played before and put them all in the same measure. Although it might be challenging to play the combination of all these things in one measure, it probably won't be as difficult as you think it will be. I don't want you to feel overwhelmed when you first try any of these

exercises; it's important that you learn to look at them in the right way, so they will not look too confusing to you.

All of the exercises in this section consist of the same basic one-measure pattern with different sixteenth-note variations attached to the beginning and end of the measure. The basic pattern that you'll add things to is your old friend Groove #6. You remember this groove, I'm sure. It's the sweet sensation that's rocking the nation, causing massive elation from station to station. Here it is in Figure 10.3.

Figure 10.3
Groove #6

To create a new groove from this, let's add a sixteenth-note variation that you already know how to play to the beginning of the basic groove (see Figure 10.4).

Figure 10.4
Sixteenth-Note Combinations Exercise #1

In the first beat of the measure, you'll play Sixteenth-Note Variation #3 on the bass drum instead of just one note on the first beat of the measure that you would play in the basic version of Groove #6. If you've gone back and played the review at the end of Chapter 6, you should have no problem playing this. It's simply a matter of getting past the first beat of the measure, where you'll be playing Sixteenth-Note Variation #3, and then moving on to play the rest of Groove #6 for the rest of the measure.

When you can play this exercise, you're ready to move on to the next one. Now you'll take the same basic groove (Groove #6) and add a different sixteenth-note variation to the beginning of the measure. In this exercise, you'll add a sixteenth-note phrase with all four possible sixteenth notes present, split up between the bass drum and the snare drum. You've played this before, back in Chapter 6, when it was called the "Big #3." In the exercise in which you learned how to play four sixteenth notes split up between the bass drum and the snare drum, you were playing that particular combination in the third beat of the measure. In this new exercise, you'll play it in the first beat of the measure to start the exercise, and then play Groove #6 for the rest of the measure. Figure 10.5 shows the exercise.

Figure 10.5
Sixteenth-Note Combinations Exercise #2

After you've worked on this exercise enough to play it at least once through, try to play it as many times in a row as possible. You should definitely try playing this exercise along to a metronome setting that's comfortable to you as soon as possible. In the next exercise, you'll play what was called "The Big #4" back in Chapter 6, in the first beat of the measure to create yet another groove using Groove #6 as its basis. Figure 10.6 shows the exercise.

Figure 10.6
Sixteenth-Note Combinations Exercise #3

Just like in the previous exercises in this section, you'll simply add a certain sixteenth-note combination (in this case, Sixteenth-Note Variation #4) to the first beat of Groove #6. Once you get past the very first beat of the measure that contains Sixteenth-Note Variation #4, the rest will be very easy because it's just Groove #6 for the rest of the measure.

Take your time when working on this exercise in case you have any trouble remembering exactly how to play Sixteenth-Note Variation #4. If it's been a while since you played it, you might need to make a few tries before it all comes back to you. The reason why I include review exercises at the end of each chapter is so you won't forget anything you already put the time in to learn how to play in the first place.

Hopefully, you've been working on those review exercises that I've put at the end of the chapters. If you have, then you should not have much trouble combining a few things that you already know how to play in one new exercise. If you haven't, then you might find yourself having to try harder. I don't want to be a nag about the reviews, but this section of the book builds on things you've already learned how to play earlier in this book, and it would be silly to let all the hard work that you already put in just slip away because you're not taking the time to review them once in a while. Wait. Now, I am sounding like a nag. Sorry.

A Deluxe Cheeseburger: Three Combinations in One Groove

Now, let's take this concept to the next level and add yet another sixteenth-note combination to a groove that has two in it already. In the first two exercises in this section of the book, you added different sixteenth-note variations to the first beat of the measure, and then used Groove #6 to complete that measure. Now, let's add some sixteenth-note variations to the fourth beat of the measure to create patterns that have a total of three different sixteenth-note combinations. Figure 10.7 shows the exercise.

Figure 10.7
Sixteenth-Note Combinations Exercise #4

The sixteenth-note variation that begins the measure is one you've played before in this very chapter. The sixteenth-note variation in the fourth beat of the measure, however, you've seen and played before, but not in this particular form. It's the sixteenth-note variation that has the last of the four possible sixteenth notes present with the last note missing. This exact sixteenth note variation can also be found in beat 3 of this measure as part of "Groove #6." When this particular sixteenth-note variation appears in Groove #6, it's split up between the bass drum in a particular fashion.

The phrase is made up of three sixteenth notes in a row, with the first note played on the bass drum, the second note played on the snare drum, and the third and last note of the phrase played on the bass drum. But in this exercise, this particular sixteenth-note variation that appears in the fourth beat of the measure will be phrased differently between the bass drum and the snare drum. The first note of the three-note phrase will be played on the snare drum on beat 4 of the measure, and the last two notes of the phrase will be played on the bass drum.

Now that you have an idea of what can be found in this measure, try to play it once through. When you've learned to play this exercise at least once through, you're ready to play it twice in a row. But before you do, I want to point out something to be aware of as you work on playing this exercise. When repeating a one-measure exercise with a sixteenth-note variation on both the first and the fourth beat of the measure, there will be two sixteenth-note variations right next to each other as you move from the end of the measure into the repeat of the measure. In other words, if you were to play this exercise more than one time through, the sixteenth-note variation that ends the measure will run right into the sixteenth-note variation that started the measure in the first place. Figure 10.8

shows an exercise made up of the same measure twice in a row, so you can see how the end of the first measure runs into the beginning of the second measure.

Now, if you feel overwhelmed before you even try this exercise, remember that you've already played three quarters of this exercise in the exercises you worked on earlier in this chapter. This exercise is simply your old pal Groove #6 with one sixteenth-note variation stuck on the front of it and a different sixteenth-note variation stuck on the end of it. If you can learn to see it this way, it can be less confusing in my opinion.

I think of Groove #6 as a hamburger. It's just a hamburger, with maybe some ketchup on it, maybe not. Sometimes a simple and plain hamburger is just what you want when you're hungry. But sometimes, you might want a hamburger with cheese on it. Now it's a cheeseburger. That's like Groove #6 with a sixteenth-note variation in the first beat of the measure. It's a regular hamburger with a little something extra. Then, if you were to take Groove #6 and add a sixteenth-note variation to the fourth beat of the measure, you'd have a cheeseburger with something else, such as bacon or pickles or whatever you might like on a hamburger. It's still just a regular old hamburger underneath all the extra stuff you're piling on it.

If you can learn to still see the regular hamburger that is Groove #6 underneath the sixteenth-note variations you add to the beginning and the end of the measure, it will be less confusing to you as you look at other new combinations you'll encounter in this chapter. Unless, of course, all this talk about hamburgers and cheeseburgers confused you even more than you might have already been. In that case, feel free to ignore my hamburger comparisons altogether. Or maybe you're a vegetarian and you can't relate to the thought of hamburgers at all. If that's the case, try to think of these exercises as tofu burgers with sprouts and celery or something. Or maybe all this talk about food has made you so hungry that you need to go eat something right now. That's how I feel. But before you go eat something, try this exercise. Go as slowly as you need to. Try to focus your concentration on the part of the exercise where you make the transition from the end of the first measure to the beginning of the second measure, because this is pretty much where all the action will be happening.

As you work on this exercise, try not to think of the end of the first measure as the goal line. You'll need to do a little bit of hustling in the first beat of the measure that comes right after the last beat of the first measure. You really won't have a whole lot of rest in this exercise because it's packed with notes.

Figure 10.8
Sixteenth-Note Combinations Exercise #5

More Deluxe Cheeseburgers

Now that you've learned how to play at least one groove that has three sixteenth-note variations in it, you're ready for more. And there's always more. Take a look at the exercise in Figure 10.9.

This exercise consists of the same one-measure groove twice in a row. In other words, the first measure of the exercise is identical to the second measure. They appear this way so you can see clearly how the end of the measure will run into the beginning of the repeat of the measure, because this is where a lot of the action and any possible difficulties you might have in learning how to play this exercise will take place.

This particular exercise is identical to the last exercise you worked on in the last section of this chapter, except for the last beat of the measure, where a different version of a particular sixteenth-note variation can be found. You might recognize this particular sixteenth-note variation as what was called Sixteenth-Note Variation #4 in a previous chapter. Figure 10.10 shows what Sixteenth-Note Variation #4 looks like in its basic form.

As it appears in the fourth beat of the measure in the exercise that you're currently working on, the notes will be split up to be played with the snare drum and the bass drum, with the first of the three notes played on the snare drum on beat 4 of the measure and the remaining two notes of the phrase played on the bass drum. The rest of the one-measure groove that makes up this exercise consists of things you've played before in the last exercise, which you worked on in the last section of this chapter, as I pointed out before.

If you spent enough time on the last exercise in this section, you won't even have to think about playing anything differently in this new exercise until you reach the fourth beat of the measure. Then, you should focus your concentration on not only the fourth measure and the new version of Sixteenth-Note Variation #4 that you find there, but how you will flow from the end of that phrase right into the first beat of the second measure of the exercise.

Figure 10.9
Sixteenth-Note Combinations Exercise # 6

Figure 10.10
Sixteenth-Note Variation #4

As I stressed to you earlier in this section, it's important not to view the end of the measure as the finish line, because you'll play quite a few notes immediately in the first beat of the second measure of the exercise. Take your time when trying this exercise for the first time, and don't be afraid to go as slowly as you might need to when first attempting it. When you can play the entire exercise at least once through, try playing it as many times in a row as you can along to your metronome. Make sure your metronome is at a setting with which you're comfortable in order to make sure that your time is as steady as it can possibly be as you play your way through the exercise.

LOOK WHERE YOU'RE GOING, WILL YA? LEARNING TO LOOK AHEAD

As the exercises get more and more complex as you make your way through this book, your only hope of learning how to play them properly lies in your ability to learn to look ahead as you're reading the exercises while playing them. As you've learned by now, many of these new exercises don't always have brand-new things in them that you've never played before. What can make some of these exercises particularly challenging is the fact that they may have two or more things that you already know how to play combined in the same measure. Often it's not a question of you being able to physically play a particular exercise, but rather a matter of the level of your understanding of that particular message. You need to keep your mind as untangled and coherent as you can when faced with an exercise that has a little more going on in it than you might be comfortable with at first glance. In that case, your ability to look ahead will come to your rescue.

When I talk about looking ahead, I'm talking about two different things. The first way to look ahead while working on a particular exercise is to study the exercise and have a full understanding of what is in it before you even pick up your sticks to even attempt to play it for the first time. Hopefully, you've been doing this all along as you've been working your way through this book. Of course, you could just pick up the sticks right away and blunder your way through an exercise, simply hoping to get lucky enough to play it right without even really looking it over. You could also run right out onto a frozen pond without asking anyone whether they think the ice is thick enough to hold you, just hoping you don't fall through.

It's perfectly natural when first playing an unfamiliar exercise to keep your eyes absolutely glued to the exact notes that you happen to be playing, as if they're going to fly away off the page if you're not staring at them. The only problem with this is that as the exercises get more and more complicated as you make your way through this book, and each measure has more and more things going on in it than ever before, you can find yourself being taken totally by surprise by the next move that you run into in a measure as you're playing it.

It's very easy to get yourself mixed up and wipe out if you're not looking ahead in the measure to see what's coming up. It would be like walking down a street that you've never been on before and looking down directly at your feet as you walk. If you never looked up, you wouldn't see the hole in the sidewalk that you might fall into or the curb coming up that would lead you right into the road, where you'd be in danger. If you walk down that same street with your head held up and your eyes looking around, you'll see what lies ahead and figure out how to avoid any hazard long before you reach it.

You can use this same approach when working on new and complex exercises on the drums. Before you even begin to play a particular exercise, take a second or two to memorize at least the first beat of the first measure of the exercise. Then, when you begin to play the exercise, keep your eyes ahead of where you're actually playing in the measure. I picture this process as two laser beams shooting on the measure. The first laser beam hits the measure at the point at which you're actually playing at any given time, and the second laser beam hits the point at which your eyes are looking ahead. Figure 10.11 shows a groove with indications of where you should be looking while you're playing.

Many times, a new exercise can be made up of things you've played many times before, but with one added different piece. When you work on playing the exercise, you don't necessarily even have to look at the parts of the measure that contain things you already know how to play. You can use your eyes to focus on the part of the measure that contains the brand-new piece.

The habit of staying at least one step ahead with your eyes when working on a brand-new exercise is an essential tool for you to keep in your growing toolbox of drumming skills, not only when reading and learning a new exercise. This skill will also help you keep your cool when you're making things up on your own. If you have a decent idea of what your next move will be and what you need to do to get there, your drumming will sound confident and strong. And that's a good thing.

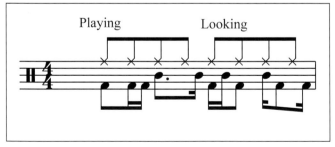

Figure 10.11
This groove shows where you should be looking while you're playing.

As you can see, it's not a very complicated process to make up new patterns out of different combinations of sixteenth-note variations. It's simply a matter of slicing and dicing and moving the parts around in different orders and combinations to create new grooves. Figure 10.12 shows another exercise consisting of a one-measure groove repeated twice:

In this exercise, I've simply taken the last exercise you worked on in this section and changed the sixteenth-note variation in the first beat of the measure. In other words, the entire exercise is identical to the last exercise except for the very beginning. As you can see, the first beat of the measure consists of a full sixteenth-note phrase played by the bass drum and the snare drum in a certain order.

You've worked on this phrasing of sixteenth notes in a previous chapter, when it went by the name of the "Big #3." To play this exercise correctly, it's simply a matter of refreshing your memory about how to play the "Big #3," and then finishing out the measure by playing exactly what you played in the last exercise you worked on in this section. Then, you'll need to focus some special attention on the transition you make from the end of the first measure of the exercise to the beginning of the second measure of the exercise, which is simply a repeat of the first measure.

As in all the exercises in this chapter, most of the action is in the area where the end of the first measure meets the beginning of the second measure. Hopefully, you've been having an easier time making these transitions as you progress through this chapter. I say "hopefully" because now you'll be moving on to even more slicing and dicing.

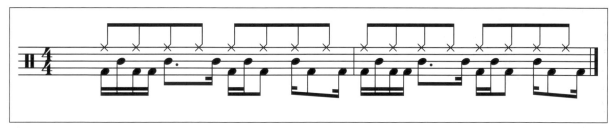

Figure 10.12
Sixteenth-Note Variations Exercise #5

More Slicing and Dicing and Some Words on Style

YOU CAN CREATE MANY DIFFERENT fills simply by taking all the sixteenth-note variations you already know and moving them around within a measure. I honestly can't even tell you the exact number of grooves you could possibly create by slicing and dicing all the variations you know. You'd have to consult your local mathematician and have him or her calculate it for you. (You could probably find your local mathematician in the Yellow Pages, under "Mathematician, Local.")

In Figures 10.13 through 10.16, I've given you at least four grooves off the top of my head using the slice-and-dice concept to finish off this chapter. Now, you don't necessarily have to able to play all of the following grooves perfectly to be a decent drummer or before you can move on in this book. However, I would like you to give each one of these grooves your best shot. This is a good idea for two reasons. First, obviously these exercises are designed to improve your coordination and help make you a better drummer by pushing your abilities to the max. Pushing yourself hard almost always will yield excellent results.

It might be a good idea to use the timer technique when working on these exercises so you don't get too frustrated if you run into any difficulties in your work. It's important to work as hard as you can for specific periods of time so you don't become frustrated enough to believe that you might never be able to play a certain groove. You can always stop when your time is up and start where you left off the next time you sit down to practice. If you approach your practice sessions with this attitude, it's only a matter of time until you can master any of those seemingly difficult exercises.

The second reason you should give these exercises your best shot is because by working on them, you will begin to develop your very own drumming style. You might find that some of these exercises come easier to you than others. If your coordination is developed to the point where it is possible for you to play all of the exercises at least decently, but one or the other of them simply feels or sounds better to you, it's perfectly fine for you to play the ones you like better more often than the ones that you don't particularly like.

Anybody who works on this book will most likely have different exercises he or she happens to like better than others. The exercises that you gravitate toward are the ones that make the most sense to you personally. I don't find that any of these exercises in this section of the book are any easier to play than any others. They are all on the same level of difficulty, in my opinion. However, there are some that I would be more likely to play if I was just playing drums for my own pleasure. The grooves that I personally gravitate toward out of the phenomenally massive number of grooves that I'm physically capable of playing are the grooves that help to make up my own personal drumming style. And the same is true of you: The grooves that you gravitate toward will help you create your own personal drumming style.

However, this doesn't mean you should just bail if you encounter a groove you're having trouble playing at first. You'll never know which grooves you like best until you try them all. We've all eaten broccoli at some point or other in our lives. I personally do not care for the taste or feel of broccoli, but other people I know love it. You have to try broccoli first in order to know whether you like it. Who knows? You may love it. Here, have some broccoli.

Figure 10.13
Sixteenth-Note Variations Exercise #7

Figure 10.14
Sixteenth-Note Variations Exercise #8

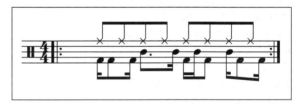

Figure 10.15
Sixteenth-Note Variations Exercise #9

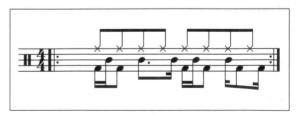

Figure 10.16
Sixteenth-Note Variations Exercise #10

Where You'll Take a Vow, Use Accents, Play in 3D, See a Ghost, and Express

Yourself

NOW THAT YOU'VE STAYED with the program in this book long enough to be able to play grooves and fills that require the advanced coordination techniques you've acquired, it's time to get detail-oriented. To become a truly great drummer, you not only need to be able to simply play grooves and fills, but you also need to be able to make those grooves and fills sound as good as you possibly can.

You might think that just being able to play something without making any mistakes automatically makes it sound as good as it can, and you would not be entirely wrong to think that. Merely playing a groove or a fill without making any mistakes is the best many drummers can do, due to limited raw talent, laziness when practicing, or simply the inability to hear the difference between drumming that just sounds okay and drumming that sounds really good. It is my solemn vow to help you become the kind of drummer who can not only tell the difference between mediocre drumming and great drumming, but who can give his or her absolute best shot at being a truly great drummer, not just a mediocre one.

What makes a drummer truly great, in my opinion? There are so many things, but the first quality that comes to mind is a drummer's attention to detail in his or her own playing. Often it's the small adjustments, the details, the little things that a good drummer does to make whatever he or she is playing at any given time sound and feel good.

Using Accents—And I Don't Mean Talking Funny

ONE OF THOSE LITTLE THINGS that a drummer can do to make any groove feel better is to use accents while playing grooves. And that doesn't mean playing a groove while talking like you're from another country. An accent is something that you do to some notes in a groove and not to others. When you play a note with an accent, you play that particular note at a louder volume than the other unaccented notes in the groove. A note with an accent is called an *accented note*; you can identify an accented note easily because it will have an accent near it in notation. Figure 11.1 shows what an accent looks like.

Figure 11.1
An accent

You will see this accent above or below any note that should be accented, or played louder than all the other unaccented notes in the particular measure or piece of music on which you happen to be working. When accents are used properly in a groove, even the simplest groove will sound quite different than it normally would when played without accents. When accents are used, two different volume levels are created within the groove, giving a more exciting feel to that groove, almost making it sound three-dimensional instead of relying on the flat and one-dimensional sound of a groove in which all the notes are played at exactly the same volume.

To show you what three-dimensional drumming sounds like, let's take a step backward in order to ultimately go forward into the new and exciting world of three-dimensional drumming. I can only hope that you're ready, because your drumming life will never again be the same after this next section.

Drumming in 3D: The Backbeat

BEFORE I UNCORK THE SECRETS of three-dimensional drumming, I feel that a few simple explanations are in order. As you learned much earlier in this book, a measure of music can be broken up into parts, or *beats* in music speak. All of the exercises that you've learned in this book have been in what is called *4/4 time*, which means that each measure of music is made up of four beats, and a quarter note is equal to the value of one beat of that same measure.

You may or may not have noticed that there has always been a snare-drum note on both beats 2 and 4 of every measure of every exercise in this book that made up a groove. Some grooves you've encountered in this book may have had more snare notes in them than just on beats 2 and 4, but even those grooves have still had snare-drum notes on beats 2 and 4. Some musicians who are so much cooler than you or I could ever hope to be refer to the snare-drum notes found on beats 2 and 4 of a groove as the *backbeat*. The term "back-beat" simply refers to accented snare notes on beats 2 and 4 of a groove. As I said earlier, you may play more notes on the snare drum than just on beats 2 and 4, but when you accent those notes on 2 and 4, you're playing a backbeat.

Although it might be true that we may never be as cool as those cooler-than-cool musicians, we can still use the term "backbeat" ourselves. (We may never be that cool, but we can at least try. Who knows? Maybe someday we can fool somebody into thinking that we're actually a little bit cool ourselves. It's so important to fantasize and have dreams.) Figure 11.2 shows a relatively simple groove you learned how to play much earlier in this book, but this time you'll accent the snare-drum notes only on beats 2 and 4, while playing the unaccented snare-drum notes at a normal volume.

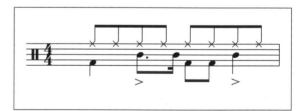

Figure 11.2
Rimshot Accent Exercise #1

Without even dealing with the accents, this groove shouldn't give you much trouble. As I pointed out, you've played this groove before. If you need to refresh your memory as to how this groove should be played, feel free to try it without the accents at first. Then, when you feel comfortable playing it, try to add the accents on the backbeat.

As you can see from looking at the exercise, there will be only one snare note besides the two snare notes found on the backbeat that will be unaccented. If you look carefully at the exercise as it's written, you'll notice that the accents appear below the hi-hat notes on beats 2 and 4 of the measure, rather than directly below the actual snare-drum notes that are to be accented. This is simply because the accent notation can't be wedged in close to the snare-drum notes without creating a mess in the notation. So, how are you supposed to know that those particular snare drum notes are to be accented and not the hi-hat notes instead? Because I told you so, that's how.

To have a volume difference between an accented snare note and an unaccented snare note, you must have two different approaches to the way you play the snare drum in the exercise. You must play the accented notes with a little bit more force than the unaccented notes, which means that you will have to adjust your attack on the snare drum with a precision that you perhaps have yet to develop.

If you give this exercise a try with the accents in place and you can naturally produce two different and distinct volume levels on the snare drum, good for you. It's hard to predict how much or how little difficulty any particular drummer will encounter when attempting to play with accents for the first time, but there is a tool I will give you that can help you create the two different volume levels that you should be playing on the snare drum as you work on this exercise. This tool is called a *rimshot.*

Drumming in 3D: The Rimshot

A RIMSHOT IS A SPECIAL WAY to strike a drum—especially a snare drum—that will instantly increase the volume and projection of the drum on which you use it at any given time. To play a rimshot, you strike the rim of the snare drum at the same time that you strike the head itself. When the rim of the snare drum is struck at the same time as the head, a unique and unmistakably sharp (and some might say) barking sound is heard from the snare drum.

To play a rimshot properly, you must adjust the angle of your wrist as you strike the snare drum. You might also have to adjust the angle of your snare drum as it sits on the snare stand to make sure that you can successfully play a rimshot every time. If, for example, your snare drum is tilted toward you, you will find it more difficult to properly play a rimshot than you would if the snare drum were in a more or less horizontal position.

If the snare drum is tilted toward you, your arm would have to be at a funny and awkward angle to strike the rim of the drum and the drumhead itself at the same time in order to properly play a rimshot. Having the snare drum placed in a horizontal manner will not require you to use a particularly weird or difficult angle of your arm in order to play a rimshot. However, you might need to adjust the overall height of the snare stand. If, for example, the entire snare stand with the snare drum on it is too high, then you are more likely to hit only the rim and not the rim and the head at the same time. A little bit of awareness and experimentation will lead you to the best height and

angle for you to play a rimshot perfectly every time. Figures 11.3 and 11.4 will give you an idea of how to play a rimshot properly.

Figure 11.3
Regular snare-playing position

Figure 11.4
Rimshot snare-playing position

The rimshot is the perfect tool for use as an accent maker. You will find as you learn to play a rimshot that a snare-drum stroke using a rimshot is louder, sharper, and more distinct than a non-rimshot stroke on the snare drum. You don't necessarily even have to use any more force when bringing your drumstick down while playing a rimshot. The mere fact that a rimshot is naturally louder than a non-rimshot stroke is enough to create the volume difference between accented and unaccented notes that you'll need to be a three-dimensional drummer.

If you play any accented snare drum notes you encounter in an exercise as rimshot strokes and the unaccented snare notes as regular, non-rimshot strokes, you'll automatically produce two distinct volume levels from your snare drum. With all this in mind, go back and try the exercise shown in Figure 11.2 while playing rimshots on the backbeat and regular, non-rimshot strokes on the unaccented snare note.

Hopefully, with some practice, you'll produce two different volume levels from your snare drum within a one-measure exercise. It may take you more than few tries to get the hang of this, but once you learn to play this exercise properly using rimshots, you'll be able to hear and get a taste of the three-dimensional type of sound that you can bring to your playing by using this technique.

Next, try using the rimshot/backbeat/accent technique on your old pal, Groove #6. As you remember, Groove #6 is the wicked sensation that's sweeping the nation with its nasty vibrations. If you thought that Groove #6 was a killer before, wait until you apply rimshots to the backbeat. I don't even think I could make up enough rhymes to properly describe the utterly funky devastation that will be unleashed upon all creation when you uncork this masterpiece. All I can say is that this is no time to be weak. Instead, it's time to stand strong and bask in the glory that will be yours when you let this one fly. Your little life will never be the same. You might even have to change your pants, your name, and your zip code all at the same time. Figure 11.5 shows Groove #6 with rimshot accents.

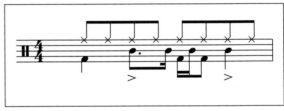

Figure 11.5
Rimshot Accent Exercise #2 (Groove #6 with accents)

As you can see, when you play Groove #6 using rimshots on the backbeat, you'll be playing the two snare-drum notes on the backbeat as rimshots and the two remaining notes on the snare drum as regular non-rimshot strokes. It may take you more than a few tries to make the quick adjustments between rimshot and non-rimshot strokes that you'll make in this exercise, but don't give up too quickly. Learning to play with two distinct volume levels on the snare drum will instantly double the number of grooves available to you. It's simply amazing, isn't it? Sure it is.

Boo! Drumming in 3D: The Ghost Note

NOW THAT YOU'VE CONCENTRATED on the accented notes in the previous exercises, it's time to take a look at the unaccented notes. You've already learned that by playing rimshots on the backbeat, you're automatically producing two distinct volume levels from your snare drum. This qualifies as 3D drumming. It's the difference between the loudest snare drum stroke and the quietest snare drum stroke that creates the three-dimensional feel. So, it stands to reason that the greater the volume difference between the loudest and the quietest snare drum strokes, the greater the three-dimensional effect on the sound.

Depending on how intense a three-dimensional feel you want to create in your drumming sound at any given time, you want to be as aware and in control of the difference between accented and unaccented strokes as possible. As you discovered earlier, using rimshots on the backbeat will pretty much take care of the louder end of the spectrum, and that may be enough to create a reasonable amount of three-dimensional effect on your drumming sound. But why settle for just a three-dimensional sound when you can go for a *really* three-dimensional sound?

You can produce a *super* three-dimensional sound by concentrating on playing the unaccented snare notes in these exercises even quieter and with even less force than just your regular unaccented snare drum stroke. This will increase the dynamic range of your drumming sound. *Dynamic range* is simply another way to describe the difference between the loudest and the quietest parts of a piece of music. In music-speak, the word "dynamics" refers to volume changes within a piece of music.

If the unaccented snare-drum notes in a groove are played even quieter than just a regular unaccented snare-drum note, they are called *ghost notes* because they are not necessarily heard as much as they are felt. (They are also called ghost notes because it's scary how much better your drumming will sound when you use them. You might even scare yourself. You definitely don't want to play too many ghost notes in a dark room. You may go mad with fright.) This does not mean that you don't play them at all; rather, you play them as quietly as you can, thereby instantly and greatly increasing the dynamic range of your drumming.

Here's an experiment for you to try that will give you an idea of the approximate volume level you should be shooting for when you try to play ghost notes. Play your old friend Groove #6. As you do, listen closely to the volume difference between the hi-hats and the snare drum. When this or any pattern is played without any particular attention paid to the relative dynamic range between the different voices of the drum kit heard in this particular pattern, the snare drum is naturally heard as being louder than the hi-hats. The snare drum has a louder and more pointed attack sound when struck than the hi-hats do. The hi-hats don't have quite the impact when struck as the snare drum does.

If you were to play rimshots on the backbeat of the same groove, those rimshot strokes would be even louder than the hi-hat than they were before. Now, as you play Groove #6 while using rimshots on the backbeats, listen carefully to the non-rimshot snare notes that remain in the measure. Try to match the volume level of those non-rimshot snare notes (or ghost notes, as we will call them) to the same volume level as the hi-hat strokes as closely as you can.

When the volume level of the ghost notes on the snare drum is matched as closely as possible to the volume level of the hi-hat, a very interesting sound presents itself within the groove. It almost sounds as if you are playing more notes on the hi-hats than just the straight eighth notes you actually are. Even though you are just playing eighth notes on the hi-hat, bringing the ghost notes on the snare drum down as close to the same volume level as the hi-hat will give the groove an undercurrent of a sixteenth-note feel, giving the overall feel of the groove a different flavor. Although this new flavor can't be described as having either an eighth or a sixteenth-note feel, it can be described as having a little bit of the feel of both. This feel can be applied anywhere that a straight eighth-note feel can be, but it has a little extra perkiness to it that can be just the feel you're searching for when Groove #6 without ghost notes is not quite right.

By understanding the usefulness of ghost notes and knowing how to apply them, you can instantly multiply the number of grooves in your arsenal not by adding any additional notes to the existing grooves, but by simply changing the volume level of certain notes within the groove itself. And that's a beautiful thing. If only everything else in life were that simple and rewarding.

By the way, the word "arsenal" means "a collection of weapons," which is what these grooves are. Believe it or not, you are the possessor of deadly weapons in the war on bad drumming. Just remember, use your powers wisely, and don't ever use those weapons against me. I'm your friend, the one who gave them to you in the first place. And besides, if you challenge me, you will be completely and utterly destroyed. Sorry, but that's just how it is.

WHAT ARE YOU TRYING TO SAY?

In my opinion, the greater the dynamic range you can create within a groove, the better that particular groove will sound. There's absolutely nothing wrong with playing every note of a groove all at the same volume if that's the sound you happen to be going for. If you were to play all the notes of a groove at the same volume, you would be producing a strong and powerful sound, but also one that might be described as flat.

When there's no contrast between any of the notes in the groove or between any of the voices of the drum kit, you're treating the drum kit as one voice instead of as the combination of voices that it actually is. For example, the snare drum is one distinct voice, as is the bass drum, the hi-hat, and so on. But not only can each piece of the drum kit be seen as a distinct voice, each distinct volume level at which you can play any of those voices can also be viewed as an additional voice available to you. The more voices that you have available overall, the greater and more precise your expression will be as you use your drumming to express yourself. In other words, the more voices you have the better, because voices are what you use to express yourself in drumming.

When drumming, you should occasionally ask yourself exactly what it is you're trying to express. Are you angry? Anxious? Peaceful and relaxed? Happy or sad? Confident or confused? Hungry? Bored? What are you trying to say? Not only does a heightened sense of dynamic range give you better tools of expression, but it also simply makes your drumming sound better. Being aware of the dynamic range of your expression can make your drumming sound more polished and in control. Creating some dynamic range within your playing, particularly in your playing of grooves, will help you go from sounding like a drummer who can play some things decently to sounding like a drummer who is much better than average. You'll sound like you might actually know what you're doing.

Don't Push Me because I'm Close to the Edge. Drumming in 3D: The Hi-Hats

WHEN IT COMES TO DRUMMING in 3D, the hi-hats can come into play in a big way. Up until now, you've probably been playing the hi-hats without paying any particular attention to how you're playing them or how the way you happen to be playing them affects the sound you're producing. But we're going to change all that as I show you how to pay attention to the way you're playing your hi-hats so you will think of the hi-hats themselves in a whole new way. There are many different ways to play the hi-hats (with drumsticks, with your face, with a flaming banana, and so on), but let's concentrate on two different ways to play the hi-hats that will enable you to instantly produce twice as many sounds from them as you could before by making some very small adjustments. The first way to play your hi-hats is by striking them with your stick on the top of the top hi-hat cymbal. Figure 11.6 shows the normal, unaccented hi-hat playing position.

This is probably the way you've been playing the hi-hats up until now, because it's the most natural way to play them when you're first starting out, and the way that makes the most sense. The second way to play the hi-hats is by striking them on the edge of the top cymbal with your stick. Figure 11.7 shows the accented hi-hat playing position.

Figure 11.7
Accented hi-hat playing position

You may be playing the hi-hats this way already, depending on the height at which you have your hi-hat stand adjusted. If your hi-hat stand is set up high enough so that it's easier for you to strike the edge of the hi-hat cymbals, then you've probably been playing them on the edge the whole time. On the other hand, if your hi-hat stand is set up low enough that you would have to reach down at an awkward angle to even play them on the edge with your stick, then you've probably been playing them on the top of the top cymbal all this time.

Figure 11.6
Normal unaccented hi-hat playing position

Now would be the right time for you to check out the height of your hi-hat stand and adjust it in such a way that you can easily strike either the top of the top cymbal or the edge of the top cymbal at any time. There's no strict rule as to the proper height for the hi-hat stand. As I suggested, the best height for you would be the height at which you can easily play either the top or the edge at any given time because in order to play the hi-hats in a 3D fashion, you'll have to be able to do just that.

Accents can be played on the hi-hat just like they can be played on the snare drum. Instead of playing accents as rimshots, as you would on the snare drum, you can play accents on the hi-hats by playing them on the edge. Playing the hi-hats on the edge produces a more intense and chunkier sound than playing them on the top. By being aware of the different sounds you can produce from the hi-hats simply by hitting them in two different places, you can take any of the grooves you already know and experiment with hi-hat accents. You can create new grooves that, although they don't contain any more notes than they did before accents on the hi-hats were added, can sound remarkably different from the same grooves being played without any hi-hat accents at all.

Figure 11.8 depicts an exercise designed to show you how big a difference the use of hi-hat accents can make in both the sound and feel of a groove. It shows the simplest drum exercise I could come up with. As a matter of fact, it's the very first groove you learned in this book, way back when you were a baby drummer. Come along and take a walk down memory lane with me and this exercise.

You should have absolutely no problem at all figuring out how to play this groove. As a matter of fact, the hardest part will be for you to reach back far enough in your memory to remember ever playing this beauty in the first place. Once you've re-familiarized yourself with that groove, take a look at the same groove with hi-hat accents (see Figure 11.9).

Figure 11.8
Groove without hi-hat accents

When playing this groove with hi-hat accents, you'll strike the edge of the hi-hats for the accents, creating a nice, chunky sound from them. For the unaccented notes, simply play the hi-hats on the top. You don't necessarily even have to strike the accented notes any harder when you play them on the edge versus the unaccented notes you play on the top. The chunky sound you produce from the hi-hats as you strike them on the edge will automatically take care of the accented sound you're going for, much the same as how a rimshot is automatically louder and sharper than a regular, unaccented snare note.

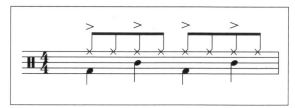

Figure 11.9
Hi-Hat Accent Exercise #1

To play every other eighth note as an accented note, as you would in this exercise, you'll need to use a somewhat peculiar levering motion with your arm as you play the hi-hat. You'll bend your wrist backward first, in order to play the first accented eighth note in the pattern, and then you'll bend your wrist forward to play the second unaccented note of the pattern, and so on throughout the exercise. It might take you more than a few tries to get the hang of the pump-like motion you'll need to make with your wrist as you play this exercise, but don't give up too easily. Give yourself enough tries to get the rhythm of the pumping motion.

After you learn how to play this exercise, try to pay close attention to the overall sound and feel of the groove with the hi-hat accents applied. You might notice that when this simple groove is played with the hi-hat accents in place, the groove now has a distinct quarter-note feel. Because the hi-hat accents are on each of the four beats in the measure (and each of the four beats of the measure represents a quarter note), the quarter notes are being brought out in the overall feel of the groove. Even though you are actually still only playing eighth notes in the groove, the quarter notes stand out much more than if the groove were played without the hi-hat accents. It's kind of like having the best of both worlds. You're playing a groove that has eighth notes on the hi-hat and the feel of forward momentum that eighth notes bring, but the groove now has a distinct quarter-note pulse to it that gives it a slight feel of heaviness because of the accents you're playing on the hi-hats on each and every beat of the measure.

If you're still not convinced that playing any kind of accents on the hi-hats will change the sound or feel of a groove, Figure 11.10 presents another little exercise that's especially designed to make a believer out of you. And if you still don't believe me, check out the DVD, where you'll see it with your own eyes. Figure 11.10 shows the exercise.

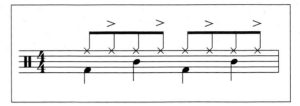

Figure 11.10
Hi-Hat Accent Exercise #2

This is the same super-simple groove as in the last exercise, but with one gigantic difference. The hi-hat accents are now on the "+" of each beat of the measure instead of on the beat. You'll still be playing eighth notes on the hi-hats, but with the accents on what we'll call the *upbeats* of each beat of the measure, a completely different sound and feel is produced. Just like with the last exercise, it might take you more than a few tries to get the feel of the pumping type of motion you'll be making with your arm as you try to play these accents where they are supposed to be within the measure. However, once you get the feel for it, I'm sure you'll notice how unbelievably different this exercise sounds and feels from the last one you worked on earlier in this section of the chapter.

Both this groove and the earlier one sound and feel almost completely different from each other, yet there is absolutely no difference between them as far as the number of actual notes in each exercise. The only difference between the two is the placement of the hi-hat accents. Hopefully, this illustrates my point and proves to you how much of a difference the use of hi-hat accents can make when creating grooves. But what about the bass drum? Can the bass drum be played with accents too? I think you already know the answer to that.

Drumming In 3D: The Bass Drum

YOU CAN ALSO PRODUCE at least two different volume levels from your bass drum by using accents. Because you can't really strike the bass drum anywhere else on the drumhead other than where the beater strikes it, you'll have to create two distinct volume levels from your bass drum by simply playing some notes louder than other notes, depending on how hard you step on the bass drum pedal.

When you step on the bass drum pedal harder than you normally would, you will produce a louder-than-normal sound from your bass drum that we will call the *accent*. Just as with the snare drum or hi-hats, when accents are added to the bass drum in any groove, that groove can take on a much different character and feel than it would if it were played without accents. We normally wouldn't go crazy with accents on the bass drum and have as many accented versus unaccented notes as we might on the snare drum, for example. That's simply because most of us don't generally have as much control over our feet as we do over our hands. Otherwise, we would brush our teeth and write or type with our feet instead of our hands. (Unless, of course, you're one of those people who can do things with your feet that most people do with their hands, such as brush your teeth or whatever. If you are one of those people, I have two things to say to you: "Congratulations, I'm very proud of you," and "Ewwww, gross!")

Accents on the bass drum are used relatively sparingly, but to great effect. Here's an exercise to give you an idea of how accents on the bass drum can affect the character and feel of a groove. The exercise will begin with a groove with no accents to get you going, and then accents will be added to the basic groove in the examples that follow the basic version. Figure 11.11 shows the basic groove with no bass-drum accents.

Figure 11.11
Basic groove with no bass-drum accents

Figure 11.12 shows the same groove with a bass-drum accent.

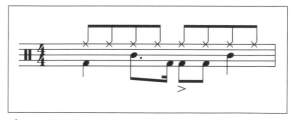

Figure 11.12
Bass Drum Accent Exercise #1

And Figure 11.13 shows the same groove with three bass-drum accents in various places.

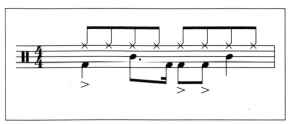

Figure 11.13
Bass Drum Accent Exercise #2

Figure 11.14 shows the same groove again, with two bass-drum accents in various places.

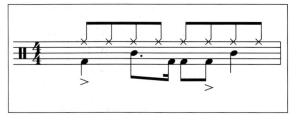

Figure 11.14
Bass Drum Accent Exercise #3

As you can see, playing accents on the bass drum can make quite a difference to the sound and feel of a groove. In this case, you're adding accents to a groove you learned much earlier in this book, which contains a particular sixteenth-note variation in the third beat of the measure. It is in this third beat of the measure where you'll focus most of your attention with regard to the playing of accents.

In the second groove of the bunch, you'll find the first accent added on the bass drum right on beat 3 of the measure. This might prove somewhat challenging because the particular bass-drum note you'll be accenting, which is on beat 3 of the measure, is surrounded by bass-drum notes that are not to be accented. But, after you give this exercise enough tries with the accent in place, I bet you'll get the hang of it in no time.

Then it would be time for you to move on to the next exercise, which should take you even less time to master than the first exercise because you'll only be adding an accent on the very first bass-drum note in the measure, right on beat 1. Having bass drum accents on both beats 1 and 3 of the measure will give this groove a distinctively heavy feel. The use of accents, whether they are played on the snare drum or the hi-hat, is essential to building your groove collection. Can you imagine how many grooves you already know that could perhaps benefit from some selective accents? Lucky for you, you don't have to imagine; Figure 11.15 presents a review exercise that includes some accent work as well as some other treats for you to work on. There's no need to thank me—I guess I'm just a generous guy by nature.

Figure 11.15
Review

Where You'll Get a Quarter, Learn How Songs Work, Hitch a Ride, and Be a

Volume Knob

UP UNTIL NOW, all the patterns or grooves you've learned in this book have revolved around eighth notes played on the hi-hats. The eighth notes on the hi-hats have served us well. The majority of grooves you'll hear in any song will probably have eighth notes played on the hi-hats, so learning grooves or patterns that have eighth notes on the hi-hat is a great place to start when you're first learning to play drums. Also, as the grooves you learned started to contain all the different sixteenth-note variations played between the snare drum and the bass drum, the hi-hat eighth notes came in extra handy because if you needed to know where any particular sixteenth note was supposed to land, you just needed to line it up with the nearest available eighth note (because any sixteenth note will either line up with an eighth note or end up exactly between any two eighth notes).

Hey...Got a Quarter?

I T IS FOR THESE REASONS that learning to play grooves with eighth notes on the hi-hat is not only the best place from which to begin playing drums, but also is a skill you will constantly use as you continue your drumming career, no matter how long your career may last. But eighth notes are not the only thing you can play on the hi-hats in a groove. Depending on the tempo or feel you might be going for, quarter notes on the hi-hat can sometimes be just the thing you're looking for. If you want to play music that is faster than what we would call normal, such as punk rock, hardcore, really fast polka, or maybe death-core bagpipe, then you should definitely have a quarter-note hi-hat technique on tap.

The faster the overall tempo, the harder time you might have with keeping eighth notes going continuously on the hi-hats. You might reach a point at which the tempo is simply too fast for you to keep up the eighth notes, and besides, if the eighth notes on the hi-hat are played too fast, they can sound like a hamster scratching itself. Also, if you find yourself having to slow down the tempo just so you can fit in every eighth note on the hi-hats, you're in hot water indeed.

Quarter Notes to the Rescue

NOTHING SHOULD EVER CAUSE you to slow down a tempo once you've established one, especially the inability to keep up the eighth notes on the hi-hat. Luckily, this is where knowing how to play quarter notes on the hi-hats instead can come to the rescue. Now, you might think that just because there are fewer hi-hat notes in a quarter-note hi-hat pattern, any groove with a quarter-note hi-hat pattern would automatically be easier to play than a groove with an eighth-note hi-hat pattern. You wouldn't be entirely wrong to think that, but you wouldn't be entirely right either. Sorry. For any groove that you learned to play while using eighth notes on the hi-hats, you will have to make some small adjustments in your coordination to play it with quarter notes instead. You really shouldn't have too much trouble making these adjustments, but you will definitely have to devote a little bit of your time to make the switch from an eighth-note pattern on the hi-hats to a quarter-note pattern. Fortunately, your overall coordination is fairly well advanced if you've made it this far in the book, so you really shouldn't have too much trouble.

To get you started, Figure 12.1 presents a very simple groove using eighth notes on the hi-hats, which you already learned much earlier in this book.

You should have absolutely no problem playing this groove. If you do, I would suggest that you go all the way back to the beginning of this book and start your drumming studies over again. Or maybe you should go play soccer or something. Now, Figure 12.2 presents the same groove, but with quarter notes on the hi-hats instead.

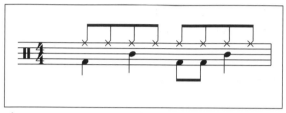

Figure 12.1
A very simple groove

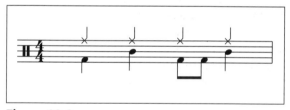

Figure 12.2
Hi-Hat Quarter Note Exercise #1

As you play this groove with quarter notes on the hi-hats instead of eighth notes, you will play an eighth note on the bass drum on the "+" of beat 3 that will not have a hi-hat note played along with it. With your advanced coordination skills, this should not pose very much of a problem for you. Remember that you've played plenty of bass-drum notes without attaching hi-hat notes to them in earlier chapters of this book, when you were playing all of those grooves that had various sixteenth-note combinations played between the snare and bass drums against a straight eighth-note hi-hat pattern. You will just have to make some very minor adjustments to play an eighth note on the bass drum against a quarter-note hi-hat pattern.

After you make those minor adjustments and are able to play this quarter-note hi-hat version of a very simple groove, try to increase the tempo as you try it again. Remember that one of the main purposes for learning to play grooves using a quarter-note hi-hat pattern instead of an eighth-note pattern is to be able to play those grooves if you're faced with a song that has a somewhat faster tempo than you've ever happened to play. My suggestion is that you practice the first version of the groove (which has eighth notes on the hi-hat) to your metronome at a tempo that is completely comfortable for you. Then, increase the tempo of the metronome at least 10 clicks and try the same groove while still playing eighth notes on the hi-hats.

Keep moving the tempo up by five or maybe ten clicks until you reach a tempo at which it is very difficult or impossible to keep the eighth notes going on the hi-hats. Or, keep moving up the tempo at least until you arrive at a tempo at which you can still play eighth notes on the hi-hats, but you're either right on the edge of being in control of your playing or the eighth notes on the hi-hats sound like a hyperactive hamster trying to scratch itself to death. That's when you'll know that it's time to try quarter notes on the hi-hats instead of eighth notes. Using quarter notes on the hi-hats instead of eighth notes will allow you to cruise along at those faster than normal tempos as you get a taste for what it feels like to play quarter notes on the hi-hats. When you feel comfortable with this first exercise, which uses quarter notes on the hi-hats, you're ready for some more. Or at least I hope you're ready. Ready or not, Figure 12.3 shows the next exercise.

Figure 12.3
Hi-Hat Quarter Note Exercise #2

I'm sure you remember the eighth-note hi-hat version of this groove from a much earlier chapter of this book. This version with quarter notes on the hi-hats should not give you much more trouble than the last exercise. It has exactly the same number of notes as the last exercise, but one eighth note on the bass drum is in a different place than in the previous exercise. Give yourself more than a few chances at figuring out this groove, and when you do, use your metronome to find the quickest tempo at which you can play this exercise.

Just like with the last exercise, the easiest way for you to find the right tempo at which to play this exercise is to start out playing the eighth-note hi-hat version of this groove to a metronome setting that is totally comfortable for you. Then, start notching up the tempo until you reach the point at which eighth notes are a near impossibility for you. Then try the groove with quarter notes on the hi-hats at that tempo. You will follow this exact procedure for all the following exercises. Figure 12.4 shows the next exercise of the bunch.

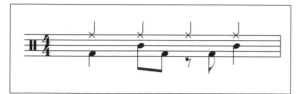

Figure 12.4
Hi-Hat Quarter Note Exercise #3

You might find this exercise slightly more challenging than the previous two, but don't let that scare you. Remember that as you advance in this chapter, your coordination will increase. You might find yourself feeling intimidated when you first look at new exercises, but that's just your silly brain trying to protect you from the disappointment of possibly not being able to play something correctly at first. What your brain doesn't actually know yet is that you are not the sad, uncoordinated person you were before you started playing drums. Have pity on your poor, slightly out-of-touch brain. It's only trying to help you; it will get the message eventually.

The exercise in Figure 12.4 contains a rest on the third beat of the measure, unlike the previous two exercises. You'll find a rest on beat 3 of the measure and a bass drum note, which will land on the "+" of beat 3, as well as a bass drum note on the "+" of beat 2. Again, you played the eighth-note hi-hat version of this groove much earlier in your studies.

Give yourself a few tries to get the hang of this groove, and then follow the procedure with the metronome that you did for the previous exercises in this section. Try the groove with eighth notes on the hi-hats at a tempo that's comfortable for you, and then gradually increase the tempo until you can't keep up the eighth notes. Then, switch over to quarter notes on the hi-hat.

This groove is a great addition to your growing collection and one that you may find yourself using a lot as you start to play in bands, so make sure you give yourself enough time to master it. You'll be glad you did. Then, when you're finished being glad, it's time to try your old pal Groove #6 with quarter notes on the hi-hats instead of eighth notes. Hey, all those other grooves are getting redone with quarter notes on the hi-hats. Why not Groove #6? Figure 12.5 shows Groove #6 with quarter notes on the hi-hat.

Figure 12.5
Hi-Hat Quarter Note Exercise #4

You might find Groove #6 quite challenging when it is redone with quarter notes on the hi-hats, but don't worry. Remember that you're better than you think you are. A certain amount of coordination is required to play this particular groove correctly, but luckily for you, you've already got the coordination. Take it slow and give this one a little bit of time, and I'm sure you'll have it down fairly quickly.

If you're confused as to exactly where the quarter-note hi-hats are supposed to be played, just look very carefully at the exercise. Study the quarter notes on the hi-hats themselves, and then look below each quarter note to determine which drum you're supposed to be playing along with each particular quarter note. When you've determined that, it's time to examine all the other notes on the snare drum and bass drum that don't line up with any particular hi-hat quarter notes. This can be a little bit tricky because, for example, there will be more than one note either on the snare drum or the bass drum that does not line up with any particular quarter note in beat 3 of this exercise.

On beat 3 of the measure, you'll play a quarter note on the hi-hats along with a bass-drum note, which is the first note of the three-note sixteenth-note variation played between the bass drum and the snare drum on beat 3. Then, you'll play the next quarter note on the hi-hats along with a single snare-drum note on beat 4 of the measure, which will bring you to the end of the measure. When you feel comfortable playing Groove #6 with quarter notes on the hi-hat, it's time to check out some more grooves that contain various sixteenth-note variation combinations between the snare drum and the bass drum that you already know how to play with eighth notes on the hi-hats, and then rework them with quarter notes on the hi-hat instead. Oh, look—here's some now (see Figures 12.6 through 12.8).

Figure 12.6
Hi-Hat Quarter Note Exercise #5

Figure 12.7
Hi-Hat Quarter Note Exercise #6

Figure 12.8
Hi-Hat Quarter Note Exercise #7

The Ride Cymbal...Finally

WE'RE ALMOST AT THE END of the book, so I figure now is as good a time as any to get into the ride cymbal. You might not even have a ride cymbal, which is why I waited so long to talk about it. But then again, you might have one, which is why we'll get into it now.

As you probably remember from earlier in this book, when you learned how to set up your drum kit, the ride cymbal is more than likely the largest cymbal in your collection. Or at least it should be. It should be not only the largest cymbal in your collection, but also the heaviest. The ride cymbal should be set up somewhere above your floor tom, way over on the right side of your drum kit as you're sitting at it. This is because you will play your ride cymbal with your right hand 99.9 percent of the time.

The ride cymbal is designed to be played as an alternative to the hi-hats. In other words, anything you can play on the hi-hats, you should be able to play on the ride cymbal also, except for any open and closed moves you might play on the hi-hats. There's not really a way to interpret open and closed hi-hat moves to the ride cymbal, so you're off the hook there. In other words, you'll just play the regular old eighth notes or quarter notes on the ride cymbal, just like you would in any groove you've already learned in which you previously played the hi-hats. This is why the ride cymbal is placed where it is in the drum kit, over and above the floor tom—so that if you want to play the ride cymbal, you will simply bring your right arm over to the ride cymbal in a straight shot, without having to cross your right arm over your left hand, as you would have to do if you were to play the hi-hats.

It's true that there's nothing stopping you from placing your ride cymbal where your crash cymbal currently resides (between and above the hi-hats and the first tom), but then where will you put that crash cymbal? Besides, you might find that if you were to put the ride cymbal where your crash cymbal should be, your right arm would cross over your left when playing the ride cymbal in a way that would restrict your left arm's ability to play the snare drum properly. Go ahead and try it if you don't believe me. Or you could take my word for it and just put your ride cymbal over and above your floor tom. That might be the best thing for both of us.

As you might remember from an earlier chapter, I informed you that crash cymbals are made to be struck mostly on the edges, while ride cymbals are made to be played on the top of the cymbal. For this reason, pay some attention to how your ride cymbal is set up on its stand. For example, you don't want the ride cymbal to be set up at a height at which it is unusually difficult for you to be able to consistently play the top of the cymbal. If the ride cymbal is set up too high, you might end up playing the edge of the ride cymbal more often than the top. You won't necessarily damage the ride cymbal by striking it at the edge, but you will not get the correct sound out of it if you play the edge instead of the top.

Feel free to experiment with the height at which you set your ride cymbal until you reach the height at which you can easily play the top of the cymbal. You also don't want the ride cymbal so low that it knocks against the floor tom when you're playing it. Again, experimentation will lead to the perfect height for you. Now all you have to do is learn how to play it.

The Ride Cymbal—Not So Much How as When

THERE REALLY ARE NO SPECIAL techniques for how to play the ride cymbal. Basically, you hit it with a stick. A little bit later, I'll show you how to get at least two different sounds out of your ride cymbal so you can bring the 3D concept to it, but for now, just concentrate on playing it in the normal place on the cymbal. The normal place for you to play is simply on the top of the cymbal, anywhere toward the middle of it, away from the edge and not quite at the dome on the very top of the cymbal. (That dome found at the top of the cymbal is called the *bell* of the cymbal, by the way.)

As I pointed out to you earlier, the ride cymbal can be played instead of the hi-hat cymbal, depending on the kind of sound you're looking to produce at any given point during a song or groove. Simply put, if you're looking for a tight, controlled sound, you should probably be playing the hi-hats. But if you're looking for a more open and airy sound, then the ride cymbal is what you should check out. There are no rules set in stone about ride cymbal usage. It's really up to the individual player as to when he or she moves from the hi-hat to the ride cymbal during any given part of a song. Maybe you'll never move from your hi-hats to your ride cymbal in a song or indeed in your whole life. Or maybe, you'll always play your ride cymbal and never go to your hi-hats at all. How can I predict what you'll do? I don't even know you. However, I don't need to know you personally to give you some ideas about when to use the ride cymbal. But to give you these ideas, I'll have to tell you a little bit about how songs work first.

How Songs Work: The Short Version

I'M SURE THAT YOU KNOW what a song is. And I'm sure you've noticed that most songs you've ever heard have drums in them. And if you've ever heard any songs that didn't have drums in them, then those songs aren't good songs. All songs are better with drums; everyone knows this. And because you play drums, you'll be playing drums in songs, so you should have at least a basic understanding of how songs are structured so you can make the most out of your part in these songs. Put in the simplest terms, most songs are made up of the following parts:

- ▶ **Intro**
- ▶ **Verse**
- ▶ **Chorus**
- ▶ **Bridge**
- ▶ **Solo section**
- ▶ **Ending**

An *intro* (short for introduction) of a song is the very beginning of the song, obviously. There's usually no singing in the intro, but of course there are exceptions to every rule, including this one. However, most of the time, the intro of a song is an instrumental piece in which either the guitar or the keyboards play part of the melody to lead into the second part of the song, called the *verse.*

The verse is usually where the singing starts. After the verse, the next part that usually comes is called the *chorus.* The chorus is part of the song that may or may not have the name of the song as part of its lyrics. For example, if the song is called "My Dog

Ate His Own Ear," the part of the song where the singer sings the words "My Dog Ate His Own Ear" would be the chorus. Now, sometimes the chorus will not have the title of the song itself in its lyrics. In this case, the chorus is likely the most memorable part of the song—the part that everyone sings along to, whether they're at a concert or listening to it at home or in the car. Usually the chorus comes after the verse, and there is typically more than one verse in a song, as well as more than one chorus.

Generally, after a song goes through the intro and at least two verses and choruses, the *bridge* comes next. The bridge is a part usually found in the middle of the song that is unlike either the verse or the chorus and is usually heard only once during a typical song, although there are, of course, exceptions to every rule. After the bridge may come a solo section, in which the guitarist, keyboardist, bagpiper, or some other instrumentalist in the band takes a solo while the rest of the band plays behind him or her. Then, the song may return to another verse and another chorus before reaching the *ending.*

There are many different ways for songs to end. Most songs have an actual ending, during which each band member plays something specific, all at the same time, in order to end the song. Sometimes, if the song is a recording, it may end with a fade out, with all of the music in the recording slowly turned down until it's inaudible. When you can't hear the song anymore, it has ended. Obviously, you wouldn't play a fade out as a band when you're playing live. As I pointed out, a fade out is usually only heard in a recorded song.

Not every song in the world has all these parts, and most songs have more than one of at least one of these parts, but almost every song has at least one of all of these parts that happens at least once in its duration. Part of the job of a good drummer is to come up with something a little bit different to play in each part or section of the song to make each of the parts stand out from the others. Sometimes the bass player or the guitarist will play something different in each part of the song, making it easy for you to come up with something different to play on the drums. Just listen carefully to whatever everyone else is playing in a particular part of a song and play a pattern on the drums that either matches or complements the rhythm of whatever your band mates are already playing in that part of the song. Sometimes, however, you might need to come up with something all by yourself for a certain section of a song in order for it to stand out against the other sections of the song.

Hi-Hats versus Ride Cymbals: The Winner Is You

THE CHOICES THAT YOU MAKE as the drummer in the band can help tremendously in creating different sounds or feels for each different section of any song on which your band is working. Sometimes something as simple as making the choice between playing the hi-hats or the ride cymbal can help to make the difference in sound that each section of the song requires. For example, you might play the ride cymbal during the intro of the song, and then move to the hi-hats for the verse. Then you might move to the ride cymbal for the solo section, and then move back to the hi-hats for the rest of the song. It's totally up to you. But do you have other choices besides just the hi-hats or the ride cymbal? Of course you do.

Half-Open (or Half-Closed) Hi-Hats, Ride Cymbals, and Infinite Possibilities

Up until now, I've only showed you how to use the hi-hats while they're closed all the way or while opening and closing them to create specific patterns, but the hi-hats can offer you so many more sounds than just these. The hi-hats can be slightly opened to create a different sound than just the regular closed sound. When you lift up your toes just a little bit while playing the hi-hats, you can produce a looser, slightly sloppy half-open or half-closed hi-hat sound.

Actually, the terms "half-open" or "half-closed" are probably the wrong ones to use in this case, because a specific position is implied by using those terms. There are as many places between

closed and open as you can create with the mere lifting of your little piggy toes. One drummer's half-open is another drummer's half-closed, and the degree to which you partially open or close the hi-hats to get a certain sound is completely up to you.

You might find yourself wondering what the difference is between a closed and a half-closed hi-hat sound, or how you're supposed to know which sound to use when. As I said before, there are no official rules for hi-hat sounds or ride cymbal sounds, but I can let you in on my ideas on the subject. These ideas might give you some guidelines to follow in your own creation of hi-hat sounds or at least give you some things to think about.

I personally view the different sounds you can create on the drum set as having different volume levels as well as different textures, in addition to their obvious differences in sound. For example, if the verse of a song is somewhat quieter in volume or lesser in intensity than the chorus of the same song, I would tend to play the verses with a closed hi-hat, creating a tighter and more focused sound. Then, when I reach the chorus of the song, which is louder or more intense, I might either open the hi-hats a little or go to the ride cymbal. Because half-open hi-hats and ride cymbal sounds are both basically louder than a closed hi-hat sound, my choice would then rely on the texture that I want to create for that chorus. For example, the half-open hi-hat sound is louder and chunkier, but still somewhat controlled-sounding. Although the hi-hats may ring out a little bit more being half-open than they would if they were fully closed, going to the ride cymbal will give me a more wide-open sound because the ride cymbal rings out much more than the half-open hi-hat sound.

Experimentation is key when determining which sound is right for each specific part of a song. I suggest you try almost every sound you can in each part of the song in order to reach the right sounds for you. There's no need for you to try every infinite possibility until you drive yourself insane or become permanently frozen in a glacier of indecision. Follow your first instincts, and if they don't quite give you the sounds you're looking for, try another two or three possibilities and settle on one. Maybe one of your band mates can help you to decide on a sound if you let them know you're searching for one. Ask for their opinions on which approach sounds better to their ears. Then do the exact opposite of what they suggest; this will keep them on their toes. (I'm kidding. Sometimes the perspective of your non-drummer band mates is invaluable. Oh, and by the way, the word "invaluable" means "very valuable.")

The Concept of Riding (and I Don't Mean in a Car)

In a typical drum groove, your right hand will most likely play eighth notes either on the hi-hats or the ride cymbal. When you happen to play eighth notes on the ride cymbal instead of the hi-hats, you are doing what I call "riding" on the ride cymbal. (When you play the hi-hats, I wouldn't say that you are "riding" on the hi-hats. You're just playing the hi-hats.)

The ride cymbal is not the only thing you can ride on in your drum kit. You could ride on your crash cymbal instead. That is to say, you could play the same eighth notes in the groove but play them on the crash cymbal instead of the ride cymbal or the hi-hats. This will give you a very loud and "washy" sound option that might come in handy for a specific part of a song.

Listen to some of your favorite music closely and try to determine what the drummer on the recording might be riding on in any particular part of a song. You might discover that he or she is, in fact, riding on a crash cymbal instead of the hi-hats or ride cymbal. (You might find that when riding on a crash cymbal, you only really have to play quarter notes because all the notes will "wash" into each other.) This is another option for you to try when making up your own drum parts if you end up in a band some day.

Another available option is to ride on one of your toms. This is another sound that you might hear somewhere. Which tom you ride on is completely up to you. Experiment with riding on each of them to get a feel for what it's like to ride on each tom on your kit. Obviously, the floor tom will give you the deepest sound out of all the other toms because it's the biggest drum, but maybe one of your other toms will give you the sound that you're looking for, so check them all out.

The Hi-Hats:
The Volume Knob of the Drum Set

THE HI-HAT MAY JUST BE THE MOST versatile voices of the drum kit. They can produce many different sounds and volume levels, and I'd like to show you yet another use for them. Picture yourself playing a verse of a song while using eighth notes on closed hi-hats. Then, when the chorus of the song arrives, you'll move over to the ride cymbal. Although it's true that you could just simply move directly from the hi-hats to the ride cymbal, moving directly from one sound to the other, you can instead use your hi-hats in a unique way to create a sort of "in between" sound while you're moving from the hi-hats to the ride cymbal. Figure 12.9 presents an exercise that introduces something called a *crescendo*.

Crescendo is a musical term for "gradually getting louder," and in this exercise, a crescendo is found over the hi-hats. As you play the second measure of the exercise, the hi-hats should be getting louder and louder as the measure goes on, until you reach the next measure of the exercise, where you'll go to the ride cymbal. (Imagine that the first two measures of the exercise are a verse of the song and the last two measures of the exercise are the chorus.)

You can make the hi-hats louder and louder as they continue through the second measure of the exercise by slowly lifting up your toes as you play through the measure, slowly opening up the hi-hats. As the hi-hats open more and more, they get louder, creating a crescendo. This can be a neat trick to use when moving from the hi-hats to the ride cymbal in a song, but it is by no means a rule. Sometimes, the quick change from the closed hi-hats to the ride cymbal is the perfect thing for some parts of songs, but you will always have the option of using a crescendo on the hi-hats to experiment. You never know when it will be just the perfect thing to bring a song dramatically into a chorus from a verse, so you should definitely practice this exercise enough to be comfortable with it so you can use it whenever you want. Or not. But at least you'll have a choice.

Figure 12.9
Ride Cymbal and Hi-Hat Crescendo Exercise

Congratulations: You're Almost a Drummer

YOU'VE COME A LONG WAY in this book, and hopefully you've learned a lot. You are now equipped with many of the tools you need to be a good drummer. Now, when you go to take private lessons with a local instructor, you can concentrate on the specific styles of music you might be interested in playing. With some guidance from your instructor, you'll be well on your way to being the drummer you always dreamed you could be. But before I let you go, I'd like you to check out one more short chapter that has some ideas about what I think makes a decent drummer a great drummer, as well as some tips that can make you the drummer who everybody wants in their band. So, if you feel lucky, turn the page and check out Chapter 13, "The Lucky Chapter: Where I'll Leave You with Some Last-Minute Advice," if you dare.

13

The Lucky Chapter: Where I'll Leave You with Some Last-Minute

Advice

S O, DO YOU FEEL LUCKY, now that you've reached "The Lucky Chapter?" I'd like to take this moment to congratulate you on reaching the end of this book. Okay, now that that moment is over, I'd like to leave you with some last-minute pieces of advice that I feel will help you to be as good a drummer as you can possibly be.

In my opinion, a good drummer is so much more than one who can merely physically play a bunch of stuff on the drums. A good drummer can develop skills and attitudes that can make him the most musically valuable player in the band and can also make him into the drummer that every band wants. Here are some of my thoughts on this very important subject, in the order in which they occur to me.

Awareness of Arrangement

YOU LEARNED A LITTLE BIT ABOUT song arrangement in the last chapter, and I'd like to expand upon some of those ideas and why it's important for the drummer to be as aware as possible of a song's arrangement.

First, having a crystal-clear vision of a song's arrangement helps you, as the drummer, know when you should play fills or when you should change up some of your voices (moving from the hi-hat to the ride cymbal, for example). As a very general rule, fills can be most effectively used to split up the song into its various different parts within the arrangement. For example, as the song moves from a verse to a chorus, a nicely timed fill can make that transition sound extra-special and right, but if you're not quite sure when that chorus is supposed to happen during the song, you're missing out on a good drummer's best opportunity to shine like a big, bright, beautiful star in the sky. (And let's face it: We would all like to shine like big, bright, beautiful stars in the sky. Or maybe that's just me.) So, make sure you're aware of the arrangement of any song you're learning or working on, so you can be ready to grab your moment to shine.

When you're at a rehearsal and you hear the other players in the band talking about where the chorus is going to come in, don't tune out and assume that they're talking about "technical" music things that don't matter to the drummer. The drummer should be every bit as aware of arrangement as anyone else in the band (if not more so). As a matter of fact, if you're more aware of a song's arrangement than anyone else in the band, you can be helpful to anyone in the band who might not be entirely sure when the chorus of the song is supposed to happen. By playing a very obvious and deliberate fill while bringing the song into a chorus, for example, you can quickly jog the memory of a confused band mate. He will hear that fill coming and remember that he is supposed to be go to the next part of the song. Hopefully, your band mate will make that transition smoothly, thanks to you and your reminder.

It's true that you could just throw a stick at your band mate and yell "Chorus!" at the top of your lungs, but that's no way to make friends. As you know, nobody likes someone who is throwing something at him unless it's money or doughnuts. And not everyone likes doughnuts.

But I digress…. Remember that most song arrangements are usually based around groupings of measures in groups of four or numbers that can be divided by four (8, 16, 32, and so on). If you pay close enough attention to the song's arrangement as it plays, with the idea of groupings of fours in your head, you shouldn't have too much trouble hearing and feeling the arrangement of that song. And when you're as fully aware of the song's arrangement as you can be, you're in the best possible position to pounce upon that song like a stealthy panther and tear it to pieces with the brutal and mighty force of your song arrangement awareness. But please don't pounce too hard. You wouldn't want to hurt yourself.

Dynamics

W E'VE TALKED ABOUT DYNAMICS before, but let's talk about them again. Awareness of dynamics (how loud or quiet parts of a song are) goes hand in hand with your awareness of the arrangement of a song. As you learn a new song, pay attention to the dynamics that may already be present if it's a song you're learning from a recording. Listen carefully to see whether there's a difference in volume or intensity as the song moves from one part to the next, and try to determine how the drummer is helping to bring out those changes in volume or intensity. Once you determine the drummer's approach to the dynamics of the song, try out that approach when your band is learning the song together.

If you're writing a brand-new song of your own with your band, listen carefully to determine where you can come into play dynamically. If the singer starts singing more intensely during the bridge of the song, for example, you might want to bring up your volume to match that intensity. Maybe the guitar player switches to a more aggressive guitar sound once the chorus of the song is reached. That would be when you bring up your volume during the chorus, and then bring your volume back down when you go to the second verse.

If you're unsure of how to approach the dynamics of a song, don't be afraid to bring it up for discussion with your band mates. In a band situation, it never hurts to talk things over. (Unless of course, your band mates don't speak to each other at all, ever. I've been in a few bands like that.) If your band is the nonverbal type, take charge of the dynamics yourself and watch in awe as your band mates follow your lead. I believe that once the drummer pays attention to the dynamics of the music he's playing, the rest of the band will follow his example. Suddenly, your music will seem three-dimensional, with peaks and valleys instead of just one boring volume groaning on and on. It's your responsibility to make sure that your band doesn't just groan on and on at the same volume, boring everybody to death. Think of yourself as a lifesaver. After all, you wouldn't want anyone to die of boredom while watching your band play, would you?

Location, Location, Location

BECAUSE THE DRUMMER IS USUALLY located in the center of the stage, easily seen by the other band members, he or she is often in the best position to relay cues to the other band members. In music, a *cue* is a signal that gets relayed through the different band members about something that is going to occur, such as another part of a song that is about to happen, or the ending of the song, or something tricky in the song, and so on. For that reason, the drummer has to be constantly watching all the different band members so he can be ready to relay a cue.

Usually the leader of the band, such as the singer or the lead guitarist (or whoever thinks he's the leader), will relay a cue to the entire band, and if everyone is on the ball , they'll catch the cue and move to the next section of the song or end the song without any major screw-ups. A good drummer can be very helpful in making sure everybody gets the cue by letting them know it's coming by a nod of the head or a dirty look. If you realize how valuable the drummer can be when it comes to relaying those cues, you can become the hero of the band when and if the going gets rough.

Relaying cues effectively is an ability that can be developed, and in some cases it's a gift. Some people are better at having an overall view of music and are just naturally better at relaying cues than the rest of us. If someone else in your band ends up being the cue person, either because he is naturally gifted or because he insists that he gives flawless cues, then let him be the cue person without an argument. There's no rule that says it has to be the drummer. Sometimes the leader of the band will give some cues and you'll end up giving some others. Whatever. But if no one in the band seems to be stepping up to the plate, let the cue person be you. As I mentioned earlier, you're in the best position geographically because you're in the center of the stage. Although it's true that some members of the band may have to turn around or turn their heads to see you, they'll get used to it. It's worth their while to get used to it.

The Last Note

IN MANY SONGS you're likely to play in your music career, the very last note of the song may be held out for a non-specific length of time while the singer leaps into the crowd, the guitar player breaks everything in sight including himself, and you play every single silly drum lick you've ever learned—including the ones that have no use except during the last note of a song.

That's wonderful, but then there's the very last short note that the entire band will play to end the madness. Who will cue that last note? Will you play the last note as the singer's vomit lands on his shoes or when the bass player falls over? Maybe, but it's a better idea for the drummer to play and cue that very last note for the rest of the band because he can be easily seen by the other band members and can make it very obvious when that last note is supposed to happen. The arms holding the sticks that have been set on fire go up, and when they come crashing down onto the cymbals, the last note is played with diamond precision, the show is over, and all that's left is the crying.

Again, some other band member could cue that last note, but if no one seems to be interested in cueing it, feel free to step in and pull the plug to end the song. Someone's got to do it. Otherwise, you might be playing that last note forever and ever, or at least until the cops come. (By the way, I don't mean to suggest that you should ever, ever set your sticks on fire or mistreat your gear in any way or even allow your band members to abuse their gear. Remember, friends don't let friends abuse their gear. Also, I didn't mean to imply that you should pull an actual plug to end a song. That's just a figure of speech.)

1...2...1, 2, 3, 4

NOW THAT YOU KNOW HOW to end a song, let's go back and talk about how to start one. There are generally two ways that a song can start. One way is for somebody in the band (sometimes the drummer) to play an intro alone, usually for four or eight measures, and then the rest of the band enters. Another way for a song to start is for all or most of the band members to start the song together. In this case, to go from complete silence to the first note of the song, someone has to count the band in. As far as determining who that someone will be, it's really no different than determining who will give the cues in the band. Sometimes the leader, or whoever thinks he's the leader, will count the songs in. But usually, that responsibility falls to the drummer.

This responsibility is not to be taken lightly, because it involves a lot more than being able to count to four in an audible voice. The count-off is directly related to the tempo, or speed, at which the song is going to be played. You don't want to count to four in one tempo and play the song in a different tempo than you counted off at. This is common sense, but you'd be surprised.

Before you count off a song, take just a couple of seconds to think about the ideal tempo of the song. Sing the melody to yourself in your head before you count off to make sure that you'll count off the song at the tempo that's best for it. I know it can be nerve-wracking and might seem impossible to collect your thoughts for long enough to do this at a show when your nerves are jumping and your adrenaline is racing, but if you can develop the ability to count that song off at the right tempo, you will have developed a skill that will make you the most valuable member of the band.

By the way, there are basically two ways to count off a song. There's a one-measure count-off in which the drummer simply counts to four, with each number representing a beat of the measure or a quarter note. The other kind of count-off is the two-measure kind. In this type of count-off, the drummer counts from one to two on the first and third beats of the first measure, and then simply counts from one to four on each beat of the second measure of the count-off. Which method you use all depends on how long you want or need the count-off to be. For some songs you might want that extra measure that the two-measure count-off will give you to settle into the groove.

Pickup Artist

SOMETIMES THE DRUMMER might play a short fill or maybe even one note before the rest of the band comes thundering in. This short phrase is called a *pickup*, and it can be one of the drummer's best moments to add to the excitement or interest of a song. Usually, if you were going to use a pickup, you would still count the band off and play the pickup as part of the count-off. In other words, you wouldn't give a full count-off and then play a pickup. The pickup should occur before the song actually starts. There are some pickups in famous and classic songs that are so distinctive that I only need to hear the pickup to name the song instantly. But, you know, I am a little weird. As I said before, some pickups are half- or full-measure fills and some are just flams on beat 4 of the measure, but a good pickup can kick start a song nicely or at least get my attention. But again, I'm weird like that.

It's About Time

NOW THAT YOU HAVE A COUPLE ideas about how to start a song, how will you keep the song at the tempo that you counted off? By paying close attention to both your own playing and the playing of all the other band members, that's how. This can be absolutely the hardest thing for a drummer to do, but it's also the most important thing about being a good drummer. This cannot be overstated: It's the drummer's job not only to keep good time, but also to be ready to help the other members of the band stay in time.

You don't have to keep perfect time like an emotionless robot. It's perfectly fine to let the feel of the song breathe a little bit as you go from one section of the song to another, but you always want to be as in control of your time as you can be. Pay particular attention to both your time and the rest of the band's time as you move from one section of a song to another, because this can sometimes prove to be the trouble area. Just because the guitar player always speeds up when he gets to a certain part of a song doesn't mean that you should speed up to match him. Ideally, he should be paying enough attention to his own playing so that he can fight his tendency to speed up, and you can help him be aware of his tendencies by not going with him.

Situations like this can be very delicate to handle and can possibly lead to harsh words and bad feelings, but be brave and strong and keep the overall goodness of your music in mind. Don't accuse or blame. Be helpful and encouraging, and you can work together to make the music better.

Be aware that you may be the one that's either speeding songs up or slowing them down according to the other band members. This can be hard to hear both emotionally and physically. No one likes to be reminded of his or her possible shortcomings, but keep your head on straight and try harder. Practice to a metronome as much as you can stand, and soon good time will be your greatest strength as a drummer. When you have good time as a drummer, you will instantly make whatever band you happen to be playing with sound better, and other bands will want you to play with them because of your excellent time-keeping skills. And that's a wonderful thing.

Hawkeye: The Nickname You Want

I F YOU WANT TO BE THE BEST drummer that you can possibly be, the drummer that every band loves, you need to learn to watch your band like a hawk. I don't mean that you should watch them to see whether they're giving you dirty looks while your back appears to be turned. I mean you should get your head out of your drum kit and look around at your other band members to see what's up while playing a gig. Do they look happy with the way the grooves are going, or are their features contorted into rictuses of pain and disapproval at the feel you're laying down?

Although it's true that some people never look like they're having a good time, the facial and body language of your band mates can give you valuable clues as to how to adjust your playing. Are you playing so loud that they appear to be wincing in pain, or do they appear to be straining to hear what you're playing? Are they hopping up and down impatiently because you might be slowing the tempo down, or are they trying to slow you down by shouting nasty things about your mother? You'll never know what they want if you don't look around to check it out.

Keep an especially sharp eye on whoever happens to be singing the song. He or she will usually be the first band member to voice an opinion on the tempo of the song since the singer has to pay close attention to his or her breathing to sing properly. If a song is moving along too fast for the singer to take deep enough breaths to get all the words out, he or she will probably let you know in either a

nice way or a not-nice way. Or, maybe the song is slower than the singer would like it, causing him or her to stretch out the words to uncomfortable lengths.

Putting yourself in the singer's shoes will go a long way toward helping you develop your awareness of how important the drummer's job is in the band. When the singer loves you, you're definitely in the band forever, so pay attention to the singer's body language. If you feel forced to change the tempo of a song while it's in progress, try to do it as smoothly as you can. This will probably sound bad no matter how smoothly you try to pull it off, but the most important thing is to learn from your mistake. The next time you play that particular song, pay closer attention to the tempo and the count-off to make sure it's closer to where it should be than last time you played it.

Paying attention is a skill that can be developed over time, so don't feel that you can get it right away. I still have to remind myself occasionally to pay attention to everything on stage, and I've been playing for a long time. Just always try to pay as much attention as you can, and you'll automatically be valuable to your band just because you're trying. By keeping a sharp eye on tempos and what's going on onstage, hopefully you will eventually earn the nickname of Hawkeye—as in, "Old Hawkeye doesn't miss a thing. At the last show, when I threw my bass at his head because I was so excited at how great his playing was, he ducked right at the last second. He's amazing."

A Fond Farewell and a Last and Most Valuable Piece of Advice

WE FIND OURSELVES AT THE END of the book, where I will send you on your way to drumming greatness. Now go find yourself a drum teacher who will check out your playing and help you to further achieve your goals. Because you took the time to learn all the basics from this book, you'll be able to move on to more specific and detailed aspects of drumming with your private instructor, saving yourself valuable time and money. This has been my purpose for writing this book, and hopefully it will pay off for you.

I want to wish you the best of luck both in your drumming career and in your life, and I thank you for hanging out with me and reading this book. I hope it has been both educational and entertaining, But before I go, I would like to give you the single most valuable piece of advice in this entire book. It is advice that will change your life and the lives of all others around you. Once you put this piece of advice into action, things will never be the same. These are words that I live by every day of my life, and it is indeed a great honor to pass these words on to you. And the words are these: Remember, always keep your... Wait. I forgot what I was going to say.

Index

A

accents, 174
  bass drums, 185–186
  hi-hats, 182–184
  paradiddles, 156
  rimshots, 175, 178
accessories, 36–38
adding
  accents to backbeats, 175
  a crash, 89
  notes, 116
adjusting
  angle of wrists to play rimshots, 177
  tempo, 192
  thrones, 27
alarm clocks, 37
awareness of song arrangements, 206

B

backbeat, 175–176
  ghost notes, 179
  rimshots, 178
bags, sticks, 37–38
bands, joining school bands, 44
bar lines, 47
basic setup, 16. *See also* setup
bass drums, 16, 22–23
  beaters, 24
  patterns, 92–93
  pedals, 24
  quadruplets, playing, 131–132
  sixteenth-note variations, 96–104
  techniques, 67
  three-dimensional drumming, 185–186
  tuning, 20–21
batter heads, 19
beaters, bass drums, 24
beats, 46–47, 49
  backbeats, 175–176
bells, 37
Big #1, 96–98
Big #2, 98–100
Big #3, 100–102
Big #4, 102–103
blank manuscript books, 37
boom stands, 25
brackets, stands, 25
bridges, 197
brushes, 38
buying
  cymbals, 29
  drum sets, 10–11
  sticks, 6–7
buzzers, 37

C

carpeting, 17
cases, 38
changing heads, speed keys, 38

choruses, 197

closed hi-hats, 68

    Groove #6, 95

clutches, cymbals, 30

combinations, sixteenth notes, 77–78, 162–169

cost

    of drum sets, 11

    of sticks, 6–7

counting

    sixteenth notes, 58

    songs, starting, 210

crash cymbals, 16, 65–67

    fills, 89

    paradiddles, 160

    quadruplets, 131

    setup, 33

    smoke and throw, 122–123

crescendos, 201

cymbals

    clutches, 30

    crash. *See* crash cymbals

    hi-hats, 182. *See also* hi-hats

    ride, 16, 34, 195–196

    setup, 33–35

    special effect, 34

    stands, 25

    thumb screws, 31

    types of, 29

D

dark version of quadruplets, 148–149

dicing, 80–82, 87

    sixteenth notes, 119–121

    style, 170–171

drum corps, 5

drumheads, 19, 22

drums

    bass, 16, 22–23

        beaters, 24

        patterns, 92–93

        pedals, 24

        quadruplets, playing, 131–132

        sixteenth-note variations, 96–104

        techniques, 67

        three-dimensional drumming, 185–186

        tuning, 20–21

    keys, 17

    pads, 8–9

    snare, 16, 26–27

        backbeats, 175–176

        ghost notes, 179–180

        notes, fills, 61–62

        quadruplets, 130

        rimshots, 177–178

        stands, 27

        throw-offs, 28

        tuning, 21

    tom toms, 32

        fills, 63

        floor, 16, 26

        tuning, 20–21

    tuning, 17, 20–21

drum sets

    accessories, 36–38

    bass drums, 22–23

    cost of, 11

    fills, 64

    hardware, 25–35

    left-handed people, setup for, 35

    lessons without, 12

    maintenance, 11

    parents, convincing them to buy, 10–11

    placement of on stage, 208

drum sets *(continued)*

    setup, 16–19

        adjusting

        cymbals, 33–35

        floor toms, 27

        hi-hat stands, 28–32

        for left-handed people, 35

        metronomes, 48

        pedals, 22

        practice routines, 110–111

        snare drums, 27–28

        thrones, 26–27

        tom toms, 32

drumsticks, 4

    bags, 37–38

    cost of, 6–7

    holding, 52

    non-standard sizes, 6

    quadruplets, 128–129

    replacing, 7–8

    standard sizes, 4–6

    sizes

        2B, 5

        3S, 5

        5A, 5

        5B, 5

        7A, 4–5

    tips, types of, 7

    triplets, 114

DVD, using with book, 2–3

dynamic range, 179, 181

dynamics of songs, 207

E

eighth notes

    hi-hat accents, 183

    quarter notes *versus,* 48–49

    smoke and throw, 122–123

    tempo, 190

    triplets, 115

emotions, expressing, 181

endings, 197

F

fills, 59–64

    #1, 59–61

    #2, 61–62

    #3, 62

    #4, 63

    #5, 63–64

    #6, 64

    crash cymbals, 65–67, 89

    creating, 88

    flam taps, 134–137

    forward quadruplets, 152

    half-measure, 121

    paradiddles, using in, 160–161

    pickups, 211

    reverse quadruplets as, 151–152

    sixteenth notes, 59, 78–79, 85

    slicing and dicing, 80–82, 87

    triplets, 115

flam taps, 134–137

    fills, 143–144

    quadruplets, 145–146

    reverse quadruplet fills, 153

floors, rugs for, 17

floor toms, 16, 26. *See also* **drums; tom toms**

    fills, 63

forward quadruplets as fills, 152

four-four time signatures, 47

G

ghost notes, 179–180
grips, sticks, 52
grooves
   #1, measure of 4/4, 50–51
   #2, "and of three," 53
   #3, moving bass drum notes, 54
   #4, sixteenth notes, 72–75
   #5, variation #2, 76–82
   #6, 77–78
      ghost notes, 179
      with open and closed hi-hats, 95
      rimshot accents, 178
      sixteenth-note combinations, 162
   accents, 174
   backbeats, 175–176
   combinations, three in one, 164–165
   dynamic range, 181
   flam taps, 134–137
   getting back after taking a fill, 60
   hi-hats, accents, 182–184
   quarter notes, playing hi-hats, 191–194
   riding, 200
   smoke and throw, 122–123
   triplets, 115
groups
   awareness of song arrangements, 206
   of notes, 127–133. See also quadruplets

H

half-closed hi-hats, 199
half-measure fills, 121
half-open hi-hats, 199
hardware, 25–35
   cymbals, 33–35
   floor toms, 26
   hi-hat stands, 28–32
   snare drums, 27–28
   thrones (seats), 26–27
   tom toms, 32
heads. See also drumheads
   drum, 19
   speed keys, 38
   tuning, 20–21. See also tuning
hearing protection, 36–37
heel down/up techniques, 67
height, hi-hats, 182
hi-hats
   eighth notes, 190
   ghost notes, 179
   half-closed, 199
   half-open, 199
   left feet positions, 68–69
   paradiddles, 161
   quarter notes, 191–194
   ride cymbals. See ride cymbals
   smoke and throw, 122–123
   stands, 28–32
   three-dimensional drumming, 182–184
   volume, 201
holding drumsticks, 52
holes in drumheads, 22

I–K

"in between" notes, 72–73
intros, 197
isolating Groove #5, 76

keys
   drum, 17
   music, 46–47
   speed, 38
kick drums, 22. See also bass drums

L

last note of songs, 209
left feet
    positions, 68–69
    repeats, 92–93
left-handed people, setup for, 35
legends, 46
lessons, 2–3
    drum pads, 8–9
    music, reading, 42–44
    without drum sets, 12
lines, measures, 47
looking ahead, 167–168

M

maintenance, drum sets, 11
matched grips, 52
measures, 46–47
    of 4/4, 50–51
    awareness of song arrangements, 206
    backbeats, 175–176
    half-measure fills, 121
    lines, 47
    paradiddles, 154
    sixteenth-note variation #4, 84–85
    smoke and throw, 122–123
    songs, starting, 210
memory, reading music, 42–44
metronomes, 36
    fills, 59
    flam taps, fills, 143–144
    quarter notes, 192
    setup, 48
    tempo, practicing, 212
music
    notes, 45
        accents, 174

        adding, 116
        contrast between, 181
        dynamic range, 181
        ghost, 179–180
        "in between," 72–73
        last note of songs, 209
        paradiddles, 154–157. *See also* paradiddles
        quadruplets, 127–133
        quarter, 47, 48–49. *See also* quarter notes
        sixteenth, 58. *See also* sixteenth notes
        triplets, 113–118
    reading, 42–44, 167–168
    rests, 45
    songs
        arrangements, awareness of, 206
        dynamics of, 207
        last note of, 209
        pickups, 211
        starting, 210
        structure of, 197–198
        tempo, keeping, 212
    stands, 37

N

nicknames, 213
non-standard stick sizes, 6
notation, 42–44
    accents, 174
    paradiddles, 154
notes, 45
    accents, 174
    adding, 116
    contrast between, 181
    dynamic range, 181
    ghost, 179–180
    "in between," 72–73
    last note of songs, 209

paradiddles, 154–157. *See also* paradiddles

quadruplets, 127–133

quarter, 47, 48–49. *See also* quarter notes

sixteenth, 58. *See also* sixteenth notes

triplets, 113–118

nylon tips, 7

O

open hi-hats, 68

groove #6, 95

P

Paiste, 29. *See also* cymbals

paradiddles, 154–156

fills, using in, 160–161

parents, convincing them to buy drum sets, 10–11

patterns

bass drums, 92–93

hi-hat accents, 183

quarter notes, 191–194. *See also* quarter notes

pedals

bass drums, 16, 24, 185

hi-hats, 28–32, 67–68

setup, 22

pickups, 211

placement of drum sets on stage, 208

playing

accents, 174

backbeats, 175–76

bass drum accents, 185–186

flam taps, 135–136

ghost notes, 179–180

hi-hats, 182–184, 191–194

music, reading, 42–44, 167–168

notes, 45

accents, 174

adding, 116

contrast between, 181

dynamic range, 181

ghost, 179–180

"in between," 72–73

last note of songs, 209

paradiddles, 154–157. *See also* paradiddles

quadruplets, 127–133

quarter, 47, 48–49. *See also* quarter notes

sixteenth, 58. *See also* sixteenth notes

triplets, 113–118

paradiddles, 154–157

quadruplets, 128–129

rimshots, 177–178

rests, 45

songs

arrangements, awareness of, 206

dynamics of, 207

last note of, 209

pickups, 211

starting, 210

structure of, 197–198

tempo, keeping, 212

positions

fills, 60

hi-hats, 182

left feet, 68–69

placement of drum sets on stage, 208

quadruplets, 130

ride cymbals, 195

rimshots, 177

sticks, holding, 52

practice

drum pads, 8–9

routines, 108–111

rudiments, 154–157

tempo with metronomes, 212

preparing drum sets for setup, 17–18
projection, rimshots, 177–178

Q

quadruplets, 127–133
   dark version of, 148–149
   flam taps, 145–146
   forward, 152
   reverse, 150–153
quarter notes, 47
   versus eighth notes, 48–49
   measures, of 4/4, 50–51
   tempo, 191–194

R

racks, 32
range, dynamic, 179, 181
reading music, 42–44
   looking ahead, 167–168
repeats, left feet, 92–93
repetition, learning by, 74, 108
replacing sticks, 7–8
researching drum sets, 10
rests, 45
   quarter notes, 193
   smoke and throw, 121
reverse quadruplets, 150–153
reversing order of flam taps, 144
reviews, 109
re-voicing, 147
rhythm, 4
   flam taps, 143
   metronomes, 36
      fills, 59
      quarter notes, 192
      setup, 48
      tempo, practicing, 212

ride cymbals, 16, 195–196
   hi-hats, comparing, 199–200
   setup, 34
riding, 200
right feet, playing quadruplets, 131–132
right hands, playing flam taps, 136
rimshots, 177–178
   accents, 175, 178
   ghost notes, 179
routines, practice, 108–111
rudiments, 154
rugs, 17

S

Sabian, 29. *See also* cymbals
school bands, joining, 44
screws, cymbals, 31
seats. *See* thrones
setup
   adjusting
      angle of wrist to play rimshots, 177
      tempo, 192
      thrones, 27
   cymbals, 33–35
   drum sets, 16–19
   floor toms, 27
   hi-hat stands, 28–32
   for left-handed people, 35
   metronomes, 48
   pedals, 22
   practice routines, 110–111
   snare drums, 27–28
   thrones, 26–27
   tom toms, 32
signatures, time, 47

sixteenth notes, 58
    combinations, 162–169
    fills, 59, 78–79
    Groove #4, taking notes out, 72–75
    Groove #5, variation #2, 76–82
    paradiddles, 154
    slicing and dicing, 119–121
    triplets, 115–118
    Variation #3, 83
    Variation #4, 84–85
    variations, using bass drums, 96–103
sizes
    non-standard sticks, 6
    standard sticks, 4–6
slicing, 80–82, 87
    sixteenth notes, 119–121
    style, 170–171
smoke and throw, 122–123
snare drums, 16, 27–28
    backbeats, 175–176
    ghost notes, 179–180
    notes, fills, 61–62
    quadruplets, 130
    rimshots, 177–178
    stands, 27
    throw-offs, 28
    tuning, 21
snare side heads, 19
solo sections, 197
songs
    arrangements, awareness of, 206
    dynamics of, 207
    last note of, 209
    pickups, 211
    starting, 210
    structure of, 197–198
    tempo, keeping, 212
special effect cymbals, 34
speed keys, 38

spurs, 22
staffs, 46–47
stages, placement of drum sets on, 208
standard stick sizes, 4–6
stands
    boom, 25
    brackets, 25
    crash cymbals, 16
    cymbals, 25
    hi-hat, 28–32
    music, 37
    ride cymbals, 16
    snare drums, 16, 27
starting
    fills, 60
    songs, 210
    stick sizes, 5
sticks, 4–9
    bags, 37–38
    cost of, 6–7
    holding, 52
    non-standard sizes, 6
    quadruplets, 128–129
    replacing, 7–8
    standard sizes, 4–6
    sizes
        2B, 5
        3S, 5
        5A, 5
        5B, 5
        7A, 4–5
    tips, types of, 7
    triplets, 114
stores, buying drum sets from, 10
style, 159
    paradiddles, using in a fill, 160–161
    sixteenth-note combinations, 162–169
    slicing and dicing, 170–171

T

taps, flam. *See* flam taps
tempo, 48
    adjusting, 192
    eighth notes, 190
    quarter notes, 191–194
    songs, keeping, 212
    triplets, 118
three-dimensional drumming
    backbeat, 175–176
    bass drums, 185–186
    ghost notes, 179–180
    hi-hats, 182–184
    rimshots, 177–178
thrones, 16, 26–27
    adjusting, 27
throw-offs, 28
thumb screws, cymbals, 31
timers, 37, 74–75
time signatures, 47
tips, types of, 7
tom toms, 32
    fills, 63
    floor, 16, 26
    tuning, 20–21
tonal keys, 46
traditional grips, 52
transitions
    crash cymbals, adding, 89
    smoke and throw, 122–123
triplets, 113–118
    slicing and dicing, 119–121
    tempo, 118
tuning drums, 17, 20–21
    bass, 20–21
    snare, 21
    toms, 20–21

types
    of cymbals, 29
    of tips, 7

V

variations
    #2, fills, 78–79
    #2, Groove #5, 76–82
    #3, sixteenth notes, 83
    #4, sixteenth notes, 84–85
    sixteenth notes, 162
        using bass drums, 96–103
        notes and groove #6, 72–75
verses, 197
volume, 189
    backbeats, 175
    eighth notes, 190
    ghost notes, 179–180
    hi-hats, 201
    ride cymbals, 195–196

W

weight, sticks, 4
wood floors, rugs for, 17
wood tips, 7

Z

Zildjian, 29. *See also* cymbals

License Agreement/Notice of Limited Warranty

By opening the sealed disc container in this book, you agree to the following terms and conditions. If, upon reading the following license agreement and notice of limited warranty, you cannot agree to the terms and conditions set forth, return the unused book with unopened disc to the place where you purchased it for a refund.

License:

The enclosed software is copyrighted by the copyright holder(s) indicated on the software disc. You are licensed to copy the software onto a single computer for use by a single user and to a backup disc. You may not reproduce, make copies, or distribute copies or rent or lease the software in whole or in part, except with written permission of the copyright holder(s). You may transfer the enclosed disc only together with this license, and only if you destroy all other copies of the software and the transferee agrees to the terms of the license. You may not decompile, reverse assemble, or reverse engineer the software.

Notice of Limited Warranty:

The enclosed disc is warranted by Thomson Course Technology PTR to be free of physical defects in materials and workmanship for a period of sixty (60) days from end user's purchase of the book/disc combination. During the sixty-day term of the limited warranty, Thomson Course Technology PTR will provide a replacement disc upon the return of a defective disc.

Limited Liability:

THE SOLE REMEDY FOR BREACH OF THIS LIMITED WARRANTY SHALL CONSIST ENTIRELY OF REPLACE-MENT OF THE DEFECTIVE DISC. IN NO EVENT SHALL THOMSON COURSE TECHNOLOGY PTR OR THE AUTHOR BE LIABLE FOR ANY OTHER DAMAGES, INCLUDING LOSS OR CORRUPTION OF DATA, CHANGES IN THE FUNCTIONAL CHARACTERISTICS OF THE HARDWARE OR OPERATING SYSTEM, DELETERIOUS INTERACTION WITH OTHER SOFTWARE, OR ANY OTHER SPECIAL, INCIDENTAL, OR CONSEQUENTIAL DAMAGES THAT MAY ARISE, EVEN IF THOMSON COURSE TECHNOLOGY PTR AND/OR THE AUTHOR HAS PREVIOUSLY BEEN NOTIFIED THAT THE POSSIBILITY OF SUCH DAMAGES EXISTS.

Disclaimer of Warranties:

THOMSON COURSE TECHNOLOGY PTR AND THE AUTHOR SPECIFICALLY DISCLAIM ANY AND ALL OTHER WARRANTIES, EITHER EXPRESS OR IMPLIED, INCLUDING WARRANTIES OF MERCHANTABILITY, SUITABILITY TO A PARTICULAR TASK OR PURPOSE, OR FREEDOM FROM ERRORS. SOME STATES DO NOT ALLOW FOR EXCLUSION OF IMPLIED WARRANTIES OR LIMITATION OF INCIDENTAL OR CONSEQUENTIAL DAMAGES, SO THESE LIMITATIONS MIGHT NOT APPLY TO YOU.

Other:

This Agreement is governed by the laws of the State of Massachusetts without regard to choice of law principles. The United Convention of Contracts for the International Sale of Goods is specifically disclaimed. This Agreement constitutes the entire agreement between you and Thomson Course Technology PTR regarding use of the software.